McGRAW-HILL MATHEMATICS

Math in my World

Douglas H. Clements

Kenneth W. Jones

Lois Gordon Moseley

Linda Schulman

McGraw-Hill School Division

New York   Farmington

PROGRAM AUTHORS

Dr. Douglas H. Clements

Kenneth W. Jones

Lois Gordon Moseley

Dr. Linda Schulman

CONTRIBUTING AUTHORS

Dr. Liana Forest

Christine A. Fernsler

Dr. Kathleen Kelly-Benjamin

Maria R. Marolda

Dr. Richard H. Moyer

Dr. Walter G. Secada

CONSULTANTS

Multicultural and Educational Consultants

Rim An

Sue Cantrell

Mordessa Corbin

Dr. Carlos Diaz

Carl Downing

Linda Ferreira

Judythe M. Hazel

Roger Larson

Josie Robles

Veronica Rogers

Telkia Rutherford

Sharon Searcy

Elizabeth Sinor

Michael Wallpe

Claudia Zaslavsky

COVER PHOTOGRAPHY Jade Albert for MMSD.

PHOTOGRAPHY All photographs are by the McGraw-Hill School Division (MMSD), Ken Karp for MMSD, Ken Lax for MMSD and Scott Harvey for MMSD except as noted below.

Table of Contents • Superstock, Inc. : iii t. • Tom and Pat Leeson/Photo Researchers : iii m. • John Yurka/The Picture Cube : iv m. • J.D. Bartlett/Bruce Coleman Inc. : v t. • Index Stock : v b. • Nancy Sheehan/The Picture Cube : vi t. • Bob Daemmrich : vi m. • Bob Daemmrich/Stock Boston : vii t. • Gary Retherford/Photo Researchers : vii b. • Jason Green/Liaison Int'l. : vii m. b. • Superstock, Inc. : ix t. • Bob Daemmrich/Stock Boston : x m. • Richard Hutchings/Photo Edit : 1 t.r. • **Chapter 1** • Lawrence Migdale : 1 b.r. • Tom & Pat Leeson/Photo Researchers : 3 • Superstock, Inc. : 7 • Fletcher & Baylis/Photo Researchers : 19 • Gregory Dimijian/Photo Researchers : 21 • Cindy Karp/National Geographic Society : 30 • John M. Roberts/The Stock Market : 32 • **Chapter 2** • Lawrence Migdale : 45 r. • T. Tracy/FPG Int'l : 48 • Richard Paisley/Stock Boston, Inc. : 53 r. • Louise Gubb/The Image Works : 62 l. • Ben Simmons/Stock Market : 62 r. • Buffalo Bill Historical Center, Cody, Wy : 66 • **Chapter 3** • John Yurka/Picture Cube. : 85 • M.W.F. Tweedie/Photo Researchers : 107 t.r. • Renee Lynn/Photo Researchers : 112 b.m. • L. West/Photo Researchers : 117 r. • Gregory K. Scott/Photo Researchers : 117 m. • J & D Bartlett/Bruce Coleman, Inc. : 117 l. • Bob Daemmrich/Stock Boston, Inc.: 123 • Henley and Savage/Uniphoto : 128 • **Chapter 5** • Lawrence Migdale/Stock Boston, Inc. : 170 t.m. • Henley and Savage/The Stock Market : 170 t.r. • Lee Boltin Picture Library : 176 • Index Stock : 182 t.r. • Phil Degginger/Tony Stone Images: 189 • Michael Busselle/Tony Stone Images : 190 • Nancy Sheehan/The Picture Cube : 191 • M. Eastcott/The Image Works : 194 • Robert Kristofik/The Image Bank : 196 t. • Spencer Jones/FPG International : 196 b. • **Chapter 6** • John Feingersh/The Stock Market : 201 • Jacob Taposchaner/FPG Int'l : 204 • Bob Daemmrich: 211 • John Lei for MMSD : 221 l. • Anne Nielsen for MMSD : 221 r. • Abe Rezny/The Image Works : 230 • **Chapter 7** • Index Stock Photography, Inc. : 237 • Photo Researchers: 238 • The Stock Market : 238 b. • Robert Ginn/Unicorn Stock Photos : 238 t. l. • Courtesy of June Acker Myers: 253 m. • The Granger Collection: 262 • Jonathan A. Meyers/FPG International: 263 t.r. • Jerry Jacka : 263 b.r. • Bob Daemmrich/Stock Boston, Inc.: 268 • **Chapter 8** • Lori Adamski Peek/Tony Stone Images : 273 • M.H. Sharp/Photo Researchers : 281 t.r. • Bill Ivy/Tony Stone Worldwide : 281 l. • Larry West/FPG International : 281 b. • Gary Retherford/Photo Researchers : 282 r. • Jason Green/Gamma Liaison : 282 l. • Grace Davies/Omni Photo Communications : 284 • Comstock : 286 b. • Patti Murray/Animals Animals : 287 t. • Clyde Smith/FPG International : 287 b. • Rolf Bettner : 296 • Stephen Simpson/FPG International : 297 t. • Erwin & Peggy Bauer/Natural Selection : 299 • Frans Lanting/Photo Researchers : 301 • **Chapter 9** • photographed courtesy permission Museum of Modern Art, New York, New York/ Pablo Picasso, "Bull," 1958 c. Estate of Pablo Picasso/Artists Rights Society, New York : 311 • Jimmy Ernst, "Another Silence," oil painting 6' x 10'3", courtesy The Rimrock Foundation : 322 • Paul Gauguin, "Still Life With Three Puppies" c. 1888 oil on wood 36 1/8" x 24 5/8" Museum of Modern Art, Mrs. Simon Guggenheim Fund : 335 • **Chapter 10** • Superstock, Inc. : 349 • Kim Robbie/The Stock Market : 356 • Bob Daemmrich/Stock Boston, Inc. : 366 • Superstock, Inc.: 384 • **Chapter 11** • Bob Daemmrich/Uniphoto : 389 • Bonnie Kamin/Photo Edit : 395 • The Granger Collection : 398 b.r. • Kindra Clineff/The Picture Cube : 405 • E. Crews/The Image Works : 425 • Michael Newman/Photo Edit : 429 • Wayne Hay/The Picture Cube : 430 • **Chapter 12** • Richard Hutchings/PhotoEdit: 443 • Superstock, Inc. : 444 • John Running/Stock Boston Inc. : 447 • Lawrence Migdale : 449 • Bob Daemmrich/Stock Boston, Inc.: 452 • Ken Kerbs for MMSD : 459 t.

ILLUSTRATION Winky Adam: 2, 3, 44, 45, 84, 85, 134, 135, 166, 167, 200, 201, 236, 237, 272, 273, 310, 311, 348, 349, 388, 389, 442, 443 • Jo Lynn Alcorn: 259, 261, 350, 364 • Bob Barner: 95, 123, 207, 208, 225, 226, 230, 232, 456, 458, 472, 474, 476 • Sue Bialecki: 398 • Ken Bowser: 29, 358, 362, 381, 385 • Hal Brooks: 46, 47, 56, 57, 64, 133, 209, 210, 224, 249, 260 • Roger Chandler: 402 • Randy Chewning: 290 • Genevieve Claire: 335, 336, 339 • Betsy Day: 103, 401 • Daniel Del Valle: 75, 118, 120, 121, 122, 184, 337 • Eldon Doty: 399, 410 • Brian Dugan: 82 • Doreen Gay-Kassel: 4, 11, 20, 23, 24, 25, 34, 168, 442, 446, 447, 448, 450, 463 • Annie Gusman: 404, 428 • Robert Hynes: 86, 108 • Stanford Kay: 28 • Jim Kelly: 56, 65, 68, 73, 74 • Rita Lascaro: 88, 130, 136, 141, 142, 150, 156, 160, 161, 202, 218, 222, 293, 473 • Tom Leonard: 283, 284, 288, 298, 301, 302 • Claude Martinot: 295, 306 • Hatley Mason: 422, 427, 431, 432, 433, 438 • Bonnie Matthews: 252 • Paul Meisel: 40 • Jonathan Milne: 9, 10, 22, 36 • Jim Paillot: 67, 143, 144, 145, 157, 179 • Hima Pamoedjo: 41, 54, 257, 271, 313, 322, 325, 331, 339, 340, 344, 346 • Miles Parnell: 182, 185, 190, 193 • Brenda Pepper: 33, 42, 175, 177, 285, 286, 315 • Mary Power: 178, 180, 186, 193 • Victoria Raymond: 240, 333, 334 • Andy San Diego: 155 • Audrey Schorr: 170, 324, 325 • Bob Shein: 7, 8, 21, 30, 394, 400, 403, 404, 416, 420, 424, 429, 430, 440 • Michael Sloan: 91, 92, 93, 94, 102, 109, 114, 119 • Matt Straub: 86, 97, 98, 100, 104, 106, 113, 119, 213, 215, 231 • Susan Swan: 146, 149, 250, 251, 256, 258, 266, 267, 453, 454, 457, 466, 469 • Peggy Tagel: 171, 173, 174, 181, 465 • Don Tate: 352, 354, 356, 373, 375, 376, 379 • Terry Taylor: 101 • TCA Graphics: 97, 98, 100, 104, 106, 119, 120, 121, 122, 123, 126, 132, 174, 187, 188, 189, 190, 191, 194, 195, 197, 199, 441 • Dale Verzaal: 15, 16, 31, 115, 116, 118, 120 • Nina Wallace: 235, 309, 365, 368, 370, 378, 382, 383, 477 • Matt Wawiorka: 293, 294, 407, 408 • Rebecca Wildsmith: 18, 278, 308.

ACKNOWLEDGMENTS "Ten Puppies (Diez Perritos)" from THE SPECTRUM OF MUSIC, Grade 1, Mary Val Marsh, Carroll Rinehart, and Edith Savage, Authors. Copyright (c) 1983 Macmillan/McGraw-Hill School Publishing Company. • Unabridged text of "Rope Rhyme" from HONEY, I LOVE by Eloise Greenfield. Text copyright (c) 1978 by Eloise Greenfield. Selection reprinted by permission of HarperCollins Publishers.

McGraw-Hill School Division

A Division of The McGraw-Hill Companies

Copyright © 1998 McGraw-Hill School Division,
a Division of the Educational and Professional Publishing Group of The McGraw-Hill Companies, Inc.

McGraw-Hill School Division
1221 Avenue of the Americas
New York, New York 10020

Printed in the United States of America
ISBN 0-02-109460-8 / 2

2 3 4 5 6 7 8 9 043/073 02 01 00 99 98 97

Contents

1 In the Rain Forest

2 Understanding Addition and Subtraction

- 4 **What Do You Know ?**
- 5 Part-Part-Whole *Explore Activity*
- 7 Addition *Explore Activity*
- 9 Addition Patterns *Explore Activity*
- 11 Count On
- 13 Related Addition Facts
- 15 **Problem-Solving Strategy** Write an Addition Sentence
- 17 **Midchapter Review**
- 18 **Extra Practice Game!** Rain Forest Climb
- 19 **Real-Life Investigation:** Applying Addition Rain to Grow On
- 21 Subtraction *Explore Activity*
- 23 Subtraction Patterns *Explore Activity*
- 25 Count Back
- 27 Related Subtraction Facts
- 29 **Extra Practice Game!** Rambling River
- 31 **Problem-Solving Strategy** Write a Subtraction Sentence
- 33 **Extra Practice Activity** What Do You See?
- 35 **Problem Solvers at Work** Read to Understand

- 37 **Chapter Review**
- 39 **Chapter Test**
- 40 **Performance Assessment • What Did You Learn?**
- 41 **Math Connection • Probability**
- 42 **Curriculum Connection • Music**
- 43 **Home Connection**

2 Pen Pals

44 Addition and Subtraction Strategies

- 46 **What Do You Know?**
- 47 Use Doubles *Explore Activity*
- 49 Add 9 *Explore Activity*
- 51 Make a 10
- 53 Three or More Addends
- 55 **Midchapter Review**

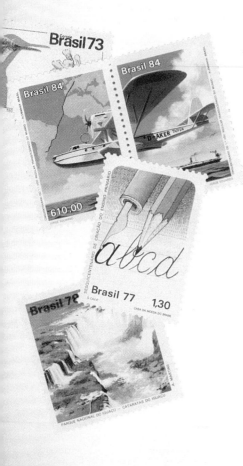

56 **Extra Practice Game!** Mailbox Drop

57 **Real-Life Investigation:**
Applying Addition **What's in the Mail?**

59 Subtract with Doubles *Explore Activity*

61 Count Up to Subtract

63 Subtract 9

65 **Extra Practice Activity** Subtraction Postcards

67 **Problem-Solving Strategy** Choose the Operation

69 Related Facts

71 Fact Families *Explore Activity*

73 **Extra Practice Activity** Secret Message

75 **Problem Solvers at Work** Choose a Strategy

77 **Chapter Review**

79 **Chapter Test**

80 **Performance Assessment • What Did You Learn?**

81 **Math Connection • Algebra**

82 **Technology Connection • Computer**

83 **Home Connection**

3 Our Backyard

84 Place Value and Graphing

86 **What Do You Know?**

87 Tens *Explore Activity*

89 Tens and Ones *Explore Activity*

91 Numbers to 50 *Explore Activity*

93 Numbers to 100 *Explore Activity*

95 **Extra Practice Game!** Schoolyard Numbers

97 Order to 100

99 Skip-Count by Fives and Tens

101 Skip-Count by Twos

103 Odd and Even *Explore Activity*

105 **Midchapter Review**

106 **Extra Practice Game!** Count on the Bees

107 **Real-Life Investigation:**
Applying Numbers **Backyard Bugs**

109 Greater and Less *Explore Activity*

111 Compare Numbers

113 **Extra Practice Game!** The Greater Number Wins

115 **Problem-Solving Strategy** Use Logical Reasoning

117 Bar Graphs *Explore Activity*

119 Pictographs *Explore Activity*

121 Use Pictographs

123 **Problem Solvers at Work** Use a Graph

125 **Chapter Review**

127 **Chapter Test**

128 Performance Assessment • What Did You Learn?

129 Math Connection • Patterns and Functions

130 Curriculum Connection • Science

131 **Cumulative Review**

133 **Home Connection**

4 Saving and Spending

134 Money

136 **What Do You Know?**

137 Pennies, Nickels, Dimes *Explore Activity*

139 Quarters *Explore Activity*

141 Count Quarters

143 **Problem-Solving Strategy** Use Guess and Test

145 **Midchapter Review**

146 **Extra Practice Game!** Save for a Rainy Day

147 **Real-Life Investigation:**
    Applying Money Skills Three-Jar Savings

149 Dollars *Explore Activity*

151 Dollars and Cents

153 Compare Money *Explore Activity*

155 **Extra Practice Game!** Money in the Bank

157 **Problem Solvers at Work** Make Change

159 **Chapter Review**

161 **Chapter Test**

162 Performance Assessment • What Did You Learn?

163 Math Connection • Probability

164 Technology Connection • Computer

165 **Home Connection**

5 Apple Pie Time

166 Telling Time

168 What Do You Know?

169 Time *Explore Activity*

171 Hour and Half Hour

173 Quarter Hour

175 Five Minutes *Explore Activity*

177 More Minutes
179 **Extra Practice Activity** Time to Shop
181 **Midchapter Review**
182 **Extra Practice Game!** Watch the Time
183 **Real-Life Investigation:** Applying Time Make a Schedule
185 **Problem-Solving Strategy** Work Backward
187 Use a Calendar
189 Ordinal Numbers
191 **Problem Solvers at Work** Use a Schedule

◦◦◦◦◦◦◦◦◦◦◦◦◦◦◦◦◦◦◦◦◦◦◦◦◦◦◦◦◦◦◦◦◦◦◦◦◦◦◦

193 **Chapter Review**
195 **Chapter Test**
196 **Performance Assessment • What Did You Learn?**
197 **Math Connection • Patterns**
198 **Technology Connection • Computer**
199 **Home Connection**

6 Fun and Games

200 Exploring 2-Digit Addition and Subtraction

202 **What Do You Know?**
203 Mental Math *Explore Activity*
205 More Mental Math
207 Count On by Tens *Explore Activity*
209 Count Back by Tens *Explore Activity*
211 Use Mental Math
213 **Extra Practice Game!** Addition/Subtraction Race
215 **Problem-Solving Strategy** Solve 2-Step Problems
217 **Midchapter Review**
218 **Extra Practice Game!** Color by Number
219 **Real-Life Investigation:**
      Applying Mental Math Play Lu-Lu!
221 Addition Strategies *Explore Activity*
223 Subtraction Strategies *Explore Activity*
225 **Problem Solvers at Work** Solve Multistep Problems

◦◦◦◦◦◦◦◦◦◦◦◦◦◦◦◦◦◦◦◦◦◦◦◦◦◦◦◦◦◦◦◦◦◦◦◦◦◦◦

227 **Chapter Review**
229 **Chapter Test**
230 **Performance Assessment • What Did You Learn?**
231 **Math Connection • Calculator**
232 **Curriculum Connection • Language Arts**
233 **Cumulative Review**
235 **Home Connection**

7 Fun at the Fair

236 Adding 2-Digit Numbers

238 **What Do You Know?**
239 Regrouping *Explore Activity*
241 More Regrouping
243 Add 2-Digit Numbers
245 More Adding 2-Digit Numbers
247 Add to Solve Problems
249 **Problem-Solving Strategy** Use Estimation
251 **Midchapter Review**
252 **Extra Practice Game!** Get to the Fair!
253 **Real-Life Investigation:** Applying Addition Patch Patterns
255 Check Addition
257 **Extra Practice Game!** Score 10
259 Add Money *Explore Activity*
261 More Adding Money
263 **Problem Solvers at Work** Choose the Method

265 **Chapter Review**
267 **Chapter Test**
268 **Performance Assessment • What Did You Learn?**
269 **Math Connection • Patterns and Functions**
270 **Technology Connection • Computer**
271 **Home Connection**

8 Animals on the Move

272 Subtracting 2-Digit Numbers

274 **What Do You Know?**
275 Regrouping *Explore Activity*
277 More Regrouping *Explore Activity*
279 Subtract 2-Digit Numbers
281 More Subtracting 2-Digit Numbers
283 Subtract to Solve Problems
285 **Extra Practice Game!** Blackbird, Fly!
287 **Problem-Solving Strategy** Make a List
289 **Midchapter Review**
290 **Extra Practice Game!** Fly South to Mexico!
291 **Real-Life Investigation:** Applying Subtraction Bird Count
293 Subtract Money *Explore Activity*
295 **Extra Practice Game!** Catch the Salmon!
297 Check Subtraction

299 Add or Subtract to Solve Problems
301 **Problem Solvers at Work** Identify Extra Information

303 **Chapter Review**
305 **Chapter Test**
306 **Performance Assessment • What Did You Learn?**
307 **Math Connection • Calculator**
308 **Curriculum Connection • Science**
309 **Home Connection**

9 Shapes in Art

310 Geometry and Fractions
312 **What Do You Know?**
313 Cubes *Explore Activity*
315 3-Dimensional Shapes
317 2-Dimensional Shapes
319 Congruent Shapes *Explore Activity*
321 Symmetry *Explore Activity*
323 **Problem-Solving Strategy** Use a Pattern
325 **Midchapter Review**
326 **Extra Practice Activity** Tangram Shapes
327 **Real-Life Investigation:**
Applying Geometry **Cover-Up Game**
329 Halves, Fourths, and Thirds *Explore Activity*
331 Fractions *Explore Activity*
333 More Fractions
335 Fraction of a Group
337 **Problem Solvers at Work** Draw a Picture

339 **Chapter Review**
341 **Chapter Test**
342 **Performance Assessment • What Did You Learn?**
343 **Math Connection • Probability**
344 **Technology Connection • Computer**
345 **Cumulative Review**
347 **Home Connection**

10 Mapping Adventures

348 Measurement
350 **What Do You Know?**
351 Measuring Length *Explore Activity*
353 Inch and Foot

355 Centimeter
357 Perimeter *Explore Activity*
359 Area *Explore Activity*
361 **Problem-Solving Strategy** Draw a Diagram
363 **Midchapter Review**
364 **Extra Practice Game!** Scavenger Hunt
365 **Real-Life Investigation:**
     Applying Measurement Make a Map
367 Pound *Explore Activity*
369 Kilogram *Explore Activity*
371 Cup, Pint, Quart *Explore Activity*
373 Liter *Explore Activity*
375 Temperature
377 Measurement Tools
379 **Problem Solvers at Work** Reasonable Answers
381 **Chapter Review**
383 **Chapter Test**
384 **Performance Assessment • What Did You Learn?**
385 **Math Connection • Graphing**
386 **Technology Connection • Computer**
387 **Home Connection**

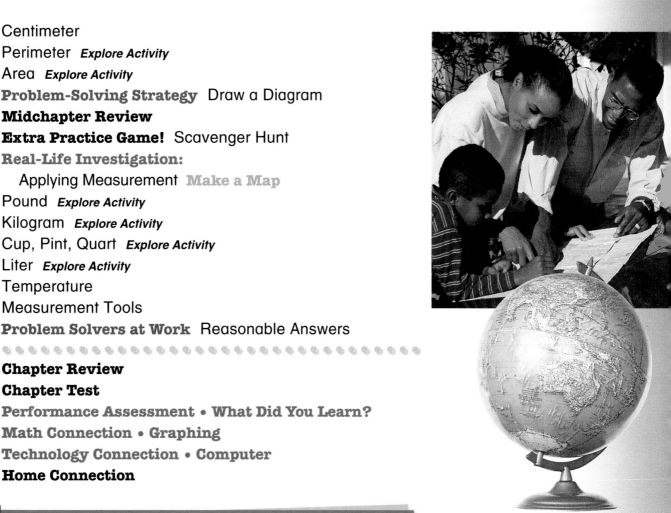

11 Math and Music

388 Numbers to 1,000 — Adding and
     Subtracting
390 **What Do You Know?**
391 Hundreds *Explore Activity*
393 Hundreds, Tens, and Ones *Explore Activity*
395 Place Value
397 Value of a Digit *Explore Activity*
399 **Extra Practice Game!** What's My Number?
401 Order to 1,000
403 Before, After, Between
405 Compare Numbers to 1,000 *Explore Activity*
407 **Extra Practice Game!** Get to the Concert!
409 **Midchapter Review**
410 **Extra Practice Game!** Comparing Cards
411 **Real-Life Investigation:**
     Applying Numbers A Music Tour
413 Regrouping for Addition *Explore Activity*
415 Add 3-Digit Numbers
417 More Adding 3-Digit Numbers

419 **Extra Practice Game!** Reach 999!

421 Regrouping for Subtraction *Explore Activity*

423 Subtract 3-Digit Numbers

425 More Subtracting 3-Digit Numbers

427 **Extra Practice Activity** Subtraction Action

429 **Problem-Solving Strategy** Solve a Simpler Problem

431 Add and Subtract Money

433 **Problem Solvers at Work** Choose the Method

435 **Chapter Review**

437 **Chapter Test**

438 **Performance Assessment • What Did You Learn?**

439 **Math Connection • Calculator**

440 **Curriculum Connection • Social Studies**

441 **Home Connection**

12 Vegetables

442 Exploring Multiplication and Division

444 **What Do You Know?**

445 Multiplication *Explore Activity*

447 Multiply by 1, 2, and 3 *Explore Activity*

449 Multiply by 4 and 5 *Explore Activity*

451 Multiplication Patterns *Explore Activity*

453 **Extra Practice Activity** Oh, Beans!

455 **Problem-Solving Strategy** Make a Table

457 **Midchapter Review**

458 **Extra Practice Game!** Multiplication Table

459 **Real-Life Investigation:**
    Applying Multiplication Plan a Garden

461 How Many Groups? *Explore Activity*

463 How Many in Each Group? *Explore Activity*

465 **Extra Practice Activity** Divide and Counters

467 **Problem Solvers at Work** Use Models

469 **Chapter Review**

471 **Chapter Test**

472 **Performance Assessment • What Did You Learn?**

473 **Math Connection • Algebra**

474 **Curriculum Connection • Health**

475 **Cumulative Review**

477 **Home Connection**

479 **Picture Glossary**

Math in my World

Welcome to your new math book!

This year you will learn about many ways to use math in your world.

How many in each bunch?

How long to bake?

How many letters?

At Home

Dear Family,

We are beginning the first chapter in our new mathematics book. During the next few weeks we will be learning to use strategies to add and subtract.

We will also be talking about rain forests and the animals and plants that live in them. Please help me complete this interview.

Your child,

_____
Signature

Interview ....

Which rain forests are you interested in?
(You may check more than one.)

❑ South American   ❑ Southeast Asian
❑ African   ❑ Central American

❑ Other _____

Do you use any products that are made of materials grown in a rain forest?
(Please list any products that you can think of, such as rubber and Brazil nuts.)

_____

_____

In the Rain Forest
Understanding Addition and Subtraction

Listen Listen to the story
In the Rain Forest.

Talk Tell what you know
about rain forests.

3

What Do You Know?

You need 10 ⬤.
Show each number with ⬤.
Draw to show how many ⬤.
Write how many in all.

5	3

_____ in all

Show this number with ⬤.
Draw to show ⬤. Cross out 3 of them.
Write how many are left.

7

_____ left

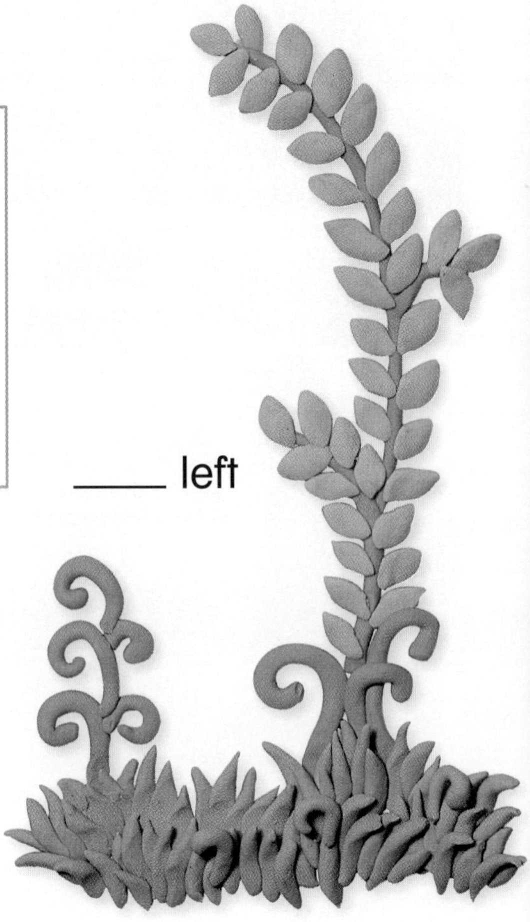

Portfolio

Show different ways to add to find how many ⬤ in all.

Show different ways to subtract to find how many ⬤ are left.

Working Together

You and your partner need 10 .
Take turns.

▶ Make a cube train for the total.

▶ Snap it into 2 parts.

▶ Write how many in each part.

▶ Find all the parts for the total.

TOTAL 3	
3	0
2	1

TOTAL 4	

TOTAL 5	

TOTAL 6	

 Critical Thinking Look at the total 6. How are the parts the same? How are they different?

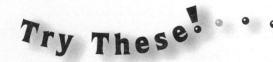

Find all the parts for the total.

Try using patterns.

TOTAL 10	
10	0
9	1

TOTAL 9	

TOTAL 8	

TOTAL 7	

Talk about the patterns you see.

We found all the parts for totals. Ask your child to name parts for 11.

Midchapter Review

Do your best!

Add.

1  $3 + 4 = $ ___

2 $4 + 2 = $ ___

3 $5 + 4 = $ ___

4
$$\begin{array}{r} 8 \\ + 3 \\ \hline \end{array}$$

5
$$\begin{array}{r} 9 \\ + 1 \\ \hline \end{array}$$

6
$$\begin{array}{r} 7 \\ + 5 \\ \hline \end{array} \qquad \begin{array}{r} 5 \\ + 7 \\ \hline \end{array}$$

7
$$\begin{array}{r} 3 \\ + 6 \\ \hline \end{array} \qquad \begin{array}{r} 6 \\ + 3 \\ \hline \end{array}$$

Workspace

Solve.

8 6 frogs are on one tree branch.
4 frogs are on another branch.
How many frogs are in the tree?

_____ frogs

9 There were 5 toucans in a tree.
7 more toucans came along.
How many toucans are there in all?

_____ toucans

10 How did you use a strategy to solve problem 9?

_____

_____

 What are some ways to use addition?

Rain Forest Climb

Climb the tree with your partner.

▶ Start at **Ground.**

▶ Write a fact for each sum.

▶ When you get to the top, check each other's work.

▶ The first player to reach the top with no mistakes is the winner.

Climb again.

Climb 1

Climb 2

12

11

10

9

8

7

6

5

4

Ground

Name _____

Rain to Grow On

A rain forest can get more than 400 inches of rain in one year.

Many plants grow very large in the rain forest. This flower is about 2 feet across.

 Talk Why do you think plants grow so large in the rain forest?

Working Together

Find out what plants need to grow.

Put soil in two cups. Label them.　　**Plant a seed in each cup. Water them.**　　**Place the cups in a sunny place.**　　**Water cup A each day.**

 Talk What do you think will happen?

▶ Measure how big the plant grows each week for three weeks.

▶ Show the data on a chart.

GROWTH OF PLANTS	
Cup A	Cup B
Week 1	
Week 2	
Week 3	

Decision Making

1 Decide how to measure your plants. Explain your method.

2 How much did the plant in cup A grow during

week 1? _____ week 2? _____ week 3? _____

3 How much did the plant in each cup grow altogether?

Cup A: _____

Cup B: _____

Write a report.

4 Tell what you learned about plants and water.

5 Tell how you found how much the plants grew each week.

More to Investigate

PREDICT Can a plant grow without light?

EXPLORE Plant more seeds. Water the seeds each day. Put one cup in a sunny place. Put one cup in a dark place.

FIND Find the total growth for each plant after three weeks. Then compare.

Rambling River

You and a partner need 2  and 2 ⬤ .

Take turns.

▶ Spin both 🔘. Find the difference.

▶ Move that many spaces.

▶ Play until someone reaches **Camp.**

Play again.

Subtract.

1
   6   10   12   8   9   5
  – 3   – 9   – 5   – 8   – 0   – 3
   3

2
   7   10   8
  – 0   – 1   – 4

3
  11   6   10
  – 3   – 6   – 6

4
   6   11   12
  – 4   – 5   – 3

Cultural Note
Rain-forest children in Mexico learn at a young age how to gather food to eat.

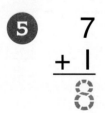

Add.

5
   7   6   2   3   9   5
  + 1   + 5   + 4   + 6   + 0   + 4
   8

6
   2   5   3   2   7   8
  + 1   + 2   + 9   + 7   + 4   + 2

7
   4   1   8   3   3   4
  + 0   + 9   + 1   + 2   + 7   + 8

Name _____

Write a Subtraction Sentence

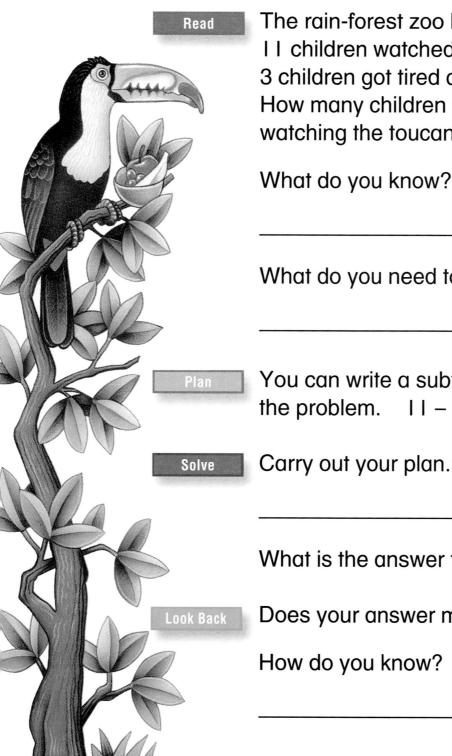

Read | Read | Plan | Solve | Look Back

Read

The rain-forest zoo has a big toucan.
11 children watched the bird eat.
3 children got tired and left.
How many children are still
watching the toucan?

What do you know? _____

_____

What do you need to find out? _____

_____

Plan

You can write a subtraction sentence to solve
the problem.   11 – 3 = ■

Solve

Carry out your plan.

_____

What is the answer to the problem? _____

Look Back

Does your answer make sense? _____

How do you know? _____

_____

_____

_____

Write a subtraction sentence to show your thinking. Solve.

Workspace

1 Rita had 9 animal crackers left after lunch.
She gave 3 crackers to Jesse.
How many crackers does Rita have now?

9 – 3 = 6

_____ crackers

2 8 children got on the zoo train.
3 children got off at the first stop.
How many children are left on the train?

_____ children

3 Greg bought 10 rain-forest stickers.
He gave 2 stickers to Lily.
How many stickers does Greg still have?

_____ stickers

4 12 friends went to the bird show.
3 left early. The rest stayed.
How many of the friends stayed at
the show?

_____ friends

At
Home

We used subtraction sentences to solve problems. You may
want to have your child make up his or her own problems.

Read to Understand

Read
Plan
Solve
Look Back

Nino plans to take a trip to the rain forest.

1 Read the problem.

Nino packs 8 T-shirts.
He packs 6 pairs of shorts.
Does he pack more shorts or T-shirts?

What do you need to find out? _____

_____

 Can you add or subtract to solve? Explain.

Does Nino pack more shorts or T-shirts? _____

Solve.

2 3 boys and 5 girls will go on the trip.
How many children will go on the trip?   ____ children

3 I boy decides to stay home.
Now how many children will go on the trip?   ____ children

 How did you solve problems 2 and 3?

Try These!

Solve.

1 Nino saw 6 toucans on Monday.
He also saw 2 red parrots.
How many birds did Nino see? _____ birds

2 What if Nino also saw 3
green parrots. How many
birds would he have seen in all? _____ birds

Write and Share

Jessica wrote this problem.

One day Sasha, Victoria, and Jenny went fishing. Sasha caught 7 fish. Victoria caught 6 fish. Jenny caught 5 fish. How many fish did they catch altogether?

Jessica Stranger
Hawthorne School
Indianapolis,
Indiana

3 Solve Jessica's problem. _____

What strategy did you choose? _____

_____

4 Write a new question for Jessica's
problem. Have a partner answer it.

Use your own paper.

What strategy did your partner use? _____

What strategy would you use? _____

 At Home Ask your child to tell you about the new
question he or she wrote for problem 4.

Chapter Review

Add.

1 ▢▢▢▢▢ $4 + 1 =$ _____

2 ▢▢▢▢▢▢ $3 + 4 =$ _____

3 ▢▢▢▢▢▢▢▢▢▢ $5 + 5 =$ _____

4 $5 + 2 =$ _____

5 $7 + 3 =$ _____

6 $3 + 1 =$ _____

7 $\begin{array}{r} 6 \\ + 5 \\ \hline \end{array}$

8 $\begin{array}{r} 6 \\ + 4 \\ \hline \end{array}$

9 $\begin{array}{r} 6 \\ + 3 \\ \hline \end{array}$

10 $\begin{array}{r} 7 \\ + 5 \\ \hline \end{array}$ $\begin{array}{r} 5 \\ + 7 \\ \hline \end{array}$

Subtract.

11 ▢▢▢▢▢▢▢▢ $8 - 3 =$ _____

12 ▢▢▢▢▢▢▢ $7 - 5 =$ _____

13 ▢▢▢▢▢▢▢▢▢ $9 - 4 =$ _____

14 $9 - 1 =$ _____

15 $12 - 3 =$ _____

16 $5 - 1 =$ _____

17 $\begin{array}{r} 10 \\ - 7 \\ \hline \end{array}$

18 $\begin{array}{r} 10 \\ - 6 \\ \hline \end{array}$

19 $\begin{array}{r} 10 \\ - 5 \\ \hline \end{array}$

20 $\begin{array}{r} 11 \\ - 3 \\ \hline \end{array}$ $\begin{array}{r} 11 \\ - 8 \\ \hline \end{array}$

Write an addition or subtraction sentence. Solve.

21 Len found 8 little frogs.
He found 3 big frogs.
How many frogs did Len find?

_____

_____ frogs

22 Ann saw 3 red birds.
She saw 9 green birds.
How many birds did Ann see?

_____

_____ birds

23 Lily bought 10 cards.
She gave 2 cards away.
How many cards does Lily have now?

_____

_____ cards

24 Nino had 12 crackers.
He ate 3 crackers.
How many crackers does Nino have left?

_____

_____ crackers

25 Kim put 6 buttons on her hat.
She put 5 buttons on her shirt.
Did she put more buttons on her hat or on her shirt?

_____

What Do You Think?

Which strategy would you use to add 9 + 2?
☑ Check one.

☐ Patterns ☐ Number line ☐ Counting on ☐ 2 + 9

Why? _____

Journal Write a list of ways you add and subtract.

Chapter Test

Add.

1

$$6 + 6 = \underline{\hspace{1cm}}$$

2

$$4 + 5 = \underline{\hspace{1cm}}$$

3
$$\begin{array}{r} 5 \\ + 6 \\ \hline \end{array}$$

4
$$\begin{array}{r} 4 \\ + 8 \\ \hline \end{array}$$

Subtract.

5

$$9 - 0 = \underline{\hspace{1cm}}$$

6

$$12 - 5 = \underline{\hspace{1cm}}$$

7
$$\begin{array}{r} 11 \\ - 6 \\ \hline \end{array}$$

8
$$\begin{array}{r} 10 \\ - 8 \\ \hline \end{array}$$

Write an addition sentence or subtraction sentence. Solve.

9 Ned saw 6 birds. Then he saw 4 more birds. How many birds did Ned see?

_____

_____ birds

10 Maria had 12 cookies. She ate 4 of them. How many cookies does Maria have left?

_____

_____ cookies

Performance Assessment

What Did You Learn?

2 groups joining

1. Write an addition sentence to show how many in all. _____

2. Write an addition word problem for the picture.

_____

_____

_____

I group leaving

3. Write a subtraction sentence to show how many are left. _____

4. Write a subtraction word problem for the picture.

_____

_____

_____

 You may want to put this page in your portfolio.

40 • forty

Name _____

Number Race

You and your partner need 2 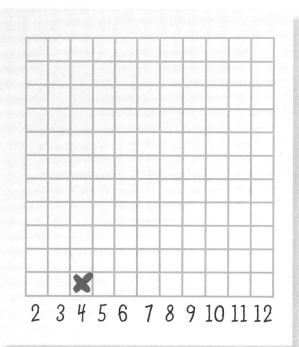 and a graph form.

Take turns.

▶ Roll the number cubes. Add.

▶ Mark an X to show the sum.

▶ Play until one sum reaches the top of the graph.

Predict the winning sum. _____

Now play.

 Talk Why did you get one or two sums more than the others?

1 When you roll a pair of number cubes, which sums are **most likely** to show?

_____

2 When you roll a pair of number cubes, which sums are **least likely** to show?

_____

3 Which sums will **never** show when you roll a pair of number cubes?

_____

Count Back

Sing this song from Puerto Rico.

Ten Puppies
(Diez Perritos)

1. Oh, I used to have ten pup - pies,
   Yo te - ní - a diez pe - rri - tos,
   yō te nế ä dyes pe rế tōs

Oh, I used to have ten pup - pies;
Yo te - ní - a diez pe - rri - tos;
yō te nế ä dyes pe rế tōs

One fell in the snow so fine,
U - no se ca yó en la nie - ve
oố nō sä kä yố en lä nyế ve

Leav - ing me with on - ly nine.
ya - no mas me que dan nue - ve.
yä nō màs mä kấ dän nooế ve

Write a number sentence to
show what happened to the puppies. _____

If one more puppy goes away,
how many puppies will be left? _____ puppies

Name

Tic-Tac-Toe Sums

PLAYERS   2

MATERIALS   game markers in two colors

DIRECTIONS   Each player chooses a color. The first player puts a marker on a number and names an addition fact for that sum. Then the other player takes a turn.

The winner is the first player to cover three numbers across, down, or diagonally.

7	9	6
5	2	1
8	3	4

At Home   Play this game to practice addition facts to 9. To practice subtraction facts, your child names a subtraction fact with that number as the difference.

Dear Family,

We are beginning another chapter in our mathematics book. During the next few weeks we will be learning new strategies for adding and subtracting and for solving problems.

We will also be talking about pen pals and writing letters. Please help me complete this interview.

Your child,

_____
Signature

Interview

To whom do you like to write letters?
(You may check more than one.)

❑ Family   ❑ Pen pal   ❑ Friends

❑ Other _____

What kinds of letters do you like to get?

_____

_____

Have you ever received a postcard from another country? If so, from where?

_____

_____

Pen Pals
Addition and Subtraction Strategies

 Listen to the story
Dear Mr. Blueberry.

 Tell about letters you write
or want to write.

What Do You Know?

Solve.

1 Nick wrote 9 letters to his pen pals.
He forgot to mail 2 of the letters.
How many letters did Nick mail? _____

Show or write about how you
solved the problem.

_____

_____

2 Lily got 3 letters last month.
She got 6 letters this month.
Did she get more than 10
letters or fewer than 10 letters? _____

Show or write about how you
solved the problem.

_____

_____

Write a word problem that uses
addition or subtraction.
Show how to solve your problem.

Name _____

Working Together

You and your partner need 9  and 9 .
Take turns.

► Make a **doubles** fact with cubes.

► Your partner adds 1 more cube.

► Record the facts.

	Double	Double Plus One
1	6 + 6 = 12	6 + 7 = 13
2	___ + ___ = ___	___ + ___ = ___
3	___ + ___ = ___	___ + ___ = ___
4	___ + ___ = ___	___ + ___ = ___
5	___ + ___ = ___	___ + ___ = ___
6	___ + ___ = ___	___ + ___ = ___
7	___ + ___ = ___	___ + ___ = ___
8	___ + ___ = ___	___ + ___ = ___
9	___ + ___ = ___	___ + ___ = ___

 Critical Thinking How can you find the sum of 10 + 11?

Try These!

Add.

1

$$\begin{array}{r} 5 \\ + 6 \\ \hline 11 \end{array}$$

Think: 5 + 5 = 10

2

$$\begin{array}{r} 3 \\ + 4 \\ \hline 7 \end{array}$$

Think: 3 + 3 = 6

3

$$\begin{array}{r} 8 \\ + 7 \\ \hline \end{array} \qquad \begin{array}{r} 6 \\ + 6 \\ \hline \end{array} \qquad \begin{array}{r} 2 \\ + 1 \\ \hline \end{array} \qquad \begin{array}{r} 8 \\ + 8 \\ \hline \end{array} \qquad \begin{array}{r} 4 \\ + 5 \\ \hline \end{array} \qquad \begin{array}{r} 3 \\ + 3 \\ \hline \end{array}$$

4

$$\begin{array}{r} 7 \\ + 6 \\ \hline \end{array} \qquad \begin{array}{r} 2 \\ + 2 \\ \hline \end{array} \qquad \begin{array}{r} 9 \\ + 8 \\ \hline \end{array} \qquad \begin{array}{r} 5 \\ + 5 \\ \hline \end{array} \qquad \begin{array}{r} 2 \\ + 3 \\ \hline \end{array} \qquad \begin{array}{r} 4 \\ + 4 \\ \hline \end{array}$$

5

$$\begin{array}{r} 4 \\ + 3 \\ \hline \end{array} \qquad \begin{array}{r} 7 \\ + 7 \\ \hline \end{array} \qquad \begin{array}{r} 6 \\ + 5 \\ \hline \end{array} \qquad \begin{array}{r} 1 \\ + 1 \\ \hline \end{array} \qquad \begin{array}{r} 7 \\ + 8 \\ \hline \end{array} \qquad \begin{array}{r} 6 \\ + 7 \\ \hline \end{array}$$

Mixed Review

6

$$\begin{array}{r} 7 \\ + 3 \\ \hline \end{array} \qquad \begin{array}{r} 2 \\ + 8 \\ \hline \end{array} \qquad \begin{array}{r} 4 \\ + 6 \\ \hline \end{array}$$

$$\begin{array}{r} 0 \\ + 9 \\ \hline \end{array} \qquad \begin{array}{r} 8 \\ + 2 \\ \hline \end{array} \qquad \begin{array}{r} 6 \\ + 4 \\ \hline \end{array}$$

At Home

We explored adding doubles-plus-one facts. Ask your child to name the doubles fact that helps find 6 + 7.

Name

Working Together

You and your partner need a ⊞ , ⊘ , and 18  .

▶ Show 9 yellow counters in a 10-frame.

▶ Spin. Show the number with red counters.

▶ Move 1 red counter to make a 10.

▶ Draw and record the addition.

	Draw	Addition Fact	Total
1		$9 + 6$	15
2			
3			
4			

McGraw-Hill School Division

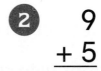

Add. Make a 10 if you forget a fact.

1   3
  + 9
  12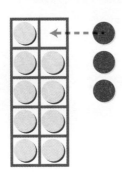

2   9
  + 5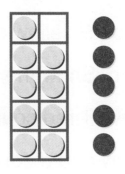

3

1	9	9	4	9	9
+ 9	+ 8	+ 3	+ 9	+ 7	+ 9

4

7	5	9	9	2	8
+ 9	+ 9	+ 6	+ 1	+ 9	+ 9

More to Explore   **Number Sense**

Another way to add with 9 is to think
of the 10 fact. Then find 1 less.

  9
+ 5

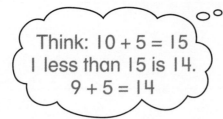

Think: 10 + 5 = 15
1 less than 15 is 14.
9 + 5 = 14

Add. Think of the 10 fact. Then find 1 less.

9	3	9	7	8	4
+ 8	+ 9	+ 6	+ 9	+ 9	+ 9

At Home — We learned a strategy for adding 9. Ask your
child to explain exercises 1 and 2 above.

Name _____

Abby has 7 stamps from Brazil.
Then she buys 5 more.
How many Brazilian stamps
does she have?

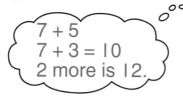

7 + 5
7 + 3 = 10
2 more is 12.

Abby has __12__ Brazilian stamps.

Draw arrows to make a 10. Add.

1 $8 + 3 = \underline{11}$

2 $7 + 4 = \underline{}$

3 $7 + 6 = \underline{}$

4 $9 + 6 = \underline{}$

5 $8 + 4 = \underline{}$

6 $8 + 6 = \underline{}$

 Critical Thinking How can you use mental math to find 8 plus 4?

McGraw-Hill School Division

Try These!

Add.

1
$$\begin{array}{r} 8 \\ +5 \\ \hline 13 \end{array}$$
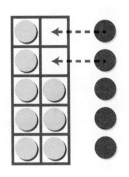

2
$$\begin{array}{r} 7 \\ +9 \\ \hline \end{array}$$
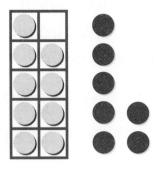

3
$$\begin{array}{r} 7 \\ +8 \\ \hline \end{array}$$
$$\begin{array}{r} 8 \\ +9 \\ \hline \end{array}$$
$$\begin{array}{r} 7 \\ +6 \\ \hline \end{array}$$
$$\begin{array}{r} 8 \\ +5 \\ \hline \end{array}$$
$$\begin{array}{r} 7 \\ +4 \\ \hline \end{array}$$
$$\begin{array}{r} 8 \\ +7 \\ \hline \end{array}$$

4
$$\begin{array}{r} 8 \\ +3 \\ \hline \end{array}$$
$$\begin{array}{r} 9 \\ +7 \\ \hline \end{array}$$
$$\begin{array}{r} 8 \\ +6 \\ \hline \end{array}$$
$$\begin{array}{r} 7 \\ +5 \\ \hline \end{array}$$
$$\begin{array}{r} 8 \\ +4 \\ \hline \end{array}$$
$$\begin{array}{r} 9 \\ +8 \\ \hline \end{array}$$

Solve.

Workspace

5 Sam sent 8 letters to her pen pal.
Then she sent 6 more.
How many letters did Sam
send in all? _____ letters

6 Ty bought 4 flag stamps.
He bought 9 bird stamps.
How many stamps did he buy?

_____ stamps

Journal Write 7 + 5 = ? Write about the strategy
you used to find the sum.

At Home We solved addition facts by making a 10. Have
your child explain how to find 8 + 6.

2   8   2

You can find out how many cards Miko has.

 Talk Which addition strategies could you use?

$$
\begin{array}{r}
2 \\
8 \\
+\,2
\end{array}
$$
10   Look for a 10 fact.   or
$$
\begin{array}{r}
2 \\
8 \\
+\,2
\end{array}
$$
4   Look for a double.

$10 + 2 = 12$ $4 + 8 = 12$

How many cards does Miko have? __12__

Add.

1

$$
\begin{array}{r}
1 \\
3 \\
+\,7 \\
\hline
11
\end{array}
$$
10

$$
\begin{array}{r}
5 \\
4 \\
+\,1
\end{array}
$$

$$
\begin{array}{r}
9 \\
2 \\
+\,2
\end{array}
$$

$$
\begin{array}{r}
8 \\
3 \\
+\,0
\end{array}
$$

$$
\begin{array}{r}
3 \\
3 \\
+\,2
\end{array}
$$

2

$$
\begin{array}{r}
3 \\
7 \\
1 \\
+\,1 \\
\hline
12
\end{array}
$$
10   2

$$
\begin{array}{r}
1 \\
2 \\
2 \\
+\,8
\end{array}
$$

$$
\begin{array}{r}
2 \\
4 \\
1 \\
+\,6
\end{array}
$$

$$
\begin{array}{r}
0 \\
3 \\
3 \\
+\,5
\end{array}
$$

$$
\begin{array}{r}
7 \\
4 \\
3 \\
+\,4
\end{array}
$$

 Critical Thinking Why is it easier to use a strategy than just to add the numbers in order?

Try These!

Add.

1

$$\begin{array}{r} 8 \\ 3 \\ +\ 1 \\ \hline 12 \end{array}$$

> 11 (Count on.)

2

$$\begin{array}{r} 6 \\ 3 \\ 3 \\ +\ 4 \end{array}$$

> 6 > 10 (Use doubles and look for a 10 fact.)

3

$$\begin{array}{r} 3 \\ 1 \\ +\ 2 \\ \hline \end{array}$$
$$\begin{array}{r} 4 \\ 8 \\ +\ 0 \\ \hline \end{array}$$
$$\begin{array}{r} 3 \\ 4 \\ +\ 3 \\ \hline \end{array}$$
$$\begin{array}{r} 9 \\ 0 \\ +\ 7 \\ \hline \end{array}$$
$$\begin{array}{r} 5 \\ 5 \\ +\ 5 \\ \hline \end{array}$$
$$\begin{array}{r} 7 \\ 3 \\ +\ 2 \\ \hline \end{array}$$

4

$$\begin{array}{r} 4 \\ 4 \\ 4 \\ +\ 4 \\ \hline \end{array}$$
$$\begin{array}{r} 3 \\ 0 \\ 8 \\ +\ 2 \\ \hline \end{array}$$
$$\begin{array}{r} 2 \\ 3 \\ 5 \\ +\ 5 \\ \hline \end{array}$$
$$\begin{array}{r} 1 \\ 2 \\ 0 \\ +\ 8 \\ \hline \end{array}$$
$$\begin{array}{r} 5 \\ 1 \\ 1 \\ +\ 5 \\ \hline \end{array}$$
$$\begin{array}{r} 3 \\ 7 \\ 3 \\ +\ 3 \\ \hline \end{array}$$

Cultural Connection — Chinese Magic Squares

Magic squares were used in China long ago.
Numbers are added in any direction.
The sum is always the same.

Complete the magic square.

What is the sum? _____

5	6	
0	4	
	2	3

Name _____

Add.

Do your best!

1   9
   + 9

2   5
   + 6

3   7
   + 9

4   8
   + 5

5   9
     1
   + 3

6   2
     5
   + 7

7   3
     0
     2
   + 2

8   4
     3
     3
   + 4

Solve.

Workspace

9 Tara mailed 9 letters.
Then she mailed 5 more letters.
How many letters did Tara mail?

_____ letters

10 How did you add for exercise 8?

_____

_____

_____

What are different strategies for adding?
Which do you like best? Why?

Mailbox Drop

You and your partner need 2  .

Take turns.

▶ Drop both  on the mailboxes.

▶ Add the two numbers.

▶ Find the sum below and write the addition under it.

▶ Play until you get all the sums.

8	9	10	11

12	13	14	15

16	17	18

Name

What's in the Mail?

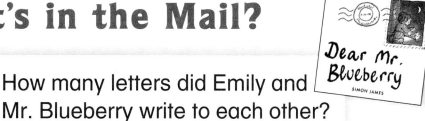

Listen How many letters did Emily and Mr. Blueberry write to each other? Listen to *Dear Mr. Blueberry.*

Do you know how much mail comes to your home?

▶ Sort the mail with your family for 2 days.

▶ Write the numbers for each day.

FAMILY MAIL CHART						
	Magazines	**Cards and Letters**	**Catalogs**	**Newspapers**	**Other**	**Total**
Day 1						
Day 2						
Total						

▶ Find the total for each day.

▶ Find the total for each kind of mail.

1 Which kind of mail did your family get most? _____

2 Which kind of mail did your family get least? _____

3 How much mail did your family get in 2 days? _____ pieces

Talk What can you tell from the **data** you collected?

Decision Making

1 Decide what kind of chart or graph to make to display the class's data. Make it.

 Talk Look at the class display. What do you notice about the totals for each kind of mail?

 Portfolio

Write a report.

2 Tell how you sorted and counted your family's mail.

3 Tell how the totals in your chart compare with the totals in the class chart.

More to Investigate

PREDICT How many pieces of mail will come to your home over 7 days?

EXPLORE Try it. Sort and count the mail with your family for 5 more days. Find the new total for each kind of mail.

FIND How did the data change over 7 days? What patterns do you see?

Working Together

You and your partner need 9  and 9 ⬛.

Take turns.

▶ Show a doubles fact with cubes.

▶ Your partner snaps the cubes into 2 equal parts.

▶ Record the facts.

Addition	Subtraction
1	$\underline{3} + \underline{3} = \underline{6}$	$\underline{6} - \underline{3} = \underline{3}$
2	___ + ___ = ___	___ − ___ = ___
3	___ + ___ = ___	___ − ___ = ___
4	___ + ___ = ___	___ − ___ = ___
5	___ + ___ = ___	___ − ___ = ___
6	___ + ___ = ___	___ − ___ = ___
7	___ + ___ = ___	___ − ___ = ___
8	___ + ___ = ___	___ − ___ = ___
9	___ + ___ = ___	___ − ___ = ___

Try These!

Solve.

1 Clint got 4 letters on Monday.
He got 4 letters on Tuesday.
How many letters did he get in all?

___8___ letters

$$\begin{array}{r} 4 \\ +4 \\ \hline 8 \end{array}$$

2 4 of Clint's letters were from
his pen pals. How many
were not from his pen pals?

_____ letters

3 Mindy bought 6 postcards.
She also bought 6 birthday cards.
How many cards did she buy?

_____ cards

4 Mindy mailed 6 of the cards
she bought. How many cards
does she have left?

_____ cards

5 Ming has 8 stamps. He buys
8 more. How many stamps
does Ming have now?

_____ stamps

6 Write a subtraction problem
about Ming.

_____

_____

At Home — We learned to use doubles to subtract. Ask your child to tell about the problem he or she wrote.

Count Up to Subtract

Sam put 9 pictures in his book.
The book can hold 12 pictures.
How many more pictures can
go into the book?

You can **count up** to subtract.
Start at 9. Count up to 12.

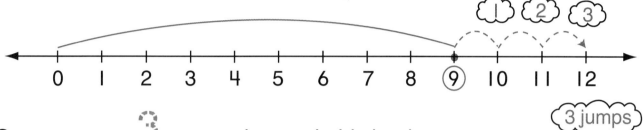

1 2 3

0 1 2 3 4 5 6 7 8 ⑨ 10 11 12

3 jumps

Sam can put __3__ more pictures in his book.

Subtract. Use the number line if you want.

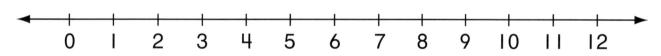

0 1 2 3 4 5 6 7 8 9 10 11 12

1 $11 - 8 =$ __3__ 〔9, 10, 11〕 $9 - 7 =$ __2__ 〔8, 9〕

2 $8 - 5 =$ ___ $10 - 8 =$ ___

3
$$
\begin{array}{cccccc}
7 & 9 & 8 & 11 & 9 & 8 \\
-5 & -6 & -6 & -9 & -8 & -7 \\
\end{array}
$$

4
$$
\begin{array}{cccccc}
10 & 7 & 5 & 10 & 6 & 7 \\
-9 & -4 & -4 & -7 & -5 & -6 \\
\end{array}
$$

Critical Thinking When would you count up to subtract?

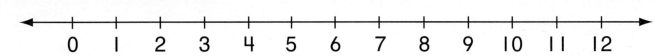

$$0 \quad 1 \quad 2 \quad 3 \quad 4 \quad 5 \quad 6 \quad 7 \quad 8 \quad 9 \quad 10 \quad 11 \quad 12$$

Subtract.
Count up if you forget a fact.

1

11	10	9	7	8	11
$-\ 9$	$-\ 9$	$-\ 6$	$-\ 5$	$-\ 7$	$-\ 8$
2					

2

12	4	7	10	5	9
$-\ 9$	$-\ 2$	$-\ 6$	$-\ 8$	$-\ 3$	$-\ 7$

3

5	10	8	6	9	7
$-\ 4$	$-\ 7$	$-\ 6$	$-\ 4$	$-\ 8$	$-\ 4$

Mixed Review

Add or subtract.

4

10	3	0	6	6	8
$-\ 3$	$+\ 1$	$+\ 8$	$-\ 3$	$+\ 3$	$-\ 5$

5

5	1	9	7	8	3
$+\ 2$	$+\ 7$	$-\ 4$	$-\ 0$	$-\ 4$	$+\ 3$

At Home We learned how to count up to subtract. Have your child explain how to count up to solve 10 − 8.

Subtract 9

Karen and her class wrote 15 letters to a pen-pal class in Canada. The pen pals wrote 9 letters. How many more letters did Karen and her class write?

Show 15. Subtract 9.

5 and 1 more is 6.

Karen and her class wrote ___6___ more letters than the pen pals.

Cross out to show how to subtract 9.

1
$$12 \atop \underline{-\ 9}$$
3

2
$$11 \atop \underline{-\ 9}$$

3
$$17 \atop \underline{-\ 9}$$
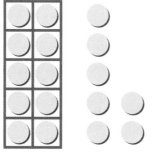

4
$$14 \atop \underline{-\ 9}$$
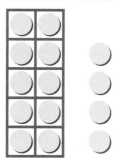

5
$$13 \atop \underline{-\ 9}$$
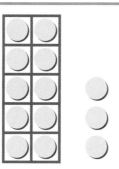

6
$$16 \atop \underline{-\ 9}$$
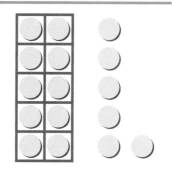

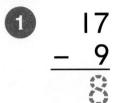

Try These!

Subtract. Use strategies if you need help.

1

17	12	10	14	18
− 9	− 9	− 9	− 9	− 9
8				

2

15	11	13	9	16
− 9	− 9	− 9	−9	− 9

Solve.

3 Cobb had 18 postcards.
He used 9 of them.
How many postcards does
he still have? _____ postcards

Workspace

4 Clara has to mail 16 cards.
She has 9 stamps.
How many more stamps
does she need? _____ stamps

5 Write a problem where you subtract 9.
Have a partner solve it.

_____

_____

Talk Tell how you solved your partner's problem.

At Home We studied subtracting 9. Talk with your child about how to solve the problem he or she wrote.

Subtraction Postcards

Use a pattern to find the differences.
Write about the pattern.

1

$13 - 4 = \underline{9}$

$13 - 5 = \underline{\hphantom{9}}$

$13 - 6 = \underline{\hphantom{9}}$

$13 - 7 = \underline{\hphantom{9}}$

$13 - 8 = \underline{\hphantom{9}}$

_____

_____

_____

_____

2

$13 - 4 = \underline{9}$

$14 - 5 = \underline{\hphantom{9}}$

$15 - 6 = \underline{\hphantom{9}}$

$16 - 7 = \underline{\hphantom{9}}$

$17 - 8 = \underline{\hphantom{9}}$

_____

_____

_____

_____

3

$15 - 9 = \underline{6}$

$15 - 8 = \underline{\hphantom{6}}$

$15 - 7 = \underline{\hphantom{6}}$

$15 - 6 = \underline{\hphantom{6}}$

_____

_____

_____

_____

Add.

1 9 + 6 = ___   5 + 9 = ___   9 + 7 = ___

2 8 + 5 = ___   7 + 5 = ___   6 + 8 = ___

3
```
  6       6       8       8       7       7
+ 7     + 6     + 9     + 8     + 8     + 7
```

4
```
  9       0       7       8       8       5
+ 8     + 8     + 9     + 7     + 6     + 8
```

Subtract.

5 17 – 9 = ___   12 – 9 = ___   16 – 9 = ___

6 11 – 8 = ___   14 – 7 = ___   17 – 8 = ___

7
```
 14      10      15      13      15       8
–  8     –  7    –  9    –  8    –  8     – 0
```

8
```
 16      13      15
–  7     –  5    –  7
```

9
```
 14      13      18
–  5     –  9    –  9
```

Cultural Note

The pony express delivered mail for only one year, from 1860 to 1861.

Name _____

Choose the Operation

Read Sal mailed 9 letters
He mailed 7 cards.
How many items did he mail?

Read
Plan
Solve
Look Back

Plan Add or subtract? $(9 + 7)$ $9 - 7$

Solve 16 items mailed.

Look Back Does your answer make sense? Yes.

Read A mail truck has 9 bags of mail.
7 bags are for the city.
How many bags are not for the city?

Plan Add or subtract? $9 + 7$ $9 - 7$

Solve _____ bags are not for the city.

Look Back Does your answer make sense? _____

Choose addition or subtraction. Solve.

1 Gary had 8 boxes to mail.
He mailed 5 of the boxes.
How many boxes still have
to be mailed?

$8 + 5$

$8 - 5$

_____ boxes

2 Ellie got 7 letters and 2 boxes
in the mail this week. How many
pieces of mail did Ellie get?

$7 + 2$

$7 - 2$

_____ pieces

Try These!

Choose addition or subtraction.
Solve.

1 Jenna gave birthday presents to 9 people.
She got 4 thank-you notes.
How many people did not send a note?

9 + 4

9 – 4

_____ people

2 May has 14 stamps.
She uses 8 of them.
How many stamps are left?

14 + 8

14 – 8

_____ stamps

3 Hank sent for 8 Yankees' autographs.
He sent for 6 Mets' autographs.
How many autographs did Hank send for?

8 + 6

8 – 6

_____ autographs

4 Justin wrote 7 letters.
His brother wrote 4 letters.
How many letters did they write in all?

7 + 4

7 – 4

_____ letters

5 Betsy wrote 11 letters.
Her brother wrote 8 letters.
How many more letters did Betsy write?

11 + 8

11 – 8

_____ letters

At Home

Today we decided whether to add or subtract to solve a problem. Ask
your child to explain how he or she solved problems 4 and 5 above.

Name _____

These are called **related facts.**

$6 + 8 = 14$ $14 - 8 = 6$

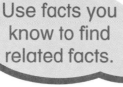
Use facts you know to find related facts.

Talk Why do you think these facts are related?

Add and subtract.

1
$8 + 9 = \underline{17}$
$17 - 9 = \underline{8}$

2
$9 + 7 = \underline{\quad}$
$16 - 7 = \underline{\quad}$

3
$0 + 8 = \underline{\quad}$
$8 - 8 = \underline{\quad}$

4
$9 + 9 = \underline{\quad}$
$18 - 9 = \underline{\quad}$

5
$8 + 8 = \underline{\quad}$
$16 - 8 = \underline{\quad}$

6
$6 + 9 = \underline{\quad}$
$15 - 9 = \underline{\quad}$

7
$7 + 4 = \underline{\quad}$
$11 - 4 = \underline{\quad}$

8
$5 + 9 = \underline{\quad}$
$14 - 9 = \underline{\quad}$

9
$7 + 6 = \underline{\quad}$
$13 - 6 = \underline{\quad}$

10
$9 + 6 = \underline{\quad}$
$15 - 6 = \underline{\quad}$

11
$5 + 7 = \underline{\quad}$
$12 - 7 = \underline{\quad}$

12
$8 + 5 = \underline{\quad}$
$13 - 5 = \underline{\quad}$

Critical Thinking Are $8 + 6$ and $8 - 6$ related facts? Why or why not?

Try These!

Add and subtract.
Then match the related facts.

1

$$7 + 8 = 15$$

$$11 - 6$$

$$9 + 4$$

$$15 - 8 = 7$$

$$5 + 6$$

$$13 - 5$$

$$9 + 7$$

$$16 - 7$$

$$8 + 5$$

$$13 - 4$$

2

$$6 + 6$$

$$17 - 8$$

$$8 + 6$$

$$12 - 6$$

$$9 + 8$$

$$14 - 6$$

$$7 + 3$$

$$13 - 7$$

$$6 + 7$$

$$10 - 3$$

More to Explore   Algebra Sense

Find the missing numbers.

$$16 - \boxed{8} = 8$$ $$11 - \boxed{} = 5$$ $$12 - \boxed{} = 4$$

$$8 + \boxed{} = 16$$ $$5 + \boxed{} = 11$$ $$4 + \boxed{} = 12$$

We learned about adding and subtracting related facts today.
Ask your child to give the related addition fact for $15 - 6 = 9$.

At Home

Name _____

Working Together

You and your partner need 9  and 9  .

▶ Make a two-color cube train.

▶ Color to show your train.

▶ Write 2 addition sentences and 2 subtraction sentences for the train.

$$6 + 5 = 11$$

$$5 + 6 = 11$$

$$11 - 5 = 6$$

$$11 - 6 = 5$$

These four facts make a **fact family.**

1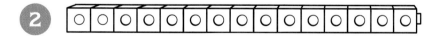

_____   _____

_____   _____

2

_____   _____

_____   _____

 Critical Thinking How many facts are in the 6 + 6 = 12 family? Why?

Complete the fact family.

1

$$
\begin{array}{r} 8 \\ + 2 \\ \hline 10 \end{array}
\qquad
\begin{array}{r} 2 \\ + 8 \\ \hline \end{array}
\qquad
\begin{array}{r} 10 \\ - 2 \\ \hline \end{array}
\qquad
\begin{array}{r} 10 \\ - 8 \\ \hline 8 \end{array}
$$

2
$$
\begin{array}{r} 9 \\ + 5 \\ \hline \end{array}
\qquad
\begin{array}{r} 5 \\ + 9 \\ \hline \end{array}
$$

$$
\begin{array}{r} 14 \\ - 5 \\ \hline \end{array}
\qquad
\begin{array}{r} 14 \\ - 9 \\ \hline \end{array}
$$

3
$$
\begin{array}{r} 7 \\ + 4 \\ \hline \end{array}
\qquad
\begin{array}{r} 4 \\ + 7 \\ \hline \end{array}
$$

$$
\begin{array}{r} 11 \\ - 4 \\ \hline \end{array}
\qquad
\begin{array}{r} 11 \\ - 7 \\ \hline \end{array}
$$

4
$$
\begin{array}{r} 8 \\ + 9 \\ \hline \end{array}
\qquad
\begin{array}{r} 9 \\ + 8 \\ \hline \end{array}
$$

$$
\begin{array}{r} 17 \\ - 9 \\ \hline \end{array}
\qquad
\begin{array}{r} 17 \\ - 8 \\ \hline \end{array}
$$

5
$$
\begin{array}{r} 4 \\ + 8 \\ \hline \end{array}
\qquad
\begin{array}{r} 8 \\ + 4 \\ \hline \end{array}
$$

$$
\begin{array}{r} 12 \\ - 8 \\ \hline \end{array}
\qquad
\begin{array}{r} 12 \\ - 4 \\ \hline \end{array}
$$

6
$$
\begin{array}{r} 8 \\ + 7 \\ \hline \end{array}
\qquad
\begin{array}{r} 7 \\ + 8 \\ \hline \end{array}
$$

$$
\begin{array}{r} 15 \\ - 7 \\ \hline \end{array}
\qquad
\begin{array}{r} 15 \\ - 8 \\ \hline \end{array}
$$

7
$$
\begin{array}{r} 7 \\ + 9 \\ \hline \end{array}
\qquad
\begin{array}{r} 9 \\ + 7 \\ \hline \end{array}
$$

$$
\begin{array}{r} 16 \\ - 9 \\ \hline \end{array}
\qquad
\begin{array}{r} 16 \\ - 7 \\ \hline \end{array}
$$

Write your own fact family.

8
$$
\begin{array}{r} \square \\ + \square \\ \hline \end{array}
\qquad
\begin{array}{r} \square \\ + \square \\ \hline \end{array}
\qquad
\begin{array}{r} \square \\ - \square \\ \hline \end{array}
\qquad
\begin{array}{r} \square \\ - \square \\ \hline \end{array}
$$

 What is a fact family?
How can it help you to add and subtract?

At Home — We learned about fact families. Have your child write the fact family for 7, 6, and 13.

Secret Message

▶ Add or subtract.

▶ Circle the facts that belong to each fact family.

▶ Write the letters in order for those facts. Use the letters to find the secret message.

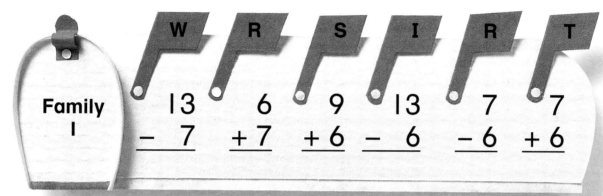

Family 1

W	R	S	I	R	T
13	6	9	13	7	7
− 7	+ 7	+ 6	− 6	− 6	+ 6

Family 2

E	T	P	E	N	T
8	8	14	6	14	14
+ 6	+ 8	− 6	+ 8	− 8	− 9

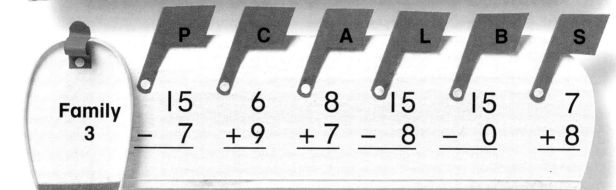

Family 3

P	C	A	L	B	S
15	6	8	15	15	7
− 7	+ 9	+ 7	− 8	− 0	+ 8

Message:

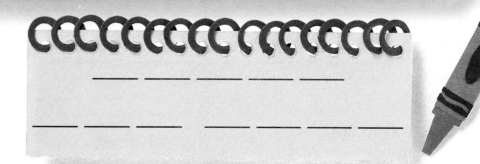

———— —— ——— ———

——— —— ———— ——————

Add or subtract.

1
9	16	8	18	5	13
+ 6	− 7	+ 8	− 9	+ 9	− 9
15					

2
8	17	9	14	5	15
+ 9	− 8	+ 9	− 9	+ 7	− 6

3
9	16	9	17	8	16
+ 8	− 9	+ 7	− 9	+ 5	− 8

Solve.

Workspace

4 Lucas sent 6 packages by mail boat. He sent 7 by airplane. How many packages did Lucas send?

_____ packages

5 Felix sent letters to 12 authors. Only 6 authors wrote back. How many authors did not write to Felix?

_____ authors

6 Sofia read 4 books one week. She read 9 books the next week. What was the total number of books Sofia read?

_____ books

Name _____

Choose a Strategy

Show how you solve this problem.

Jill made 15 cards.
Jack made 8 cards.
Who made more cards? _____

How many more cards? _____ cards

Explain your strategy. _____

_____

_____

Solve.

1 Corey asked 9 friends to his party.
Then he asked 5 more friends.
How many friends did Corey ask
to his party?   _____ friends

2 Alana has 7 cards to mail.
She has 4 boxes to mail.
Does she have more boxes
or cards to mail?   _____

Try These!

Solve.

1 Betty wrote 10 letters last month.
Ted wrote 8 letters last month.
Who wrote more letters? _____

How many more letters? _____

2 Luis packed 14 boxes today.
Tomorrow he has to pack 9 boxes.
How many more boxes did he
pack today than he will tomorrow? _____

Write and Share

Ashley wrote this problem.
I wrote 3 letters to Jessica in
July. I wrote 5 more in August.
How many letters did I
write in all?

Ashley Gruner
O'Rourke School
Mobile, Alabama

STUDENT TO STUDENT

3 Solve Ashley's problem. _____

What strategy did you choose? _____

_____

4 Write a problem about pen pals.
Have a partner solve it.

Use your own paper.

What strategy did your partner use? _____

 At Home — Ask your child to tell you about the problem he
or she wrote.

Name _____

Chapter Review

Add.

1　7
　　+ 8

2　9
　　+ 5

3　8
　　+ 9

4　7
　　+ 6

5　5
　　+ 8

6　9
　　+ 9

7　6
　　+ 8

8　9
　　+ 6

9　1
　　2
　+ 7

10　4
　　3
　+ 7

11　2
　　6
　　2
　+ 6

12　8
　　1
　　2
　+ 1

Subtract.

13　18
　　− 9

14　10
　　− 7

15　9
　　− 8

16　16
　　− 9

17　17
　　− 8

18　14
　　− 8

19　15
　　− 9

20　13
　　− 8

Solve.

21 Billy mailed 9 cards. He mailed 12 boxes.
Did Billy mail more cards or boxes? _____

How many more? _____

Choose addition or subtraction. Solve.

22 Ling bought 6 stamps.
Jen bought 8 stamps.
How many stamps do
they have in all?

$6 + 8$ ____ stamps

$8 - 6$

23 Jen had 9 boxes.
She mailed 3 boxes.
How many boxes does
she have left?

$9 + 3$ ____ boxes

$9 - 3$

Solve.

24 Lynn sent 15 letters.
Joe sent 9 letters.
How many more letters
did Lynn send than Joe?

____ letters

25 Rob got 4 postcards.
He also got 9 letters.
How many pieces of
mail did Rob get?

____ pieces of mail

What Do You Think?

Which strategy would you use to subtract $18 - 9$?
☑ Check one.

☐ Use doubles. ☐ Count up. ☐ Use a fact family. ☐ Subtract 9.

Why? _____

 Choose a fact family.
Write two word problems using two of the facts.

Chapter Test

Add.

1   7
    + 9

2   9
    + 8

3   1
       3
    + 6

4   3
       7
       6
    + 2

Subtract.

5   14
     − 9

6   10
     − 8

7   11
     − 7

8   17
     − 9

Choose addition or subtraction.
Solve.

9 Lu wrote 9 letters to Kim.
      She wrote 6 letters to Robin.
      How many more letters did she
      write to Kim than to Robin?

      _____ letters

      9 + 6

      9 − 6

---

10 George bought 9 postcards.
      He also bought 6 birthday cards.
      How many cards did George buy?

      _____ cards

      9 + 6

      9 − 6

What Did You Learn?

Make a train of 13 cubes.
Use two different colors.

Color to show the train you made.

Write two addition sentences for
the train you made.

_____

_____

Write two subtraction sentences for
the train you made.

_____

_____

Look at a partner's train.
How is it the same as your train?

How is it different? _____

_____

 You may want to put this page in your portfolio.

Name _____

Variables

You can use related facts to find ■.

$7 + ■ = 15$

$7 + 8 = 15$

Think: $15 - 7 = 8$
■ $= 8$

$■ - 9 = 4$

$13 - 9 = 4$

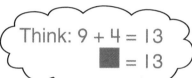
Think: $9 + 4 = 13$
■ $= 13$

Add or subtract.
Find the missing numbers.

1 | $■ + 6 = 12$ | $17 - ■ = 9$ | $5 + ■ = 12$
$6 + 6 = 12$
_____ | _____ | _____

2 | $9 + ■ = 10$ | $■ - 5 = 9$ | $8 + 6 = ■$
_____ | _____ | _____

3 | $16 - ■ = 8$ | $11 - 5 = ■$ | $■ + 8 = 8$
_____ | _____ | _____

Write your own.

4 _____ | _____

_____ | _____

Technology Connection
Computer

Picture a Problem

 Talk How can making a picture help you write and solve a problem?

The screen shows a picture made with counter stamps.

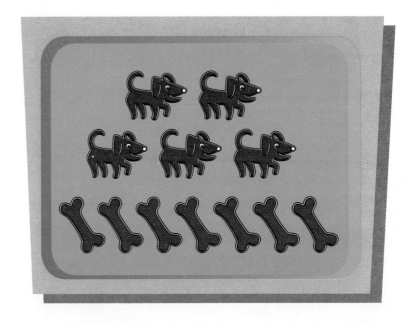

Use the picture to complete and solve.

Betsy has _____ dogs.

There are _____ bones.

How many more bones are there than dogs?   _____ bones

At the Computer

1 Use counter stamps to make a picture.

2 Write an addition word problem for ___ picture. Solve it.

3 Write a subtraction word problem ___ picture. Solve it.

Name

Drop It!

PLAYERS 2

MATERIALS 2 pennies or counters

DIRECTIONS Take turns. Drop the 2 pennies or counters on the board below. Add the two numbers.

0	3	7	5	4	2
8	5	1	7	6	9
8	7	6	4	2	6
4	9	1	8	3	0
0	9	3	2	5	1

Play this game to help your child practice basic addition facts. To practice subtraction facts, choose a number from 11 to 18. Take turns dropping 1 penny on the game board. Then subtract that number from the number chosen.

At
Home

Dear Family,

Our new chapter in mathematics will be about place value and graphing. I will learn more about numbers to 100 and how to make graphs.

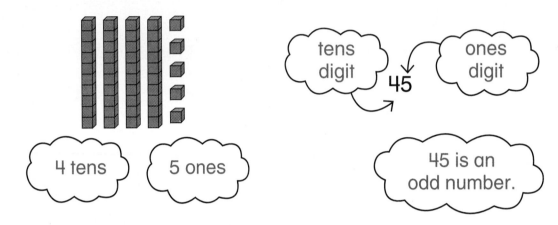

tens digit

ones digit

45

4 tens

5 ones

45 is an odd number.

We will also be talking about things we can count. Please help me complete this interview.

Your child,

_____
Signature

Interview ·····································

Did you like to count things when you were a child?   _____

Did you ever count bugs?   _____

Do you think bugs are:

❏ icky?   ❏ cute?   ❏ interesting?

❏ other? Explain. _____

_____

Our Backyard
Place Value and Graphing

 Listen to the story *The Icky Bug Counting Book.*

 Tell about things that live in your backyard.

What Do You Know?

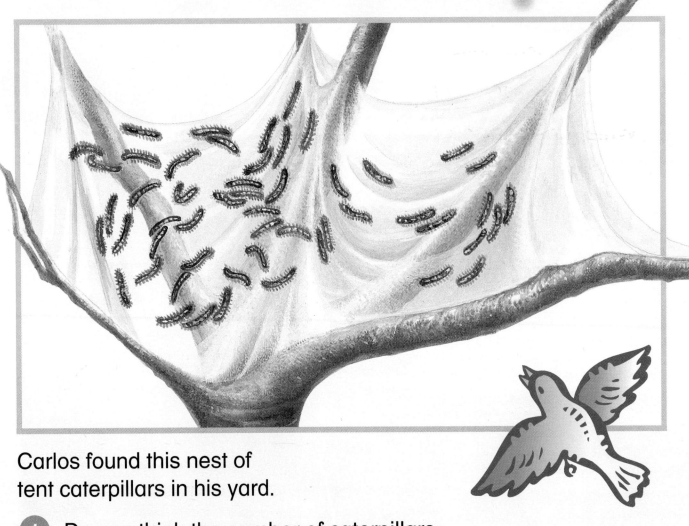

Carlos found this nest of
tent caterpillars in his yard.

1 Do you think the number of caterpillars
is more than 100 or less than 100? _____

2 Estimate how many. Estimate: ____

Then count the number of caterpillars. Count: ____

3 Was your estimate more or less than the
number you counted? _____

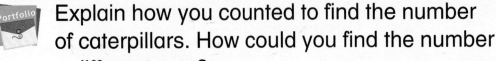 Explain how you counted to find the number
of caterpillars. How could you find the number
a different way?

Working Together

You and your partners need 100 .

▶ Use cubes to make tens.

▶ Show one more ten each time.

▶ Write how many tens.

▶ Write the numbers.

Show.	Write.		
/	1 ten	10	ten
//	2 tens	20	twenty
///	_____	___	thirty
	_____	___	forty
	_____	___	fifty
	_____	___	sixty
	_____	___	seventy
	_____	___	eighty
	_____	___	ninety
	10 tens	100	one hundred

 Critical Thinking What pattern do you see?

Try These!

Ring groups of ten.
Write how many tens. Write the number.

B 2.18.08

1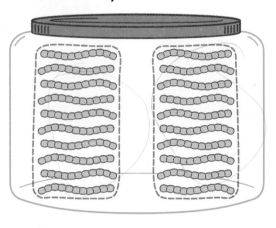

2 tens   20

2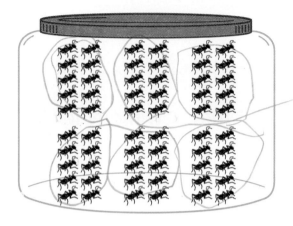

2 tens   20

3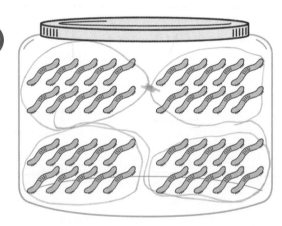

4 tens   40

4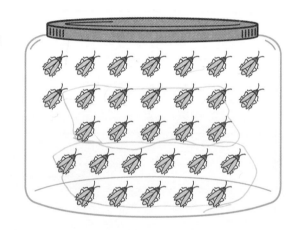

2 tens   20

5

7 tens

6

_____ tens

At Home

We grouped things in tens. Have your child tell you about making tens.

Name ___ B 2-18-08

Working Together

You and your partner need 40 .

▶ Use two hands to take a bunch of cubes.

▶ Estimate how many cubes. Count.

▶ Make tens. Count again.

▶ Write how many tens and ones.
Write the number.

1 __3__ tens __2__ ones __32__

I hundreds
2 __8__ tens __I__ ones __181__

3 __5__ tens __0__ ones __50__

I hundred
4 __10__ tens __0__ ones __110__

5 __7__ tens __0__ ones __70__

Critical Thinking Which is easier to count: 40 cubes
or 4 trains of 10? Explain.

McGraw-Hill School Division

Try These!

Write how many tens and ones.
Write the number.

B 2-18-08

1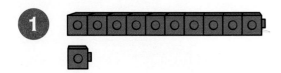

___ ten   ___ one

___ eleven

2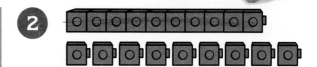

_1_ ten   _9_ ones

_19_ nineteen

3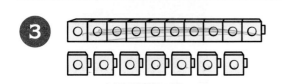

_1_ ten   _7_ ones

_17_ seventeen

4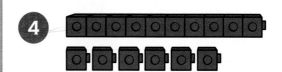

_1_ ten   _6_ ones

_16_ sixteen

5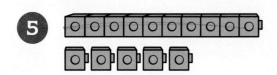

_1_ ten   _5_ ones

_15_ fifteen

6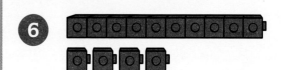

_1_ ten   _4_ ones

_14_ fourteen

7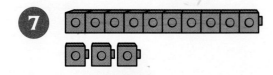

_1_ ten   _3_ ones

_13_ thirteen

8

_1_ tens   _10_ ones

_20_ twenty

At Home

Today we learned about tens and ones. Have your child tell the number of tens and ones in 16 and in 36.

Name _____

The **digit** 3 means 30.

The **digit** 2 means 2.

3 tens   2 ones

B
2-18-08

Working Together

You and your partner need 5 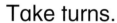,

9 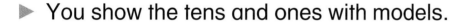, and a 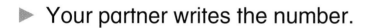.

Take turns.

▶ You show the tens and ones with models.

▶ Your partner writes the number.

1	4 tens 7 ones	47	2	2 tens 1 one	21
3	1 ten 9 ones	19	4	4 tens 8 ones	48
5	0 tens 6 ones	6	6	4 tens 0 ones	40
7	3 tens 5 ones	35	8	0 tens 9 ones	9
9	1 ten 3 ones	13	10	2 tens 6 ones	26
11	2 tens 4 ones	24	12	4 tens 5 ones	45

Critical Thinking What is the value of the 4 in 43?

Try These!

Count. Write how many tens and ones.
Write the number.

1 <u>4</u> tens <u>6</u> ones

<u>46</u>

2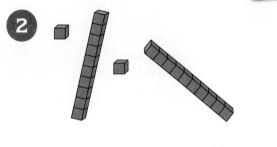

____ tens ____ ones

____

3 ____ tens ____ ones

____

4 ____ tens ____ ones

____

Write how many tens and ones.

5 29 <u>2</u> tens <u>9</u> ones

6 34 ____ tens ____ ones

7 50 ____ tens ____ ones

8 12 ____ tens ____ ones

9 43 ____ tens ____ ones

10 38 ____ tens ____ ones

11 17 ____ tens ____ ones

12 25 ____ tens ____ ones

At Home

We identified tens and ones in numbers to 50. Ask your child how many tens and ones are in the number 40.

Numbers to 100

Name _____

The digit 6 means 60.

67

The digit 7 means 7.

6 tens   7 ones

Working Together

You and your partner need 9 ,

9 , and a .

Take turns.

▶ You show the tens and ones with models.

▶ Your partner writes the number.

1 5 tens 4 ones   54   **2** 8 tens 1 one   ____

3 9 tens 6 ones   ____   **4** 6 tens 9 ones   ____

5 5 tens 8 ones   ____   **6** 8 tens 4 ones   ____

7 7 tens 0 ones   ____   **8** 3 tens 7 ones   ____

9 6 tens 5 ones   ____   **10** 5 tens 2 ones   ____

11 9 tens 3 ones   ____   **12** 4 tens 3 ones   ____

 Critical Thinking   What is the value of the 4 in 74?

Try These!

Count. Write how many tens and ones.
Write the number.

1
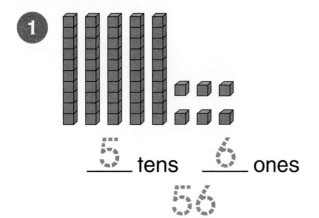
_5_ tens _6_ ones

_56_

2
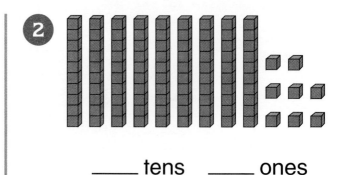
___ tens ___ ones

___

3
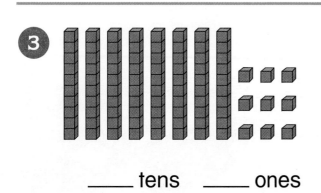
___ tens ___ ones

___

4
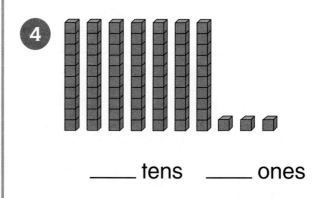
___ tens ___ ones

___

5
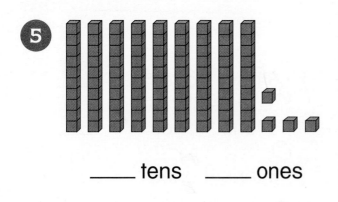
___ tens ___ ones

___

6
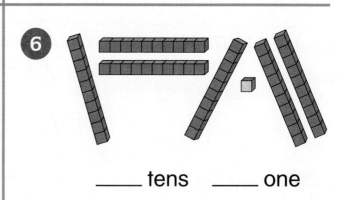
___ tens ___ one

___

Write how many tens and ones.

7 85 _8_ tens _5_ ones

8 68 ___ tens ___ ones

9 99 ___ tens ___ ones

10 77 ___ tens ___ ones

At Home

We identified tens and ones in numbers to 100. Ask your child to tell what the 4 means in the numbers 42 and 34.

Schoolyard Numbers

You and your partner need a ⬤ and 60 ▢.

Take turns.

▶ Drop the ⬤ on the board.

▶ Pick up that many cubes.

▶ For each turn, add more cubes to your set.

▶ Make a ten when you can.

▶ Write how many tens and ones after each turn.

Be the first to reach 30!

Total	
____ tens	____ ones
____ tens	____ ones
____ tens	____ ones
____ tens	____ ones
____ tens	____ ones
____ tens	____ ones
____ tens	____ ones
____ tens	____ ones
____ tens	____ ones
____ tens	____ ones
____ tens	____ ones

Write the number.

1 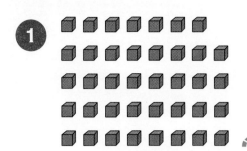 _39_

2  ____

3 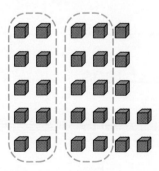 ____

4 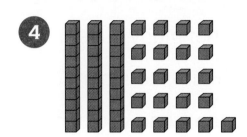 ____

---

5 6 tens 5 ones ____

6 1 ten 3 ones ____

7 0 tens 8 ones ____

8 5 tens 6 ones ____

9 8 tens 8 ones ____

10 4 tens 1 one ____

Write how many tens and ones.

11 68 _6_ tens _8_ ones

12 94 ____ tens ____ ones

13 12 ____ tens ____ ones

14 43 ____ tens ____ ones

15 35 ____ tens ____ ones

16 90 ____ tens ____ ones

---

17 ____ tens ____ ones

18 ____ tens ____ ones

Write the missing numbers.

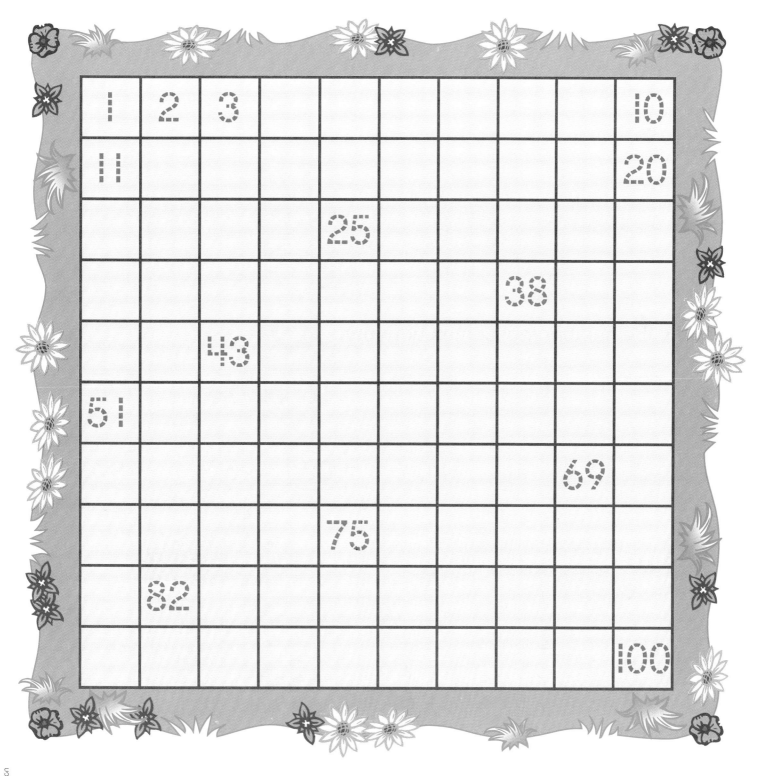

1	2	3							10
11									20
				25					
						38			
		43							
51									
							69		
			75						
82									
									100

 Critical Thinking What is the number pattern going →?
What is the number pattern going ↓?
What is the number pattern going ←?

Try These!

Write the number that comes just after.

1 21 22 | 93 ☐ | 56 ☐ | 39 ☐

2 99 ☐ | 60 ☐ | 85 ☐ | 72 ☐

Write the number that comes just before.

3 39 40 | ☐ 95 | ☐ 48 | ☐ 70

4 ☐ 21 | ☐ 89 | ☐ 76 | ☐ 37

Write the number that comes between.

5 41 42 43 | 14 ☐ 16 | 76 ☐ 78

6 89 ☐ 91 | 80 ☐ 82 | 55 ☐ 57

Mixed Review

Add.

7

$$\begin{array}{r} 4 \\ +8 \\ \hline \end{array} \qquad \begin{array}{r} 9 \\ +9 \\ \hline \end{array} \qquad \begin{array}{r} 7 \\ +6 \\ \hline \end{array} \qquad \begin{array}{r} 8 \\ +7 \\ \hline \end{array} \qquad \begin{array}{r} 9 \\ +1 \\ \hline \end{array} \qquad \begin{array}{r} 6 \\ +8 \\ \hline \end{array}$$

8

$$\begin{array}{r} 7 \\ +7 \\ \hline \end{array} \qquad \begin{array}{r} 8 \\ +9 \\ \hline \end{array} \qquad \begin{array}{r} 6 \\ +5 \\ \hline \end{array} \qquad \begin{array}{r} 5 \\ +8 \\ \hline \end{array} \qquad \begin{array}{r} 0 \\ +7 \\ \hline \end{array} \qquad \begin{array}{r} 8 \\ +8 \\ \hline \end{array}$$

At Home — Ask your child to tell you a number that comes just after 60, a number between 43 and 45, and a number just before 93.

You can **skip-count** the coins by tens.

 50¢

___¢

You can **skip-count** the coins by fives.

 20¢

___¢

1 Skip-count by tens. Write the numbers.

10, 20, 30, ___, ___, ___, ___, ___, ___, ___

2 Skip-count by fives. Write the numbers.

5, 10, 15, 20, 25, 30, ___, ___, ___, ___, ___,

___, ___, ___, ___, ___, ___, ___, ___, ___

Critical Thinking How was counting the stacks of pennies like counting the dimes or nickels?

Try These!

Skip-count by tens. Write the numbers.

1. 3, 13, 23, ___, ___, ___, ___, ___

2. 29, 39, ___, ___, ___, ___, ___

3. 16, 26, ___, ___, ___, ___, ___

4. ___, ___, 28, 38, 48, ___, ___

5. ___, ___, ___, 62, ___, ___, ___

Skip-count by fives. Write the numbers.

6. 35, 40, 45, ___, ___, ___, ___

7. 20, 25, ___, ___, ___, ___, ___

8. ___, ___, 80, 85, 90, ___, ___

9. ___, ___, ___, 50, ___, ___, ___

More to Explore Patterns

Fill in the blanks. Use patterns to help.

21	22	23	24	25	26	27				
31										
								58		60

At Home — We skip-counted by fives and tens to 100. Ask your child to skip-count by tens from 42.

Name _____

Talk What is an easy way to count the rabbit ears?

2, 4, 6, ____, ____, ____, ____

How many ears? ____

Skip-count by twos. Write the numbers.

1 How many spots? ____

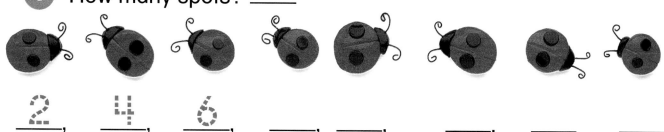

2, 4, 6, ____, ____, ____, ____ ____

2 How many eyes? ____

3 How many wings? ____

Try These!

Connect the dots. Skip-count by twos.

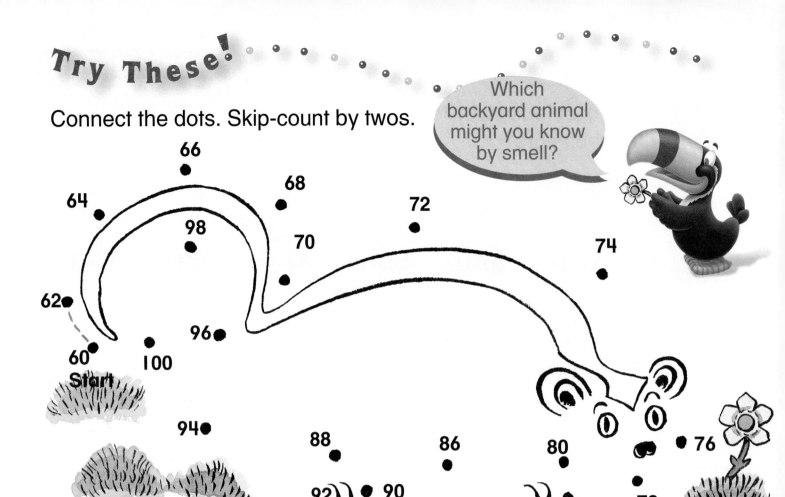

Which backyard animal might you know by smell?

66 68 72 74 64 98 70 62 96 60 Start 100 94 88 86 80 76 92 90 84 82 78

Cultural Connection

Numbers Around the World

4 twenties and four

Numbers are said in different ways around the world. This is how 84 is said in some languages.

French	4 twenties and four	Arabic	four and eighty
Japanese	8 tens and four	Spanish	eight four

Can you say 84 in other languages? Try it with a partner.

At Home

We skip-counted by twos to 100. Ask your child to start at 48 and skip-count by twos to 80.

Working Together

You and your partners need 55 .

Build this tower of trains.   Write the number of cubes.

1   __
2   __
        __
        __
        __
        __
        __
        __
        __

1 Color the trains that can be split into 2 equal parts.

2 How many cubes are in trains with 2 equal parts?

   2 , 4 , ___ , ___ , ___

   *These numbers are **even** numbers.*

3 How many cubes are in trains without 2 equal parts?

   1 , 3 , ___ , ___ , ___

   *These numbers are **odd** numbers.*

Write *odd* or *even* for each number.
You may use cubes to help.

1 ☐☐☐☐ 4

even

☐☐☐☐☐☐☐ 7

_____

2 ☐☐☐☐☐☐☐☐☐ 9

☐☐☐☐☐☐ 6

_____

3 ☐☐☐☐☐☐☐☐☐☐☐ 11 _____

4 ☐☐☐☐☐☐☐☐☐☐☐☐☐☐☐☐☐☐ 18 _____

5 Color the even numbers. Circle the 10s.

1	2	3	4	5	6	7	8	9	10
11	12	13	14	15	16	17	18	19	20
21	22	23	24	25	26	27	28	29	30
31	32	33	34	35	36	37	38	39	40
41	42	43	44	45	46	47	48	49	50

 Write about how you know when a number is odd or even.

 We learned about odd and even numbers. Have your child name two odd numbers and two even numbers.

Midchapter Review

Do your best!

Write how many tens and ones.
Write the number.

1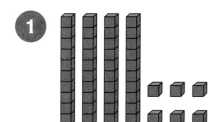

___ tens ___ ones

___

2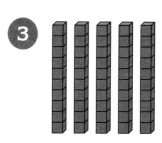

___ tens ___ ones

___

3

___ tens ___ ones

___

Write the number just before, between,
or just after.

4 ___, 30   **5** 87, ___, 89   **6** 74, ___

Skip-count. Write the numbers.

7 10, 20, 30, ___, ___, ___, ___, ___

8 30, 35, 40, ___, ___, ___, ___, ___

9 66, 68, 70, ___, ___, ___, ___, ___

10 Is the number 5 even or odd?
How can you tell?

Write about skip-counting by tens, fives, and
twos. Tell why you count this way.

Count on the Bees

1	2	3	4	5	6	7	8	9	10
11	12	13	14	15	16	17	18	19	20
21	22	23	24	25	26	27	28	29	30
31	32	33	34	35	36	37	38	39	40
41	42	43	44	45	46	47	48	49	50
51	52	53	54	55	56	57	58	59	60
61	62	63	64	65	66	67	68	69	70
71	72	73	74	75	76	77	78	79	80
81	82	83	84	85	86	87	88	89	90
91	92	93	94	95	96	97	98	99	100

You and your partner need 5 .

Take turns.

▶ Look for a skip-counting pattern.

▶ Cover 5 numbers in the pattern.

▶ Your partner says the hidden numbers.

▶ Color 1 point for saying the pattern.

Play until you reach 5 points.

Points	1	2	3	4	5
Player 1					
Player 2					

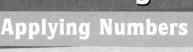

Name

Backyard Bugs

Bugs, insects, and other creatures live everywhere. Some are easy to see. Some hide.

 Talk Where could you find bugs, insects, and other creatures living in your backyard?

Cultural Note

Harvester ants store seeds in their nests. The Tuareg people of the Sahara Desert collect the ants' seeds.

Working Together

▶ You and a partner need gloves, cups, some paper, and a pencil.

▶ Find a place to look for bugs, insects, and other creatures.

▶ Draw a picture of each kind of living thing you find.

▶ Keep a tally of how many of each living thing you find.

▶ Find the total for each living thing.

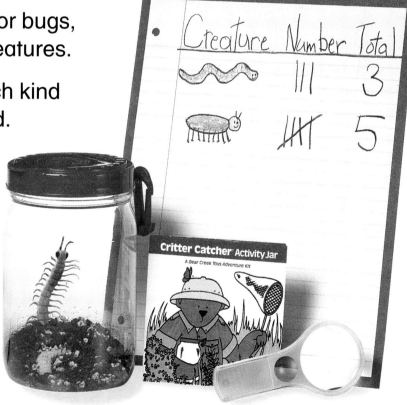

McGraw-Hill School Division

Decision Making

1 Decide how to show what you found. You can make a picture, a graph, or another kind of display.

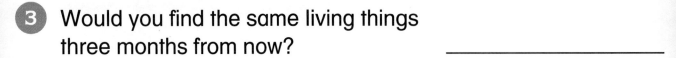

2 How many bugs, insects, and other creatures did you find in all? _____

3 Would you find the same living things three months from now? _____

4 How might the numbers of living things change?

Explain. _____

_____

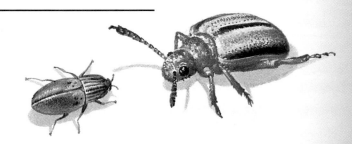

Portfolio

Write a report.

5 Tell what you learned about the numbers of living things in your backyard.

6 Tell how you decided to show what you found.

More to Investigate

PREDICT Will the numbers or kinds of living things be different someplace else?

EXPLORE Look in another place. Record the new information.

FIND Find a library book about insects. Share what you learn with the class.

Name _____

Compare 25 and 37.

> I compare the tens to see which number is greater.

25 is less than 37. 37 is greater than 25.

Talk How would you compare 25 and 27?

Working Together

You and your partner need 18 and 18 ▪.

▶ You show one number with models.

▶ Your partner shows the other number.

▶ Compare.

1 21 ⟨ is greater than ⟩ 11
is less than

2 39 is greater than 22
is less than

3 59 is greater than 68
is less than

4 36 is greater than 37
is less than

 Critical Thinking How would you compare 47 and 43 without models?

McGraw-Hill School Division

Try These!

> You may use models to help.

Compare.

1 11 is greater than 21
        (is less than)

2 41 is greater than 40
        is less than

3 85 is greater than 25
        is less than

4 53 is greater than 62
        is less than

5 94 is greater than 98
        is less than

6 92 is greater than 76
        is less than

More to Explore — Estimation

Choose the estimate you think is best.

The number of cars in a large parking lot.

(greater than 100)

less than 100

The number of books in a library.

greater than 100

less than 100

The number of children in your class.

greater than 100

less than 100

The number of pencils that you have.

greater than 25

less than 25

 At Home

We compared numbers to 100. Ask your child to tell whether 45 is greater than or less than 29.

Name _____

Ernesto gathered 46 acorns and 64 pine cones. Which did he gather more of?

Compare 46 and 64 and find out.

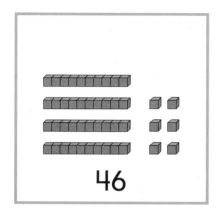

46

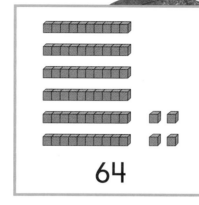

64

46 < 64

64 > 46

46 **is less than** 64.

64 **is greater than** 46.

Ernesto gathered more pine cones than acorns.

___

Compare. Write > for *is greater than*.
Write < for *is less than*.

Use models to help.

1 37 < 39   58 ◯ 43   80 ◯ 77

2 25 ◯ 5   68 ◯ 63   39 ◯ 40

3 66 ◯ 63   12 ◯ 21   58 ◯ 85

Critical Thinking How would you compare 14, 41, and 44? Which number is greatest? Which is least?

Try These!

Compare.
Write > or <.

> is greater than

< is less than

1. 9 ⟫ 2   0 ◯ 3   12 ◯ 18

2. 42 ◯ 45   90 ◯ 97   71 ◯ 68

3. 27 ◯ 20   6 ◯ 13   54 ◯ 49

4. 15 ◯ 25   79 ◯ 69   55 ◯ 71

5. 87 ◯ 86   24 ◯ 34   98 ◯ 89

6. 46 ◯ 51   8 ◯ 18   34 ◯ 43

Mixed Review

Subtract.

7.
$\begin{array}{r} 17 \\ -\ 8 \\ \hline \end{array}$
$\begin{array}{r} 13 \\ -\ 5 \\ \hline \end{array}$
$\begin{array}{r} 16 \\ -\ 7 \\ \hline \end{array}$
$\begin{array}{r} 18 \\ -\ 9 \\ \hline \end{array}$
$\begin{array}{r} 11 \\ -\ 4 \\ \hline \end{array}$
$\begin{array}{r} 14 \\ -\ 8 \\ \hline \end{array}$

8.
$\begin{array}{r} 12 \\ -\ 9 \\ \hline \end{array}$
$\begin{array}{r} 16 \\ -\ 8 \\ \hline \end{array}$
$\begin{array}{r} 17 \\ -\ 9 \\ \hline \end{array}$
$\begin{array}{r} 15 \\ -\ 6 \\ \hline \end{array}$
$\begin{array}{r} 13 \\ -\ 7 \\ \hline \end{array}$
$\begin{array}{r} 10 \\ -\ 4 \\ \hline \end{array}$

At Home

We used the symbols > and < to compare numbers to 100.
Have your child tell you which number is greater: 22 or 12.

The Greater Number Wins

You and your partner need cards for 1 to 100.

▶ Each player gets 50 cards.

▶ Turn over your top card. The player with the greater number takes both cards.

▶ Place winning pairs in your box below. Continue until the last card is played.

Winner: the player with more cards

Winning Cards Player 1

Winning Cards Player 2

Play again.

This time, the player with the lesser number takes both cards.

Winner: the player with more cards

Color even numbers)) orange)) .

Color odd numbers)) black)) .

Compare. Write > for *is greater than*.
Write < for *is less than*.

2 83 ◯ 79   38 ◯ 41   60 ◯ 65

3 92 ◯ 99   18 ◯ 8   74 ◯ 82

4 27 ◯ 28   10 ◯ 11   43 ◯ 34

5 16 ◯ 17   22 ◯ 12   74 ◯ 75

6 4 ◯ 44   65 ◯ 55   81 ◯ 80

Problem-Solving Strategy

Use Logical Reasoning

Read | Which one is the centipede?
The number of its legs has 2 ones.
The tens digit is an odd number
between 1 and 4.

Read
Plan
Solve
Look Back

Plan | Can you add or subtract to
find the answer? __NO.__

Solve | What is a 2-digit number
with 2 ones?

12, 22, 32, 42, 52,
62, 72, 82, 92

Which numbers have a
tens digit between 1 and 4?
Which tens digit is odd?

22, 32

3

Look Back | The centipede is the one with __32__ legs.

Solve.

1 Which one is the millipede?
The number of its legs has
6 in the tens digit. _____

The ones digit is just before 7. ____

The millipede is the one with ____ legs.

2 Which one is the sow bug?
The number of its legs
is between 16 and 20. _____

The ones digit is even. ____

The sow bug is the one with ____ legs.

Try These!

Solve.

1 How many eggs are in the nest?
The number of eggs is greater than 70.
The number is less than 80.
The tens and ones digits are
the same.

_____ eggs

---

2 How many caterpillars are in the "tent"?
The number has 5 tens.
The ones digit is greater than 3.
The number is less than 55.

_____ caterpillars

---

3 How many ants are under the rock?
The number is between 33 and 46.
The ones digit is greater than the tens digit.
There are 4 tens in the number.

_____ ants

---

4 Write your own problem about critters.
Give it to a partner to solve.

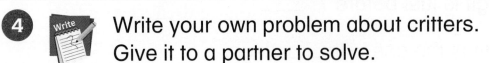

_____

_____

_____

Working Together

You will need a , a 📷, and a 📷.

Find out which bird your class likes best.

🔊 Listen to the names of the birds.

1 Give your teacher the cube whose color is the same as the bird you like best.

2 Count. Write the total number of votes for each bird.

 **Cardinal**

 Goldfinch

Blue Jay

3 Use the totals to complete the **bar graph.**
Color one space to show each vote.

OUR FAVORITE BIRD

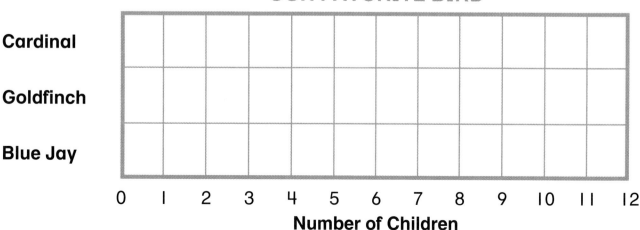

	0	1	2	3	4	5	6	7	8	9	10	11	12
Cardinal													
Goldfinch													
Blue Jay													

Number of Children

Mira counted how many times she saw cardinals at her feeder.
Here are the totals for each season.

Cardinals seen

winter:	1
spring:	12
summer:	10
fall:	4

1 Use the totals to complete the bar graph.

CARDINALS SEEN AT MIRA'S FEEDER

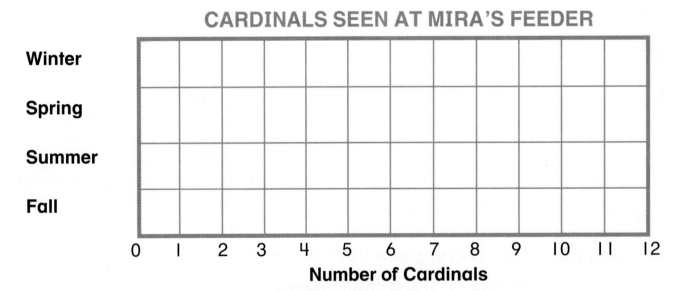

Winter

Spring

Summer

Fall

0 1 2 3 4 5 6 7 8 9 10 11 12

Number of Cardinals

Use the graph to answer these questions.

2 When were the most cardinals seen? _____

3 When were the fewest cardinals seen? _____

4 How many more cardinals were seen in

summer than in fall? _____

5 How many cardinals were seen altogether? _____

At Home

Ask your child to explain how to tell how many cardinals were seen in the spring.

Name _____

Working Together

Which insect does your class like most?
Survey your class to find out.

1 Record each vote with a **tally mark** (|).

 Firefly

 Bee

 Butterfly

 Grasshopper

Other

2 Use your data to make a **pictograph.**

Draw one for each vote.

OUR FAVORITE INSECT	
Firefly	
Bee	
Butterfly	
Grasshopper	
Other	

Each stands for I vote.

 Critical Thinking Why is it important to line up the pictures in a pictograph?

Carrie counted the butterflies she saw.
She used tally marks to show each kind.

Butterflies seen

copper: |||

monarch: ||||| ||

swallowtail: |

white: ||||| |||

1 Complete the pictograph.

Draw one for each butterfly.

BUTTERFLIES CARRIE SAW	
Copper	
Monarch	
Swallowtail	
White	

Each stands for 1 butterfly.

Use the graph to answer these questions.

2 Which butterfly did Carrie see most? _____

3 How many monarchs did she see? _____

4 How many more whites than coppers did she see? _____

5 What was the fewest number of butterflies seen? _____

At Home

Your child took a survey and put the data on a graph.
Have your child explain the graph on page 119.

Name _____

Ely's school sold flower bulbs
to raise money. Help Ely graph
the sales.

 How could you show so many
bulbs on a graph?

Flower Bulb Sales
Day 1   20 bulbs
Day 2   50 bulbs
Day 3   60 bulbs
Day 4   40 bulbs

1 Decide how many bulbs you will
show for each 🔸 picture.
Complete the pictograph.

FLOWER BULB SALES	
Day 1	
Day 2	
Day 3	
Day 4	

Each 🔸 stands for _____ flower bulbs.

2 Complete the key to tell what each
picture means.

3 How did you show 40 bulbs?

_____

4 How did you use counting as you
drew pictures for 40 bulbs? _____

_____

Here are the kinds of flower bulbs that were sold.

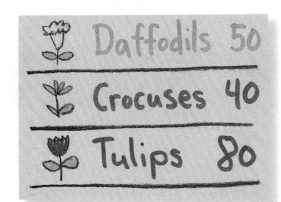

Daffodils 50

Crocuses 40

Tulips 80

1 Decide on a title for the graph. Complete the pictograph.

Daffodils	

Each stands for 10 bulbs.

2 How many bulbs does each picture stand for?   _____ bulbs

3 How many pictures would you draw to stand for 90 tulips?   _____

4 How many more tulips than crocuses were sold?   _____

 Write about how to make a pictograph.

 Your child learned about using a key on a graph. Ask your child to explain the key for the pictograph on this page.

Use a Graph

Children at the Pleasant Valley School planted trees for Arbor Day.

The pictograph shows what they planted.

Read
Plan
Solve
Look Back

TREES PLANTED FOR ARBOR DAY	
Locust	🌳 🌳 🌳 🌳
Oak	🌳 🌳 🌳 🌳 🌳 🌳 🌳 🌳 🌳 🌳
Maple	🌳 🌳 🌳 🌳 🌳 🌳
Pine	🌳 🌳 🌳

Each 🌳 stands for 1 tree.

Solve.

1 How many more oak trees than locust trees were planted? ____

2 How many maple trees and pine trees were planted altogether? ____

3 How many trees were planted in all? ____

 Critical Thinking How did you use the graph to solve the problems?

Try These!

This pictograph shows how many children planted trees on Arbor Day.

CHILDREN WHO PLANTED TREES	
Grade 1	👤 👤
Grade 2	👤 👤 👤 👤
Grade 3	👤 👤 👤

Each 👤 stands for 5 children.

Solve.

1. How many more grade 2 children planted trees than grade 1 children?

   _____ children

2. What if 20 grade 4 children helped plant trees. Would there be more grade 4 children or grade 2 children? _____

Write and Share

Michael wrote this problem.

How many children planted trees in grades 1, 2, and 3?

Michael Hughes
Snowden School
Memphis,
Tennessee

STUDENT TO STUDENT

3. Solve Michael's problem. _____
   What strategy did you use?

   _____

4. Write a problem using information from the graph. Have a partner solve it.

Use your own paper.

At Home

We used a graph to solve problems. Talk with your child about how to solve the problem that he or she wrote.

Name _____

Write the number.

1

_____ tens _____ ones

_____

2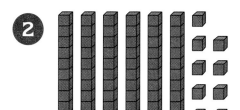

_____ tens _____ ones

_____

3 eighty

_____

Write the number just before, between, or just after.

4 ___, 96   **5** 59, ___   **6** 19, ___, 21

7 41, ___   **8** 76, ___, 78   **9** ___, 54

Skip-count. Write the numbers.

10 60, 65, 70, ___, ___, ___, ___, ___, ___

11 40, 42, 44, ___, ___, ___, ___, ___, ___

Write *odd* or *even* for each number.

12 12 _____   **13** 7 _____   **14** 21 _____

Compare. Write > for *is greater than*.
Write < for *is less than*.

15 78 ◯ 81   **16** 39 ◯ 29   **17** 58 ◯ 85

18 40 ◯ 38   **19** 55 ◯ 51   **20** 16 ◯ 27

Solve.

21 How many acorns are there?
The number is odd.
The tens digit is 2.
The ones digit is less than 3.

_____

22 How many seeds are there?
The ones digit is 5.
The tens digit is between 3 and 6.
The number is greater than 45.

_____

Use the graph to answer these questions.

SEEDS IN FRUIT	
Cherry	⟋
Lemon	⟋ ⟋ ⟋ ⟋ ⟋ ⟋
Melon	⟋ ⟋ ⟋ ⟋ ⟋ ⟋ ⟋ ⟋ ⟋ ⟋ ⟋ ⟋ ⟋ ⟋ ⟋

Each ⟋ stands for 1 seed.

23 How many seeds are in the lemon? _____

24 How many seeds would be in 10 cherries? _____

25 Which fruit has the most seeds? _____

What Do You Think?

What do you like most about graphing?
☑ Check one.

☐ Bar graphs   ☐ Pictographs   ☐ Tally marks

Why? _____

Journal Is 59 greater than or less than 63?
Draw or write to explain.

Chapter Test

Write the number.

1 ____

Write the missing number.

2 54, ____, 56

____

Skip-count. Write the numbers.

3 26, 28, ____, ____, 34, ____, ____, ____, ____

Write *odd* or *even* for the number.

4 18 ____

5 23 ____

Compare. Write < for *is less than*.
Write > for *is greater than*.

6 56 ◯ 72

7 45 ◯ 41

Use the graph to answer these questions.

8 Are there more elm trees or maple trees?

_____

9 How many trees are there in all?

_____

TREES IN MY BACKYARD	
Elm	🌳 🌳 🌳 🌳
Maple	🌳 🌳 🌳 🌳 🌳
Willow	🌳

Each 🌳 stands for 1 tree.

Solve.

10 How many bugs are there? The number is even. The tens digit is 3. The ones digit is between 0 and 4. How many bugs?

____ bugs

What Did You Learn?

Work with a partner.

▶ Put some  and 🔳 in a bag.

▶ Pick some ▦ and 🔳 from the bag.

▶ Color to show what you picked.
Write the number.

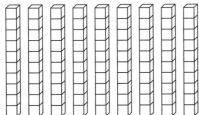

_____

▶ Color to show what your partner picked.
Write the number.

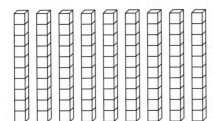

_____

▶ Compare the numbers that you and your
partner picked. Write about comparing numbers.

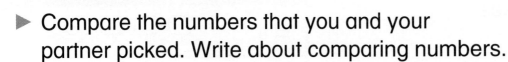

_____

_____

_____

 You may want to put this page in your portfolio.

Math Connection

Patterns and Functions

Name _____

Cubes and Numbers

Continue the pattern. Use .
Then write the pattern with numbers.

2   4   6   ___   ___   ___

3   6   9   ___   ___   ___

    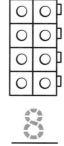 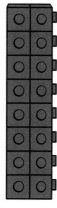

2   4   8   ___   ___

Critical Thinking How is the last pattern different from the others?

McGraw-Hill School Division

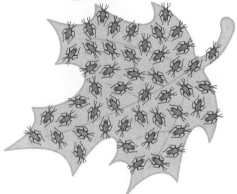

Estimation

This is what it looks like to find
50 bugs under a leaf!

How many bugs are under each leaf?
Choose your estimate.
Then count and write the total.

50 bugs

1

more than 50

(less than 50)

Total: _____

2

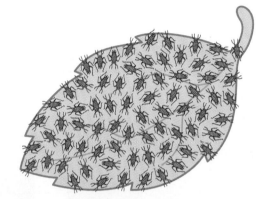

more than 50

less than 50

Total: _____

3

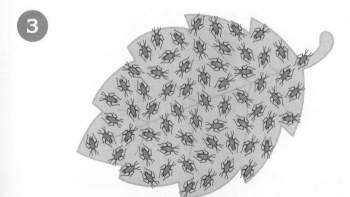

more than 50

less than 50

Total: _____

4

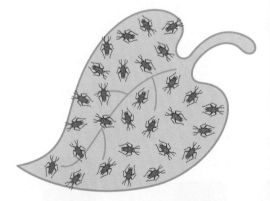

more than 50

less than 50

Total: _____

Cumulative Review

Choose the letter of the correct answer.

1

$$9 + 5$$

- (a) 4
- (b) 13
- (c) 14
- (d) 15

6

$$6 + 8 = \underline{?}$$
$$8 + 6 = \underline{?}$$
$$\underline{?} - 8 = 6$$
$$\underline{?} - 6 = 8$$

- (a) 14
- (b) 8
- (c) 6
- (d) 2

2

8 tens 6 ones

- (a) 68
- (b) 80
- (c) 81
- (d) 86

7

$$6 + 5$$

- (a) 12
- (b) 11
- (c) 3
- (d) 1

3

$$13 - 6$$

- (a) 19
- (b) 8
- (c) 7
- (d) 5

8 43

- (a) 3 tens 4 ones
- (b) 4 tens
- (c) 4 tens 3 ones
- (d) not here

4

10, 15, 20, __?__

- (a) 25
- (b) 15
- (c) 10
- (d) 5

9

$$4 + 4 = \underline{?}$$

- (a) 0
- (b) 8
- (c) 44
- (d) not here

5

67 is less than __?__

- (a) 56
- (b) 66
- (c) 67
- (d) 70

10

__?__, 50, 51

- (a) 59
- (b) 58
- (c) 50
- (d) 49

11 There were 15 birds flying. 9 landed. How many are still flying?

(a) 15
(b) 9
(c) 7
(d) 6

16 Ani saw 5 birds and 3 flies. Which did she see more of?

(a) birds
(b) flies
(c) bugs
(d) not here

12 26 is greater than ___?___

(a) 36
(b) 38
(c) 25
(d) not here

17 Bob has 8 big bugs and 6 small bugs. How many does he have in all?

(a) 2
(b) 6
(c) 8
(d) 14

13 32, ___?___, 34

(a) 33
(b) 31
(c) 30
(d) 22

18 There are 3 mice and 4 more join them. How many mice altogether?

(a) 8
(b) 7
(c) 4
(d) 3

14 The number is odd. The tens digit is between 3 and 5. What is the number?

(a) 24
(b) 31
(c) 45
(d) 46

19

17
− 8

(a) 6
(b) 7
(c) 8
(d) 9

15

Our Favorite Drinks

Milk
Juice
0 1 2 3 4 5 6 7
Number

How many people like milk and juice?

(a) 4
(b) 6
(c) 9
(d) 10

20

Bugs Found	
Ants	🐞🐞🐞🐞🐞🐞🐞
Bees	🐞🐞🐞🐞

Each 🐞 stands for 1 bug.

How many more ants than bees were found?

(a) 2
(b) 4
(c) 6
(d) 8

Name _____

Estimate, Count, Graph!

DIRECTIONS Ask your child to estimate the number of each of the pictured objects in your home. Then count and record how many of each. Compare. Talk about the estimates and the counts.

| Estimate: _____ windows | Estimate: _____ doors | Estimate: _____ chairs |
| Count: _____ windows | Count: _____ doors | Count: _____ chairs |

Show the counts on the graph.
Color the boxes.

OUR HOME COUNT

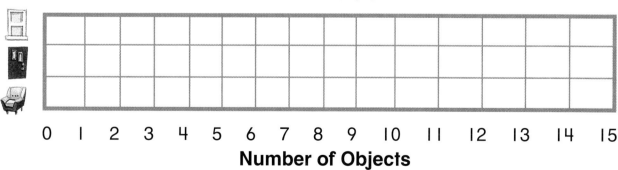

0 1 2 3 4 5 6 7 8 9 10 11 12 13 14 15

Number of Objects

Your child has been learning about numbers to 100 and graphing. This activity will reinforce these skills and also develop estimating skills. You may extend the activity by asking questions about information shown in the graph.

At
Home

Dear Family,

We are beginning a new chapter in mathematics. During the next few weeks I will be learning about coins and their value.

We will also be talking about saving and spending money. Please help me complete this interview.

Your child,

_____
Signature

Interview ....

What did you save for when you were a child?

❑ Toys   ❑ Games

❑ Snacks   ❑ Clothes

❑ Other _____

_____

Saving and Spending
Money

 Listen to the story
A Chair for My Mother.

 Tell about something you want to save for.

What Do You Know?

Count the money.

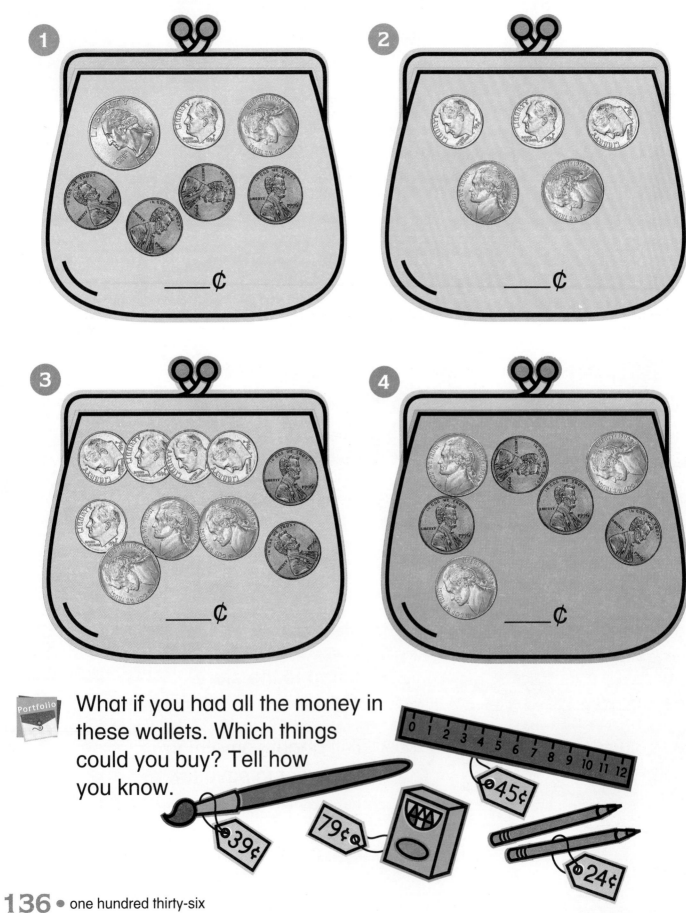

1 _____ ¢

2 _____ ¢

3 _____ ¢

4 _____ ¢

Portfolio

What if you had all the money in these wallets. Which things could you buy? Tell how you know.

39¢ 79¢ 45¢ 24¢

Name _____

dime
10¢
10¢

nickel
5¢
15¢

penny
1¢
16¢

16¢

Working Together

You and your partner need
10 , 10 , and 5 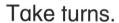.

Take turns.

▶ Pick up a handful of coins.

▶ Write how many of each coin.

▶ Your partner writes how much money.

▶ Return the coins to the pile.

Count dimes by tens.

Count nickels by fives.

1 ____ dimes ____ nickels ____ pennies ____¢

2 ____ dimes ____ nickels ____ pennies ____¢

3 ____ dimes ____ nickels ____ pennies ____¢

4 ____ dimes ____ nickels ____ pennies ____¢

 Talk Tell your partner how you count coins.

McGraw-Hill School Division

Try These!

Count. Write how much money.

1

40¢   45¢   50¢   55¢   56¢ 57¢ 58¢   _58¢_

2      _____

3   _____

4   _____

Cultural Connection

Moroccan Coins

In Morocco coins are called **dirham** and **centimes.**

100 centimes = 1 dirham

Count. Write how many dirham.

____ centimes   ____ centimes   ____ dirham

At Home

We are learning to count money. Ask your child to count the sets of coins on this page.

Name _____

 or  **quarter**
25¢

Working Together

You and your partner need a ,

1 , 4 , 10 🪙, and 20 🪙.

Take turns.

▶ Toss the cube.

▶ Put that much money on your money sorter.

▶ Trade coins when you can.

Play until someone can trade for a quarter.

Lose your coins if you forget to trade.

MONEY SORTER			
Quarter	**Dime**	**Nickel**	**Penny**

How many different ways can you show 25¢?
Make a list like this.

MAKE 25¢

Quarter	Dime	Nickel	Penny
1			
	2		5
	1	3	

McGraw-Hill School Division

Try These!

Count. Write how much money.

Remember to count on from 25.

1

25¢   35¢   40¢   45¢   46¢ 47¢ 48¢   48¢

2

_____

3

_____

4

_____

5

_____

Mixed Review

Skip-count. Write the numbers.

6 65, 70, 75, _____, _____, _____, _____, _____

7 30, 40, 50, _____, _____, _____, _____, _____

8 27, 37, 47, _____, _____, _____, _____, _____

At Home

We counted sets of coins. Have your child tell the total amount for 1 quarter, 2 dimes, and 5 pennies.

How much did Rita save?
Count by twenty-fives to find out.

25¢   50¢   75¢

Rita saved __75¢__.

Count. Write how much money.

1

25¢   50¢   60¢   65¢   70¢

2

    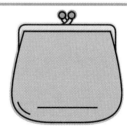

3

Critical Thinking There are 2 coins in your pocket. What is the most you could have? What is the least?

Try These!

Count. Write how much money.

1

97¢

2

3
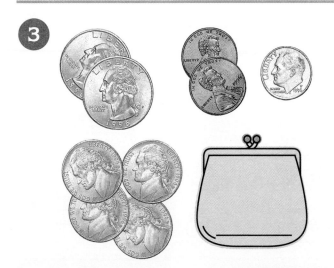

4
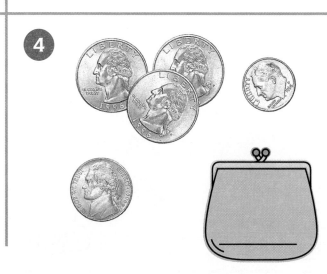

More to Explore   Money

Count. Write how much money.

    **half dollar**
50¢

 50¢   75¢   85¢   90¢

_____

_____

At Home

We counted sets of coins. Have your child count a group of 2 quarters, 2 dimes, and 4 pennies.

Name _____

Use Guess and Test

Read   Melody spent 15¢ at the pet store. Which two things did she buy?

Read
Plan
Solve
Look Back

Plan   What plan could you use to find the answer?

You can use a **guess-and-test** strategy.

ball 7¢

brush 9¢

Solve   Guess that she bought a ball and a brush.

$$7¢ + 9¢ = 16¢$$

(16¢ is 1 ¢ too much.)

Try the ball and the bone.

___ + ___ = ___

mouse 5¢

bone 8¢

YUMMY
dog biscuit 4¢

Look Back   What is the answer to the problem? _____

Solve. You may use , , or .

1   Andy spent 9¢.
Which two things did he buy?

_____

2   Chris spent 17¢.
Which two things did she buy?

_____

Try These!

Pencil 3¢

doll 9¢

boat 4¢

book 7¢

cards 6¢

B

hat 8¢

toy car 5¢

Solve. You may use ⬤, Mental Math, or ▱.

1 Barry has 12¢ to spend.
Which two things can he buy?

_____

2 Find two other things Barry can buy.

_____

3 Juan spent 11¢.
Which two things did he buy?

_____

4 Tawana has 15¢ to spend.
Which three things can she buy?

_____

5 Write about how you solved problem 4. _____

_____

_____

 Write your own rules for using guess and test.

At Home

We used a guess-and-test strategy to solve problems.
Ask your child to explain how to solve problem 1 above.

Midchapter Review

Count. Write how much money.

Do your best!

1  _____

2 _____

3 _____

4  _____

5  _____

6  _____

7  _____

Solve.

 whistle 9¢

 jump rope 7¢

 bubbles 6¢

8 Roberto spent 13¢.
Which things did he buy?

_____

9 Fran spent 16¢.
Which things did she buy?

_____

10 How did you solve problem 9? _____

_____

 Explain how you would count 2 quarters, 3 dimes,
1 nickel, and 8 pennies.

Save for a Rainy Day

You and your partners need a  and a ⊠.

You each need 1 🪙, 3 🪙, 4 🪙,
and 20 🪙.

Take turns.

▶ Put all of your coins in this pocket.

▶ Roll the cube. Spin the spinner.

▶ Move the amount rolled on the cube
to the **Store** to spend money. Move
to the **Bank** to save money.

▶ Play until one player has no money
left in the pocket.

Play again.

Name

Three-Jar Savings

 Listen to *A Chair for My Mother.*

 What would you buy with the money in the jar?

Working Together

You and your partner need , , and .

What if you get 30¢ allowance each week?

▶ Let **Jar 1** be for money to spend on little things, like snacks.

▶ Let **Jar 2** be for money you save for bigger things, like toys.

▶ Let **Jar 3** be for money you save for really big things, like a vacation.

▶ Write how much of the 30¢ you would put in each jar each week.

____¢

____¢

____¢

Decision Making

1 How much would be in each
jar after 4 weeks?
Decide how to find out. You can use

 ,  , or a .

Jar I: _____ ¢   **Jar 2:** _____ ¢   **Jar 3:** _____ ¢

2 Decide on a toy you want.
Make up its cost. _____

3 Which jar would have enough money
in it first to buy the toy? Why? _____

_____

 Write a report.

4 Tell what you learned
about saving money.

5 Tell how you found
the amount in each
jar after 4 weeks.

More to Investigate

PREDICT How long will it take you to
save for the toy in problem 2?

EXPLORE What other ways are there
to save money?

FIND Find out how to start a savings
account at a bank.

Toy Fund

Name _____

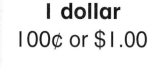

I dollar
100¢ or $1.00

Working Together

You and your partner need coins, a , and a ⊗.

Take turns.

▶ Spin the spinner.

▶ Take one of that coin. Put it on your wallet workspace.

▶ Trade coins when you can.

▶ Continue until one partner has exactly enough to trade for a one-dollar bill.

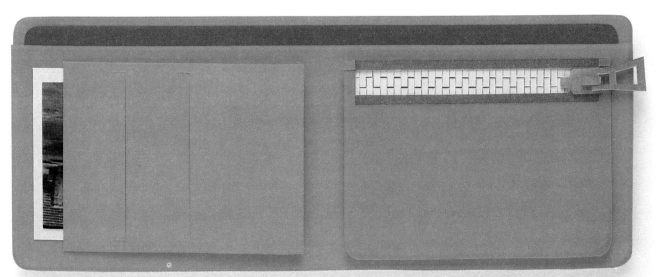

Critical Thinking What if you have 8 coins and your partner has 5 coins? Who has more money? Explain.

Try These!

Remember to write $1.00 for 100¢.

Count. Write how much money.

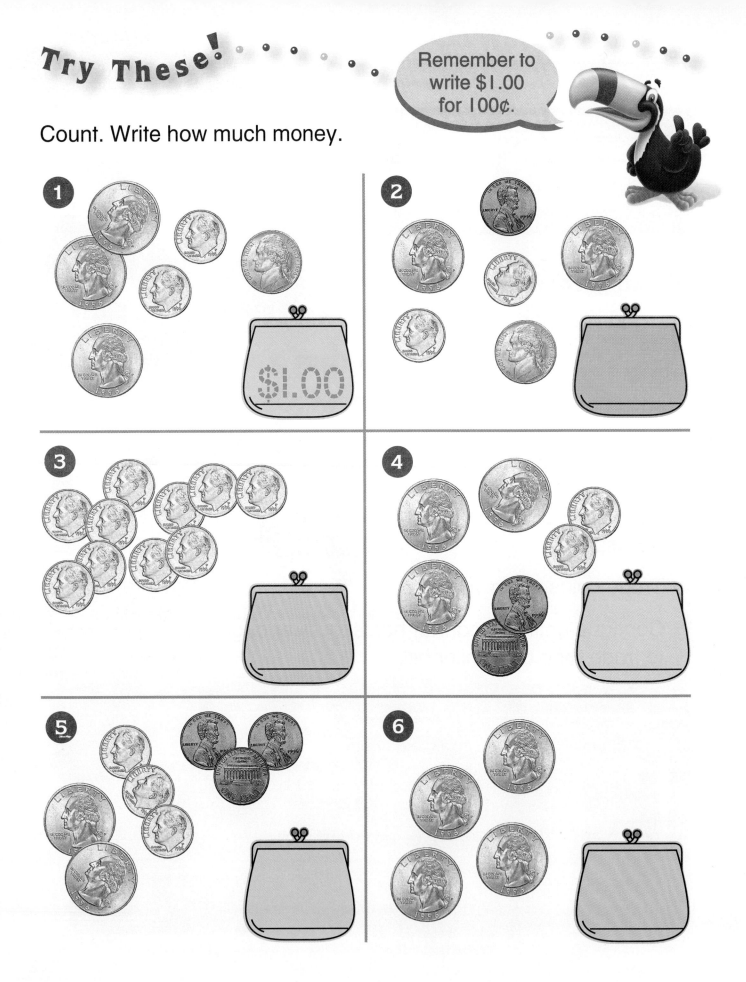

1

2

3

4

5

6

$1.00

 Journal How many different ways can you make $1.00 using all of the same coin? Draw or write to show how.

 At Home Today we made $1.00 with coins. Have your child place more coins in each purse so that every problem shows $1.00 in coins.

How much did the children
earn washing cars?

First count the
dollars. Then
count the cents.

$1.00 $1.25 $1.35   **$1.35**

Count. Write how much money.

1

$1.00, $2.00, $3.00 $3.05 $3.10 $3.10

2

25¢   50¢   75¢ $1.00 $1.10 $1.15   _____

3

_____

Critical Thinking Why do you think people use dollar bills?

Try These!

Count. Write how much money.

1

$2.80

2

_____

3

_____

4

_____

Mixed Review

Compare. Write > for *is greater than*.
Write < for *is less than*.

5 42 ⃝> 36   20 ◯ 24   69 ◯ 70

6 33 ◯ 45   86 ◯ 59   31 ◯ 30

 At Home

We learned to count dollars and cents. Have your child tell the amount of money shown by 3 dollars, 2 quarters, and 4 nickels.

Name _____

Working Together

You and your partner need 6 🪙, 6 🪙,
8 🪙, and 10 🪙.

Take turns.

▶ Scoop up some coins.

▶ Your partner counts and writes
how much money.

▶ Do you have enough money
to buy the object?
Choose *yes* or *no*.

▶ Return the coins to the pile.

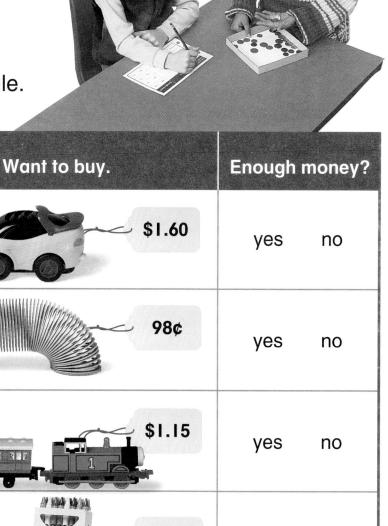

	How much money?	Want to buy.	Enough money?
1	_____	$1.60	yes no
2	_____	98¢	yes no
3	_____	$1.15	yes no
4	_____	$1.50	yes no

 Critical Thinking When can you buy an item?

Count. Is there enough money?
Choose *yes* or *no*.

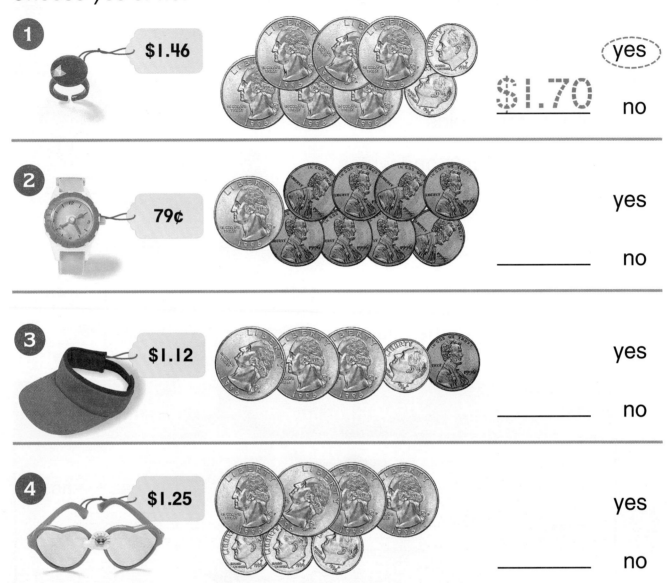

1    $1.46   (yes) $1.70   no

2   79¢   yes   _____ no

3    $1.12   yes   _____ no

4    $1.25   yes   _____ no

More to Explore   Estimation

Choose the estimate you think is best.

Joe has 2 quarters, 30 pennies. He has	Inez has 8 dimes, 7 nickels. She has
more than $1.00.	more than $1.00.
less than $1.00.	less than $1.00.

At Home

Ask your child if 4 quarters, 1 dime, and 1 penny is enough to buy the object in problem 3.

Money in the Bank

You and your partner each need 2 dollars in coins and a 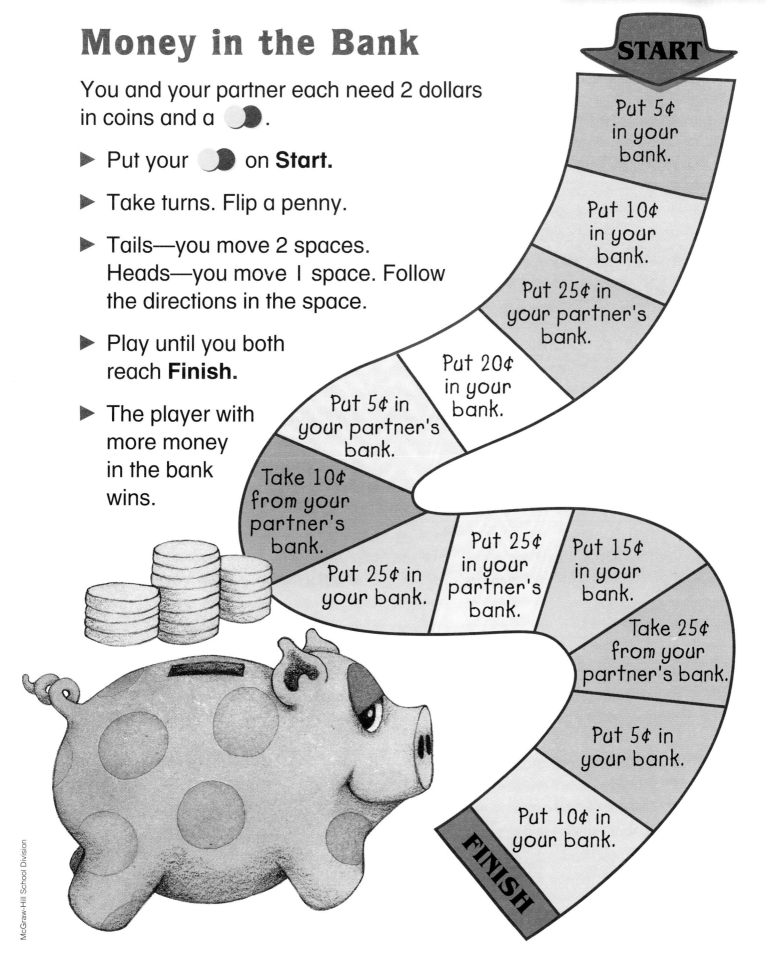 .

▶ Put your ⬤ on **Start.**

▶ Take turns. Flip a penny.

▶ Tails—you move 2 spaces. Heads—you move 1 space. Follow the directions in the space.

▶ Play until you both reach **Finish.**

▶ The player with more money in the bank wins.

START

Put 5¢ in your bank.

Put 10¢ in your bank.

Put 25¢ in your partner's bank.

Put 20¢ in your bank.

Put 5¢ in your partner's bank.

Take 10¢ from your partner's bank.

Put 25¢ in your bank.

Put 25¢ in your partner's bank.

Put 15¢ in your bank.

Take 25¢ from your partner's bank.

Put 5¢ in your bank.

Put 10¢ in your bank.

FINISH

Count. Write how much money.

_____   _____

eraser 7¢   game $1.50   pencils 8¢ each   notepad 9¢   book $1.29

Solve. Use the picture.

3 Chuck has 17¢.
   Can he buy a pad and a
   pencil?

   _____

4 Sue spent 15¢.
   Which things did she buy?

   _____

5 Cara has $1.45.
   Can she buy the game?

   _____

   What could she buy?

   _____

6 Bill has $1.00.
   What can he buy?

   _____

   _____

Cultural Note
Rice, beads, shells,
and stones have all
been used as money
at different times in
history.

Make Change

Diwa bought a pin at the museum gift shop. He gave the clerk $1.00. What should the change be?

toy 87¢   rock 23¢   pin 78¢   Shell 43¢

Read
Plan
Solve
Look Back

 Talk   Why should Diwa get **change**?

To find the change, start with the cost.
Then **count up** to the amount given.

Cost of Pin					Gave the clerk:
78¢	79¢	80¢	90¢	$1.00	$1.00

Then count the coins.

Diwa should get ___22¢___ change.

Use coins to find the change.
Show how you count up.

1 Jasper bought a shell.
He gave the clerk 50¢. ___44¢___ _____ change

2 Terry bought a toy.
She gave the clerk $1.00. _____ _____ change

 Critical Thinking   You give the clerk 3 quarters, 1 dime, and 1 nickel for a toy. Is 2¢ the correct change? Explain.

McGraw-Hill School Division

Try These!

Use coins to count up to make change.

1 Rosa bought a ball for 42¢. She gave the
clerk 50¢. What was her change? _____ change

2 What if the ball Rosa bought was on sale
for 32¢. How much change would she get? _____ change

 Talk How did you solve problem 2?

Write and Share

Ahmed wrote this problem.

Robert bought a turtle
for 97¢.
He gave the clerk $1.00.
What was his change?

Ahmed Kamal
Mandarin Oaks
School
Jacksonville, Florida

3 Solve Ahmed's problem. _____

4 **Write** Write a problem about buying an item and
getting change. Have a partner solve it.

How did your partner solve your problem? _____

_____

How did you solve your partner's problem? _____

_____

At Home Ask your child to tell you how to
solve the problem he or she wrote.

Name _____

Match.

1

penny   dime   quarter   nickel

Count. Write how much money.

2  _____

3  _____

4  _____

Is there enough money? Choose *yes* or *no*.

5  $1.20    yes

no

6  82¢    yes

no

Solve. Which two items did they buy?

7 Mallory spent 17¢.

_____

_____

8 Tyrone spent 13¢.

_____

_____

Write the amount of change.

9 Miguel bought milk.
He gave the clerk 40¢.

_____ change

10 Faith bought juice.
She gave the clerk $1.00.

_____ change

What Do You Think?

Which is the easiest way to count a lot of coins?

☑ Check one.

☐ Count them one at a time.

☐ Group the same coins and count.

☐ Use a calculator.

Why? _____

 Draw a group of coins. Draw or write to explain how to find the amount you have.

Name _____

Draw lines to match.

1

dime   penny   quarter

2

1¢   5¢   10¢   25¢

Count. Write how much money.

3  _____

4   _____

5  _____

6  _____

Is there enough money? Choose *yes* or *no*.

7    yes

no

8    yes

no

Solve. Which two items did they buy?

9 Erin spent 14¢.

_____

10 Abdul spent 10¢.

_____

Performance Assessment

What Did You Learn?

Complete the chart.
Show different numbers of coins to make $1.00.

Use coins if you want to.

1	Use 4 coins.				
2	Use 6 coins.				
3	Use 7 coins.				
4	Use 10 coins.				
5	Use 12 coins.				
6	Use 24 coins.				

 You may want to put this page in your portfolio.

Name _____

Coin Toss

 If you toss a penny, is it more
likely to land heads up or tails up?

Try it with a partner.
Toss a penny 10 times. For each
toss, make a tally mark (|) to
show heads or tails.

 1

		Totals
Heads		
Tails		

Your total
should
equal 10.

If you toss 20 times, will the penny
land more on one side than the other?

_____

Try it. Show your results with tally marks.

2

		Totals
Heads		
Tails		

  Write what you think is likely to happen
if you toss the penny 100 times.

Use your own paper.

McGraw-Hill School Division

Show the Same Amount

 How do you find different ways to show the same amount of money?

You can use a computer to help you.

1 Count. Write how much money. _____

At the Computer

2 How many different ways can you show the amount in the picture? Make a list like this.

Dollar	Quarter	Dime	Nickel	Penny
	1	12	1	

3 What happens if you keep trading up until you cannot trade anymore?

_____

4 Show a money amount. Have a partner show it another way.

Name

Buy It!

MATERIALS coins, dollar bills, paper for price tags

DIRECTIONS Work with your child to make price tags for several food items in your home. Keep prices under $5.00.

Give your child coins and bills to "buy" the items. Have your child show you the exact amount needed to buy each item.

 At Home Play "store" with your child. Switch roles and have your child tell you if you have shown the correct amount.

McGraw-Hill School Division

At Home

Dear Family,

We are starting a new chapter in mathematics. We will be learning about time, from a minute to a year.

We will also be talking about making apple pies and the ingredients that are used. Please help me complete this interview.

Your child,

_____
Signature

Interview ....

What kinds of pies do you like?

❑ Apple   ❑ Lemon   ❑ Sweet potato

❑ Pumpkin   ❑ Pecan   ❑ Peach

❑ Other _____

Did you ever make a pie? _____

If so, what kind? _____

What ingredients did you use? _____

_____

Apple Pie Time
Telling Time

CHAPTER 5

🔊 **Listen**
Listen to the story *How to Make an Apple Pie and see the world.*

💬 **Talk**
Tell about what is in pies that you like.

What Do You Know?

1 Write the number for each hour on the clock.

2 What time is shown? _____

 Write a morning time. Draw or write about something you do at this time. Write the time you finish.

Name _____

Working Together

You and your partner
need a  or class clock.

only
10 seconds
left

Take turns.

▶ Estimate how many times you
can do the activity in 1 **minute.**

▶ Your partner says "Go!" and
watches the clock.

▶ Record the actual number
of times.

ACTIVITY	ESTIMATE	ACTUAL
Write your whole name.	_____ times	_____ times
Say the ABCs.	_____ times	_____ times
Hop on 1 foot.	_____ times	_____ times
Say a rhyme.	_____ times	_____ times
Count by ones to 100.	_____ times	_____ times
Snap your fingers.	_____ times	_____ times

Critical Thinking Why did some minutes seem longer than others?

Try These!

Ring things that take less than 1 minute to do.

1 Read a book.

2 Brush teeth.

3 Eat a cookie.

4 Sleep at night.

5 Count to 10.

6 Play tag.

Talk Talk about your answers with a partner.

Mixed Review

How many pieces of pie? Skip-count by fives.

7     _____ pieces

8   _____ pieces

9   _____ pieces

 At Home We explored how many times we could do an activity in 1 minute. Ask your child to answer exercise 2 above.

Name _____

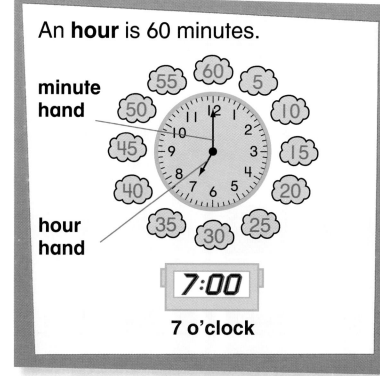

An **hour** is 60 minutes.

minute hand

hour hand

7:00

7 o'clock

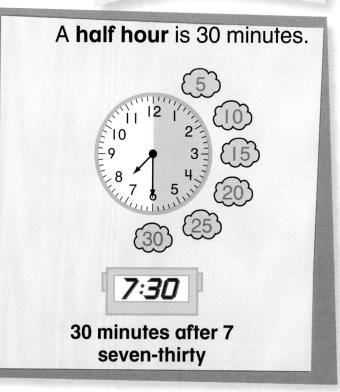

A **half hour** is 30 minutes.

7:30

**30 minutes after 7
seven-thirty**

Talk How does each kind of clock show the time?

Write the time.

1   6:00

2   :

3   :

4   :

5   :

6   :

Critical Thinking Why can you also say *half past seven* for 7:30?

McGraw-Hill School Division

Try These!

Draw the missing minute hand to show the same time.

1

2

3

4

5

6

7

8

Solve.

9 The apple pie will bake for one hour.
At what time will it be done?

_____

 Draw clock hands to show 3:30.
Why does the minute hand point to 6?

 Ask your child to tell you the time at various points in the evening.

2:00

2 o'clock

A **quarter hour** is 15 minutes.

2:15

15 minutes after 2
a quarter after 2

2:30

30 minutes after 2
half past 2

2:45

45 minutes after 2
a quarter to 3

Show the same time.
Draw the missing minute hand.

 **1** 3:45

 **2** 11:15

 3  8:30

 4  7:45

 Critical Thinking What is the difference between *a quarter after* and *a quarter to*?

Try These!

Write the time.
Write the time 15 minutes later.

1   15 minutes later

7:00

2   15 minutes later

___:___

3  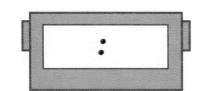 15 minutes later

___:___

4  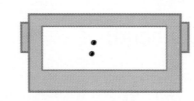 15 minutes later

___:___

More to Explore   Patterns

Find the pattern. Complete the train schedule.

Leave:	2:30	2:45	3:00	:	:	:
Arrive:	4:00	4:15	:	4:45	:	:

174 • one hundred seventy-four

At Home

Have your child count from 6:00 to 6:45 in 5-minute intervals.

Name _____

Working Together

You and your partner need a and a ⏰.

Take turns.

▶ Start with 11 o'clock.

▶ Roll the number cube.

▶ Write that many minutes later.

▶ Draw the new time on the clock.

Talk Could you get a time later than 12:00 on your first roll? Explain.

Turn 1

____ minutes later

Turn 2

____ minutes later

Turn 3

____ minutes later

Turn 4

____ minutes later

Turn 5

____ minutes later

Turn 6

____ minutes later

Critical Thinking What is the latest time that you could get? What is the earliest time? Explain.

Try These!

Write the time.

1

10:05   __:__   __:__   __:__

2

__:__   __:__   __:__   __:__

 Cultural Connection   **Maya Monuments**

Long ago the Maya people carved monuments to record important dates.

Look at these Maya symbols for numbers.

•	••	•••	••••	⎯
one	two	three	four	five

•	••	•••	••••	═
six	seven	eight	nine	ten

Write the Maya symbol.

7 _____   10 _____

Design a Maya monument.

At Home — We learned to tell time to 5-minute intervals. Ask your child to tell you the time when it is 7:20.

Name _____

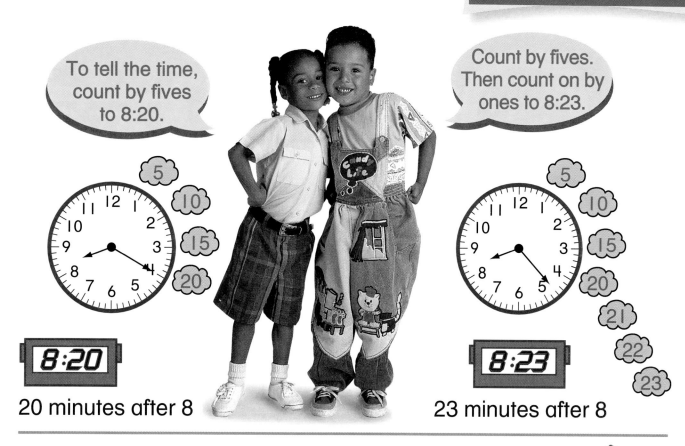

To tell the time, count by fives to 8:20.

Count by fives. Then count on by ones to 8:23.

8:20

20 minutes after 8

8:23

23 minutes after 8

Write the time.

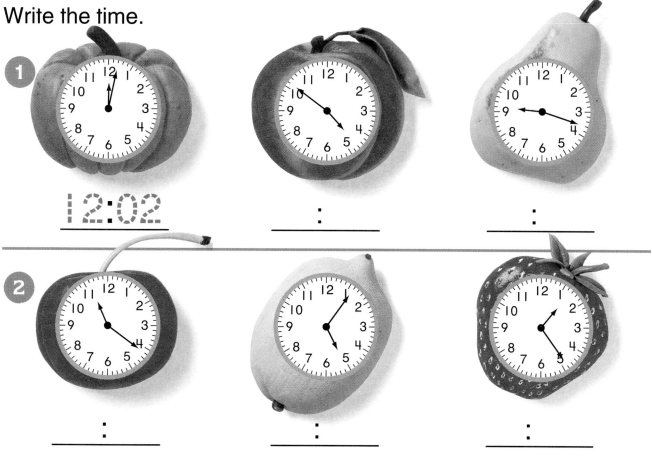

1

12:02

___ : ___

___ : ___

2

___ : ___

___ : ___

___ : ___

Critical Thinking The time is 11:59. How would you write the time for 1 minute later?

CHAPTER 5 *Lesson 3*

one hundred seventy-seven • **177**

Try These!

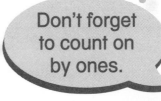 

Don't forget to count on by ones.

Write the time.

1

4 minutes later

 3:17   3:21

2

2 minutes later

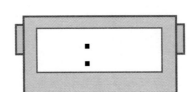 :   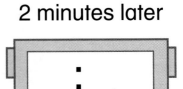 :

3

3 minutes later

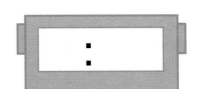 :   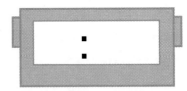 :

4

5 minutes later

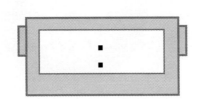 :   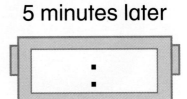 :

Mixed Review

Count. Write how much money.

5  _____

6  _____

178 • one hundred seventy-eight

 We learned to tell time to the minute. Ask your child to explain exercise 4 to you.

Time to Shop

The clocks show the time that
Josie got to each store.

▶ Write the time.

▶ Draw a line to connect the
clocks in order.

McGraw-Hill School Division

Write the time.

 1

4 : 45   __ : __   __ : __   __ : __

2

__ : __   __ : __   __ : __   __ : __

Write the time. Write the later time.

3

15 minutes later

3:00   3:15

4

10 minutes later

__ : __   __ : __

5

30 minutes later

__ : __   __ : __

6

5 minutes later

__ : __   __ : __

Midchapter Review

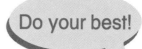

Do your best!

Write the time.

1

:
_____

2

:
_____

3

:
_____

4

:
_____

5

:
_____

6

:
_____

Show the same time. Draw the missing minute hand.

7

1:30

8

9:45

Write the time.

9

15 minutes later

:
_____

:
_____

10

3 minutes later

:
_____

:
_____

 Journal How do you find 5 minutes later than 3:21?

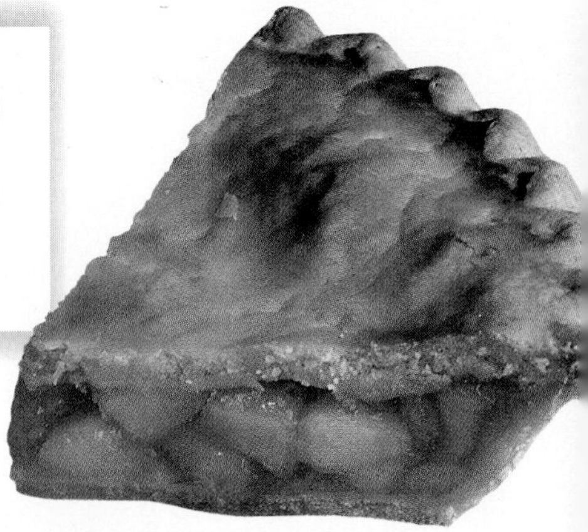

Watch the Time

You and your partner need 14 ⬤⬤ .

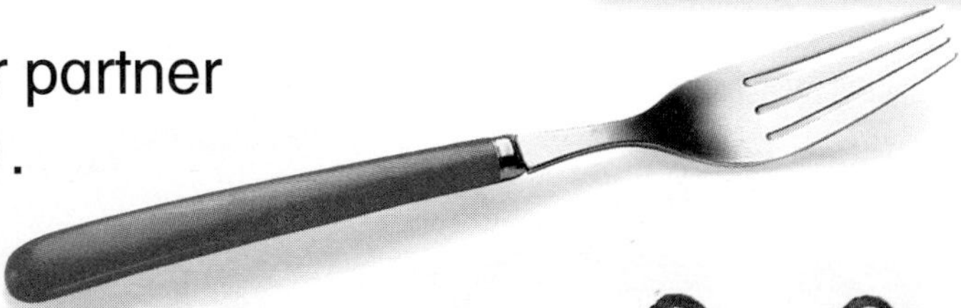

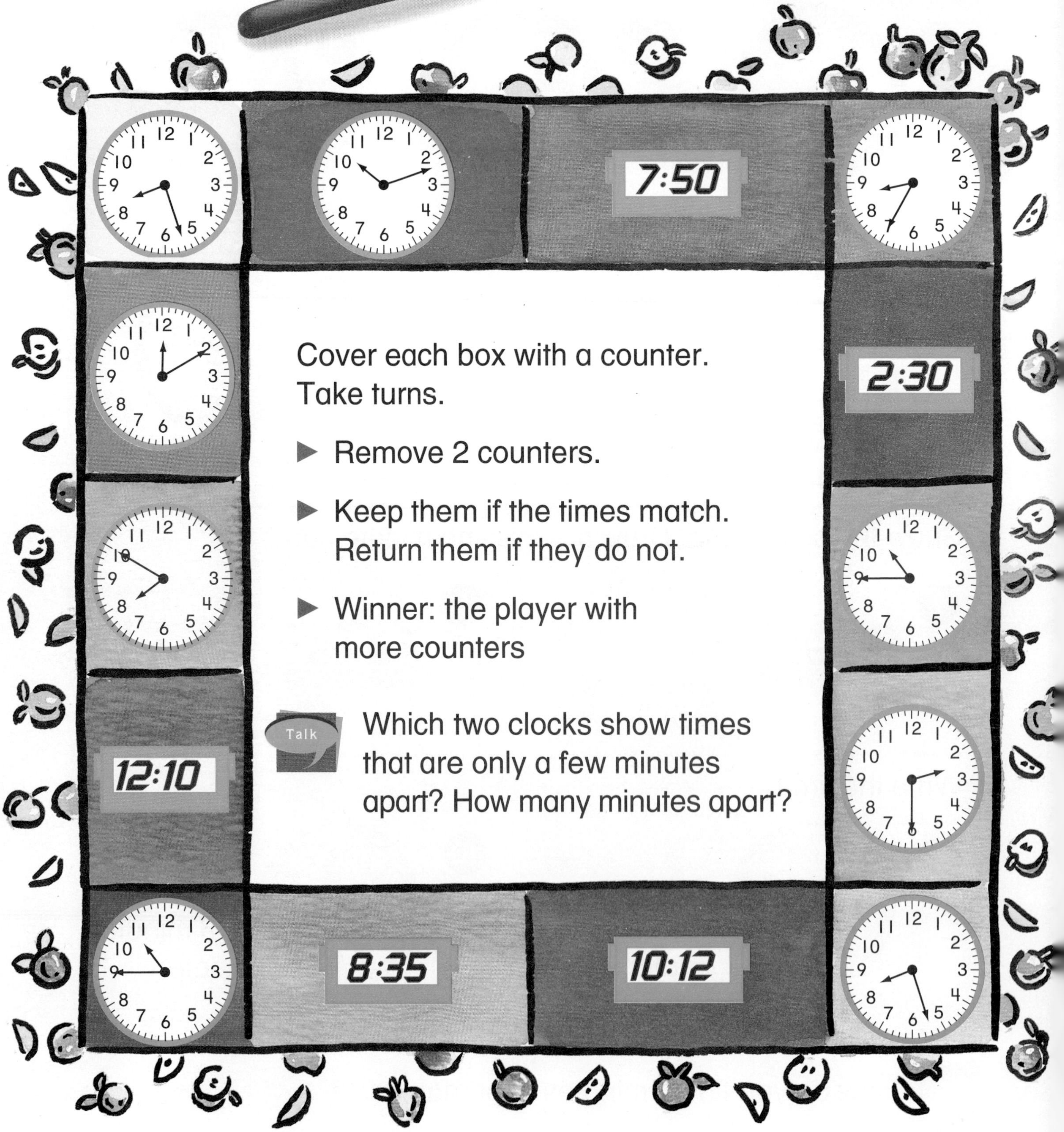

Cover each box with a counter. Take turns.

▶ Remove 2 counters.

▶ Keep them if the times match. Return them if they do not.

▶ Winner: the player with more counters

Talk Which two clocks show times that are only a few minutes apart? How many minutes apart?

7:50

2:30

12:10

8:35

10:12

Name _____

Make a Schedule

A schedule helps people look at information quickly.

Talk What are some different kinds of schedules that people use?

Working Together

Work with a partner. Make up a schedule for a school day.

▶ Write the day.

▶ Write the time you would do each activity.

▶ Write the name of the activity.

Day of the week _____	
Time	**Activity**

Decision Making

Talk How do you think a teacher would change your schedule?

Portfolio **Write a report.**

1 Tell how you decided what to put on your schedule.

2 How does your schedule compare to your teacher's schedule?

Day of the week	Monday
Time	**Activity**
9:30	Math
10:00	Recess
11:00	Reading
12:00	Lunch
1:00	Gym

More to Investigate

PREDICT What if you made a schedule for a Saturday. How might it be the same? How might it be different?

EXPLORE Make a Saturday schedule.

FIND Compare the schedules.

Name _____

Work Backward

Read   The bake sale starts at 12:00. The bakers need to arrive 2 hours before it starts. At what time should the bakers arrive?

Plan   You can **work backward** to solve the problem.

Solve   Start with 12 o'clock. Count back 2 hours.

_11_ o'clock, _10_ o'clock

The bakers should arrive at _10_ o'clock.

Look Back   Does your answer make sense? Explain.

Solve.

1   Miguel took his cupcakes out of the oven at 3:30. They took 1 hour to bake. When did he put them in the oven?   ____ : ____

2   Sunny left the bake sale at 2:00. She was there for 2 hours. When did she arrive?   ____ : ____

Talk   Tell a partner how you solved problems 1 and 2.

Try These!

Solve.

1 Tanya finished baking raisin squares at 9:00.
It took 3 hours altogether.
At what time did Tanya start?

6:00

2 It took Aaron 2 hours to peel apples for his pies.
He finished at 3:00.
When did he begin?

___:___

3 The class made pies until 3:00.
Paula helped for the last 4 hours.
When did she start helping?

___:___

4 Taro wants his cookies to be ready by 10:30.
It will take 2 hours in all.
At what time should he start?

___:___

5 Write Write your own problem.
Have a partner solve it.

_____

_____

_____

At Home

We counted backward to solve problems. Ask your child to tell you what time it was 2 hours ago.

Use a Calendar

January

Sun	Mon	Tues	Wed	Thurs	Fri	Sat
				1	2	3
4	5	6	7	8	9	10
11	12	13	14	15	16	17
18	19	20	21	22	23	24
25	26	27	28	29	30	31

February

Sun	Mon	Tues	Wed	Thurs	Fri	Sat
1	2	3	4	5	6	7
8	9	10	11	12	13	14
15	16	17	18	19	20	21
22	23	24	25	26	27	28

March

Sun	Mon	Tues	Wed	Thurs	Fri	Sat
1	2	3	4	5	6	7
8	9	10	11	12	13	14
15	16	17	18	19	20	21
22	23	24	25	26	27	28
29	30	31				

April

Sun	Mon	Tues	Wed	Thurs	Fri	Sat
			1	2	3	4
5	6	7	8	9	10	11
12	13	14	15	16	17	18
19	20	21	22	23	24	25
26	27	28	29	30		

May

Sun	Mon	Tues	Wed	Thurs	Fri	Sat
					1	2
3	4	5	6	7	8	9
10	11	12	13	14	15	16
17	18	19	20	21	22	23
24 31	25	26	27	28	29	30

June

Sun	Mon	Tues	Wed	Thurs	Fri	Sat
	1	2	3	4	5	6
7	8	9	10	11	12	13
14	15	16	17	18	19	20
21	22	23	24	25	26	27
28	29	30				

July

Sun	Mon	Tues	Wed	Thurs	Fri	Sat
			1	2	3	4
5	6	7	8	9	10	11
12	13	14	15	16	17	18
19	20	21	22	23	24	25
26	27	28	29	30	31	

August

Sun	Mon	Tues	Wed	Thurs	Fri	Sat
						1
2	3	4	5	6	7	8
9	10	11	12	13	14	15
16	17	18	19	20	21	22
23 30	24 31	25	26	27	28	29

September

Sun	Mon	Tues	Wed	Thurs	Fri	Sat
		1	2	3	4	5
6	7	8	9	10	11	12
13	14	15	16	17	18	19
20	21	22	23	24	25	26
27	28	29	30			

October

Sun	Mon	Tues	Wed	Thurs	Fri	Sat
				1	2	3
4	5	6	7	8	9	10
11	12	13	14	15	16	17
18	19	20	21	22	23	24
25	26	27	28	29	30	31

November

Sun	Mon	Tues	Wed	Thurs	Fri	Sat
1	2	3	4	5	6	7
8	9	10	11	12	13	14
15	16	17	18	19	20	21
22	23	24	25	26	27	28
29	30					

December

Sun	Mon	Tues	Wed	Thurs	Fri	Sat
		1	2	3	4	5
6	7	8	9	10	11	12
13	14	15	16	17	18	19
20	21	22	23	24	25	26
27	28	29	30	31		

Use the **calendar.**

1 How many days in each month?

July _31_   May ____   March ____   June ____

2 On what day of the week is the date?

August 15 _____   June 1 _____

January 18 _____

Critical Thinking

What is the same about April and July?
What is different?

Try These!

Complete the calendar.
Then solve.

JANUARY

Sunday	Monday	Tuesday	Wednesday	Thursday	Friday	Saturday
				1	2	3
4	5	6	7	8	9	10
11	12	13	14			

1 January has _____ days.

2 January has _____ Fridays.

3 The play is on January 13. The class will practice on the Friday before. What is the date of the practice?

_____

4 The drama club meets every Thursday. How many times will they meet in January?

_____

5 Yuri's birthday is one week after January 21. When is his birthday?

_____

6 On which day of the week does January begin?

_____

At Home

Ordinal Numbers

You can use **ordinal numbers** to tell about the days and the weeks in a month.

fourth Tuesday

May **twenty-first**

third week

Janell will visit the doctor the fifth Friday in May.

That date is

May 29
_____.

MAY						
Sun	Mon	Tues	Wed	Thurs	Fri	Sat
					1	2
3	4	5	6	7	8	9
10	11	12	13	14	15	16
17	18	19	20	21	22	23
24/31	25	26	27	28	29	30

---

1 On what date does the second week in May begin?

_____

2 What is the date of the third Tuesday?

_____

3 What is the sixth day of the week?

_____

4 What day of the week is the thirty-first of May?

_____

5 What date is the fourth Tuesday in May?

_____

6 What date is the first Monday in May?

_____

 Critical Thinking Why are the twenty-fourth and the thirty-first of May shown in the same box?

Ring the date.

1. first Thursday  blue
   third Tuesday red

2. nineteenth of February green
   twenty-third of February yellow

3. second Monday orange
   fourth Wednesday purple

FEBRUARY

Sun	Mon	Tues	Wed	Thurs	Fri	Sat
1	2	3	4	5	6	7
8	9	10	11	12	13	14
15	16	17	18	19	20	21
22	23	24	25	26	27	28

More to Explore   Logical Reasoning

Draw lines to show order.

Slice the apples. Watch out for seeds.	1st
Bake the pie until it is done.	2nd
Buy apples and flour and other good things.	3rd
Put the apples in a nice crust.	4th

 At Home

Have your child tell you on which day of the week the fifteenth of this month falls.

Use a Schedule

The Saturday TV shows before
12:00 noon are A.M.

The Saturday TV shows after
12:00 noon are P.M.

SATURDAY TV							
Channel	10:00 A.M.	10:30 A.M.	11:00 A.M.	11:30 A.M.	12:00 noon	12:30 P.M.	1:00 P.M.
48	French for Kids	Wild Animals	Learn Japanese		English Is Easy	Chinese Cooking	Spanish Cartoons
53	Gym-nastics	Fly a Kite		Science Fun	Basketball Tips	Sing-Along	Make It Yourself

How many choices do you have at 12:00 noon?

To find out, look across the chart to 12:00 noon.
Then read the show titles under 12:00 noon.

*English Is Easy
Basketball Tips*

There are __2__ choices.

Solve.

1 How long is the TV show *Learn Japanese*? _____

2 Can you watch *Wild Animals* and
Fly a Kite? Explain.

_____

3 Yoko wants to watch *Science Fun*.
Tami wants to watch *English Is Easy*.
Can they each watch their shows? Explain.

_____

Critical Thinking Why do people use schedules?

Channel	11:30 A.M.	12:00 noon	12:30 P.M.	1:00 P.M.
1	Cartoons	Figure Skating		Computer Whiz
9	Superkid	TV Weekly	Sea World	

Solve.

1 Which shows are 1 hour long? _____

2 Can you watch *Computer Whiz* and *Sea World*? Explain. _____

Write and Share

Jessica wrote this problem.

Tina wants to watch "Figure Skating." Jessica wants to watch "Computer Whiz." Can they each watch their program? Explain.

Jessica Boullosa
O'Rourke School
Mobile, Alabama

3 Solve Jessica's problem. _____

4 Write a problem using information from the schedule. Have a partner solve it and explain the answer.

Use your own paper.

How did your partner explain his or her answer? _____

_____

At Home

Have your child use the schedule above and tell you which shows are on at 12:00 noon.

Chapter Review

Write the time.

1

____:____

2

____:____

3

____:____

Write the time.
Write the time 5 minutes later.

4

____:____   ____:____

Solve.

5 Louie got to the train station
at 11:00. It took him 1 hour
to get to the station.
At what time did he leave? ____:____

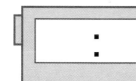

6 Una got to her grandmother's
house at 3:30. She
traveled for 3 hours.
At what time did she leave? ____:____

McGraw-Hill School Division

Use the calendar to solve.

7 How many days in April?

_____ days

8 What day of the week is April 27?

_____

9 What day of the week is the twenty-ninth of April?

_____

10 What date is the fifth Wednesday in April?

_____

APRIL

Sun	Mon	Tues	Wed	Thurs	Fri	Sat
			1	2	3	4
5	6	7	8	9	10	11
12	13	14	15	16	17	18
19	20	21	22	23	24	25
26	27	28	29	30		

What Do You Think?

Which one do you use most often?
 Check one.

DECEMBER						
Sun	Mon	Tues	Wed	Thurs	Fri	Sat
			1	2	3	4
5	6	7	8	9	10	11
12	13	14	15	16	17	18
19	20	21	22	23	24	25
26	27	28	29	30	31	

1:40

Why? _____

 Write the time.
Explain how you can use counting to find the time.

Name _____

Write the time.

_____ : _____

_____ : _____

_____ : _____

Write the time and the time 5 minutes later.

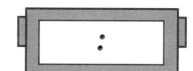

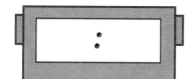

Use the calendar to solve problems 5 to 8.

JULY						
Sun	Mon	Tues	Wed	Thurs	Fri	Sat
			1	2	3	4
5	6	7	8	9	10	11
12	13	14	15	16	17	18
19	20	21	22	23	24	25
26	27	28	29	30	31	

5 On what day of the week is the Fourth of July? _____

6 What date is the fourth Sunday in July? _____

7 On which day of the week is the twenty-second of July?

_____

8 How many Fridays are there in July?

_____

9 Percy rides the bus for 1 hour to get to school. He gets to school at 8:30. What time does he leave?

_____

10 Luke got to his sister's house at 2:30. It took him 2 hours to get there. What time did he leave?

_____

What Did You Learn?

Complete the train schedule.

Then add two more stops to the schedule. Show the times for each.

TRAIN SCHEDULE

Train Leaves	Train Arrives	How Long Does It Take?
Ashville 9:30	Dover 9:45	_____
Dover 9:55	Liberty _____	25 minutes
Liberty 10:30	Suntown 11:01	_____
Suntown 11:10	Blue Valley 12:00	_____
_____	_____	_____
_____	_____	_____

 You may want to put this page in your portfolio.

Name _____

Calendar Detective

You can find number patterns on a calendar.

4, 5, 6, 7, 8, 9, 10
The pattern is +1.

AUGUST

Sun	Mon	Tues	Wed	Thurs	Fri	Sat
						1
2	3	4	5	6	7	8
9	10	11	12	13	14	15
16	17	18	19	20	21	22
23/30	24/31	25	26	27	28	29

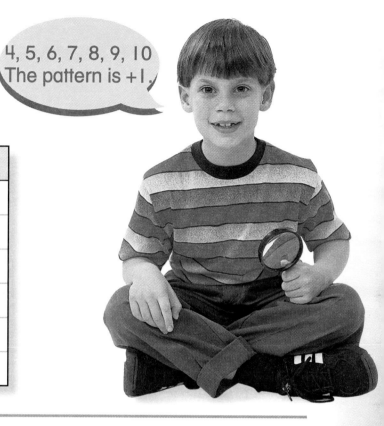

Look for number patterns on the calendar. You may want to use a calculator to help.

	Write the numbers	Name the pattern
1 Ring some numbers that go ➡.		
2 Ring some numbers that go ⬇.		
3 Ring some numbers that go ↙.		
4 Ring some numbers that go ↘.		

Technology Connection

Make a Schedule

In what ways can a schedule change?

You can use a computer spreadsheet to help you make and change a schedule quickly.

PARTY SCHEDULE			
Activity	**Start Time**	**How Long It Takes**	**End Time**
Welcome guests	12:30	10 minutes	12:40
Musical chairs	12:40	20 minutes	
Sing songs		10 minutes	
Play games		20 minutes	
Eat cake		10 minutes	
Open presents		10 minutes	
Give out party favors		5 minutes	
Say goodbye		5 minutes	

At the Computer

1. Complete the spreadsheet.
   When will the party be over? _____

2. Change the start of the party to 1:00.
   What happens to the schedule? _____

   _____

3. Change the length of time for playing games to 40 minutes.
   What happens to the schedule? _____

   _____

Name _____

Picture Clock

MATERIALS paper, crayons, scissors, clasp

DIRECTIONS Make a clock. Draw a picture for each activity you do. Tell about the activity. Show the time you do it.

As you and your child do this activity, it will help him or her develop a sense about the sequence of events that occur during the day.

McGraw-Hill School Division

At Home

Dear Family,

We are beginning an exciting new chapter in mathematics. I will be learning more about mental math and how to use what I know to add and subtract bigger numbers. Some of my work will look like this:

$$40 + 40 \qquad 36 + 20 \qquad 80 - 40 \qquad 56 - 20$$

We will also be talking about games we play. Please help me complete this interview.

Your child,

_____
Signature

Interview ....

What kinds of games do you like to play?
(You may check more than one.)

❑ Ball games   ❑ Board games

❑ Sidewalk games   ❑ Video games

❑ Other _____

What was your favorite game
when you were a child? _____

What were your rules for the game? _____

_____

Fun and Games
Exploring 2-Digit Addition and Subtraction

Listen Listen to the stories from *Hopscotch Around the World.*

Talk Do you ever play a game like this? What are your rules?

What Do You Know?

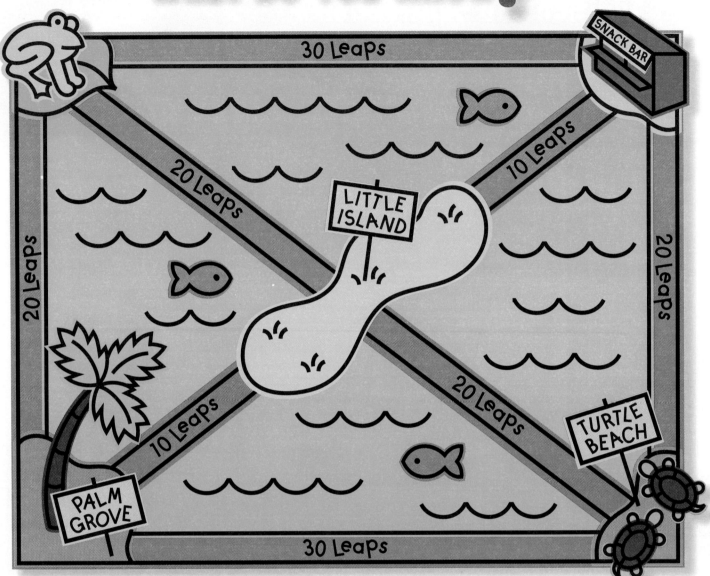

30 Leaps

SNACK BAR

20 Leaps

10 Leaps

20 Leaps

20 Leaps

LITTLE ISLAND

10 Leaps

20 Leaps

TURTLE BEACH

PALM GROVE

30 Leaps

The frog must leap on the paths.
Find the total number of frog leaps.
Use mental math.

1 Find the shortest way for Frog to get from his pad to Turtle Beach.

How many leaps? _____

2 Frog wants to stop at the Snack Bar and then Little Island on his way to Turtle Beach.

How many leaps? _____

Write a problem about frog leaps.
Explain how to solve it.

Name

Working Together

You and your partner need a .

Take turns.

▶ Choose a starting number. Write it in the first arrow.

▶ Spin. Write the + or – sign and the number.

▶ Your partner makes up a problem with the numbers.

▶ You solve the problem and write the total.

Start with 62 points. Lose 3 points. How many points are left?

59

	Starting Number	Spin + or –	Total Points
1			
2			
3			
4			
5			
6			

Starting Numbers

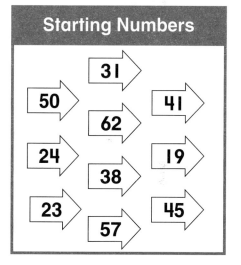

31
50
41
62
24
19
38
23
45
57

Use a starting number only once.

Try These!

Find the total number of points.

	Starting Number	+ or –	Total Points
1	28 ▶	– 2	26
2	31 ▶	+ 3	___
3	49 ▶	+ 1	___
4	64 ▶	– 1	___

	Starting Number	+ or –	Total Points
5	20 ▶	– 2	___
6	45 ▶	+ 2	___
7	56 ▶	+ 3	___
8	32 ▶	– 3	___

 Talk Tell a partner how you found the total points.

Mixed Review

Count on or count back to complete.

9 90, 80, 70, ___, ___, ___, ___, ___

10 22, 32, 42, ___, ___, ___, ___, ___

11 9, 19, 29, ___, ___, ___, ___, ___

12 85, 75, 65, ___, ___, ___, ___, ___

13 77, 67, 57, ___, ___, ___, ___, ___

At Home We counted on and counted back to add and subtract 1, 2, and 3. Ask your child how to add 52 + 3.

Name _____

You know
I + I = 2,
so you know
10 + 10 = 20.

You know
3 − I = 2,
so you know
30 − 10 = 20.

You can use **mental math** to solve these problems.

1 There are 4 red counters and 4 blue counters.
How many counters in all?

 counters

What if there were 40 red counters
and 40 blue counters.
How many counters in all?

 counters

2 There are 8 balloons.
2 of the balloons are green.
The rest of them are pink.
How many balloons are pink?

_____ balloons

What if there were 80 balloons
and 20 were green.
How many balloons would be pink?

_____ balloons

3 There are 2 big balls and 3 small balls.
How many balls in all?

_____ balls

What if there were 20 big balls
and 30 small balls.
How many balls in all?

_____ balls

 Critical Thinking How is 40 + 40 different from 4 + 4?
How is 80 − 20 different from 8 − 2?

Try These!

Complete the problems.
Use mental math to solve.

1 There are __4__ orange balls.

There are __2__ green balls.

How many balls in all? _____ balls

What if there are __40__ orange balls

and __20__ green balls?

How many balls in all? _____ balls

---

2 There are _____ kites.

_____ kites fly away.

How many kites are left? _____ kites

What if there are _____ kites

and _____ fly away?

How many kites are left? _____ kites

Add or subtract.

3 6 – 2 = _____   1 + 4 = _____   8 – 3 = _____

60 – 20 = _____   10 + 40 = _____   80 – 30 = _____

4 3 + 4 = _____   5 + 4 = _____   7 – 7 = _____

30 + 40 = _____   50 + 40 = _____   70 – 70 = _____

At Home

We are learning how to use facts to solve problems with tens. Have your child explain problem 2 above.

Find how many of each toy the store has.

Working Together

You and your partner need 6 .

Take turns.

▶ Put a counter on one of the boxes below.

▶ Write the number in the addition sentence.

▶ Count on by tens to find the total.

▶ Your partner checks your work.

You may use a box only once.

	On the Shelf	In Boxes	Total
1		41 + ___ = ___	
2	CHESS	23 + ___ = ___	
3		18 + ___ = ___	
4	VIDEO	35 + ___ = ___	
5		26 + ___ = ___	
6		34 + ___ = ___	

Critical Thinking What is the greatest total you could get? Explain.

Try These!

You can count on by tens: 46, 56, 66.

Solve.

1 Mr. Tong had 46 games to sell.
He got a box with 20 more games.
Now how many games does he have to sell?

_66_ games

2 There are 32 dolls in a store window.
Another window has 10 more dolls
than the first window.
How many dolls are in the second window?

_____ dolls

3 Mr. Tong placed 25 toy cars on one shelf.
He placed 30 cars on another shelf.
How many cars did he place on the
two shelves?

_____ cars

Add.

4 43 + 10 = _____

5 27 + 30 = _____

6 65 + 20 = _____

7 72 + 10 = _____

8 10 + 17 = _____

9 39 + 30 = _____

10 54 + 20 = _____

11 83 + 10 = _____

12 76 + 20 = _____

13 30 + 44 = _____

14 51 + 30 = _____

15 62 + 10 = _____

At Home

We counted on 10, 20, or 30 to add. Ask your child
to tell you how to solve problems 1 to 3 above.

Name _____

Working Together

You and your partner need a and 2 ⬤ .

Take turns.

You may use a number only once.

▶ Put a counter on the wheel.

▶ Write the number to start a subtraction sentence.

▶ Your partner spins to get tens and writes the number in the sentence.

▶ Count back by tens to find the difference.

1 ____ – ____ = ____   2 ____ – ____ = ____

3 ____ – ____ = ____   4 ____ – ____ = ____

5 ____ – ____ = ____   6 ____ – ____ = ____

7 ____ – ____ = ____   8 ____ – ____ = ____

9 ____ – ____ = ____   10 ____ – ____ = ____

Critical Thinking What is the least difference you could get? Explain.

Try These!

You can count back by tens: 65, 55, 45.

Solve.

1 Alana scored 65 points.
Then she lost 20 points.
How many points does she have now?

_45_ points

2 To win a game takes 77 points.
Ryan has 30 points.
How many more points does he need?

____ points

3 Ella has 29 points.
Her brother has 20 points.
How many more points does Ella have?

____ points

Subtract.

4 88 − 30 = ____   **5** 37 − 30 = ____

6 45 − 20 = ____   **7** 61 − 20 = ____

8 58 − 10 = ____   **9** 82 − 10 = ____

10 72 − 20 = ____   **11** 56 − 20 = ____

12 97 − 30 = ____   **13** 75 − 30 = ____

14 64 − 10 = ____   **15** 99 − 10 = ____

Journal

Write about how you use mental math to solve some problems.

At Home

We counted back 10, 20, or 30 to subtract. Ask your child to tell you how to solve problems 1 to 3 above.

There were 67 people at the game.
Then 30 more people came.
How many people are at the game now?

 Talk Which mental math strategy would you use to solve this problem?

There are __97__ people at the game.

Cultural Note
Boys and girls in 81 countries around the world play on Little League teams.

Solve.

1 There are 75 children who play ball.
This week 20 of them did not play.
How many children played ball this week?   ____ children

2 The home team made 30 points.
Then they made 40 more points.
How many points did they make in all?   ____ points

3 The class had 83 tickets to sell.
They have 30 tickets left.
How many tickets did they sell?   ____ tickets

The class sold the tickets for $1 each.
How much money did they make?   ____

Solve.

1 There are 36 bags of popcorn.
There are 20 bags of chips.
How many more bags of popcorn
are there than bags of chips?

_16_ bags

---

2 The children sold 38 hot dogs.
Then they sold 3 more.
How many hot dogs did they sell?

_____ hot dogs

---

3 The children made 24 cookies to sell.
Someone ate 2 cookies.
How many cookies do they have to sell?

_____ cookies

---

4   Choose a pair of numbers.
Write a problem.
Have a partner solve it.

48	2

36	20

30	62

_____

_____

_____

More to Explore — Number Sense

54 people are going to the
game.
Each bus holds 30 people.
How many buses are needed?

_____ buses

The school has 36 helmets.
Each team needs 10 helmets.
How many teams can use the
helmets at one time?

_____ teams

At Home — Ask your child to tell you about
problem 4 above. Try to solve it.

Addition/Subtraction Race

You and your partner need a , a 📱, and 2 ⚪⚫.

Take turns.

▶ Put your counter on **Start.**

▶ Roll a number cube.
Move that many spaces.

▶ Tell the sum or difference.
Check your answer with a calculator.

▶ If correct, stay in the space.
If wrong, move back one space.

▶ The winner is the first player to reach **End.**

START

| 28 – 10 |
| 55 + 30 |
| 37 + 3 |
| 79 – 2 |
| 64 + 20 |

| 75 + 3 | 80 – 2 | 46 – 30 |
| 21 + 2 |

| 19 – 10 | 53 + 1 | 34 + 2 | 99 – 20 | 47 + 20 |

| 30 + 30 |

WINNER

| End | 10 + 70 | 80 – 80 | 24 + 2 | 65 + 3 | 73 – 2 |

Add or subtract.

1 $14 + 3 = \underline{17}$ $20 + 40 = \underline{\hspace{1cm}}$ $38 - 10 = \underline{\hspace{1cm}}$

2 $80 - 1 = \underline{\hspace{1cm}}$ $95 - 3 = \underline{\hspace{1cm}}$ $47 + 20 = \underline{\hspace{1cm}}$

3 $63 + 1 = \underline{\hspace{1cm}}$ $18 + 30 = \underline{\hspace{1cm}}$ $73 - 20 = \underline{\hspace{1cm}}$

4 $30 + 26 = \underline{\hspace{1cm}}$ $52 - 30 = \underline{\hspace{1cm}}$ $81 + 2 = \underline{\hspace{1cm}}$

5 $24 - 2 = \underline{\hspace{1cm}}$ $10 + 68 = \underline{\hspace{1cm}}$ $45 - 10 = \underline{\hspace{1cm}}$

6 $70 - 20 = \underline{\hspace{1cm}}$ $96 - 30 = \underline{\hspace{1cm}}$ $25 + 20 = \underline{\hspace{1cm}}$

7 $87 + 3 = \underline{\hspace{1cm}}$ $30 + 2 = \underline{\hspace{1cm}}$ $72 - 30 = \underline{\hspace{1cm}}$

Mixed Review

Count. Write how much money.

8

_____

9

_____

10

_____

11

_____

Name _____

Solve 2-Step Problems

Read — Dana put 25 stars on her notebook.
Her cat licked off 10 of the stars.
Then Dana put 3 new stars on the book.
How many stars are on Dana's notebook now?

Read
Plan
Solve
Look Back

Plan — What strategies can you use?
Do you need more than one?

Solve

Step 1

25 stars
10 licked off
How many left?

____ stars

Step 2

____ stars left
3 more stars
Now how many stars?

____ stars

How did you do Step 1? _____

_____

How did you do Step 2? _____

_____

Look Back — Does your answer make sense? Why?

_____

_____

Try These!

Solve.
Show how you found your answer.

1 Kim made 39 cards.
She sent out 10 cards yesterday.
Today she sent out 20 cards.
How many cards does Kim have left? _____ cards

Step 1: _____ Step 2: _____

---

2 Mary put 27 flowers on a shirt.
10 flowers fell off in the wash.
3 flowers fell off when she wore the shirt.
How many flowers are still on the shirt? _____ flowers

Step 1: _____ Step 2: _____

---

3 Joel had 31 points.
He scored 20 more points.
Then he lost 3 points.
How many points does Joel have now? _____ points

Step 1: _____ Step 2: _____

---

4 Mario owned 56 baseball cards.
He gave 2 cards to Kareem.
Kareem gave Mario 10 cards.
How many cards does Mario have now? _____ cards

Step 1: _____ Step 2: _____

At Home

We solved two-step problems. Ask your child how to solve problem 3 above.

Name _____

Do your best!

Add or subtract.

1 26 + 3 = ____

2 65 − 2 = ____

3 50 − 30 = ____

4 30 + 30 = ____

5 17 + 30 = ____

6 58 − 20 = ____

7 46 + 20 = ____

8 96 − 10 = ____

Solve.

9 Simon had 51 cards.
He gave 20 of them to his brother.
How many cards does Simon have now?   ____ cards

Solve. Show how you found your answer.

10 Lucie put 68 beads on a string.
Then she put 3 more beads on the string.
The string broke and 20 beads fell off.
How many are on the string now?   ____ beads

Step 1: _____   Step 2: _____

 Write about how you use mental math
to subtract 74 − 30.

Color by Number

You and your partner need a  ,
, and .

Choose red or yellow.

Take turns.

► Drop the counter on the board. This number is your starting number.

► Spin to get another number.

► Add or subtract. Your partner checks.

► If correct, color the space with your color. If wrong, color the space with your partner's color.

The player with more spaces colored wins.

35	36	63	70	42
75	45	47	39	68
72	52	66	59	72

Red score: ____

Yellow score: ____

Name

Play Lu-Lu!

Working Together

You and your partners need a , 4 cardboard circles, and a cup.

▶ Take turns. Each player gets two tosses a turn.

▶ Shake the four circles in a cup and toss them. Count the dots.

▶ If all four pieces land faceup, toss them all again.

▶ If some pieces land facedown, toss only the facedown pieces on your second toss.

▶ Use mental math to add the points to your score. Use the calculator to check.

▶ The winner is the first player to score 100 points.

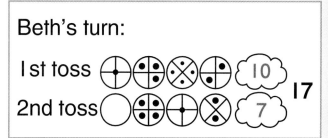

Beth's turn:

1st toss ⊕ ⊕ ⊡ ⊕ 10

2nd toss ◯ ⊕ ⊕ ⊗ 7   17

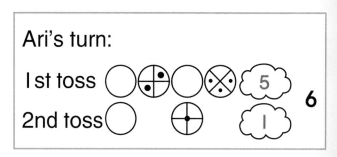

Ari's turn:

1st toss ◯ ⊕ ◯ ⊗ 5

2nd toss ◯ ⊕ 1   6

SCORE CARD

Beth	Ari
10	12
+17	+ 6
27	18

Decision Making

1 What if you have 48 points and you score 15 more points?
What strategy would you use to add? _____

_____

2 Make up new rules for the game.
Then try it.
How does the game work now? _____

_____

Write a report.

3 Tell how you added the scores for each round.

4 Tell how you changed the game.

More to Investigate

PREDICT What kind of a game could you make up that uses mental math to subtract?

EXPLORE Work with your group.
Make up a subtraction game.
Write the rules. Play the game.

FIND How is your game like the Lu-Lu game? How is it different? Trade games with another group and play.

There are 45 big marbles.
There are 23 small marbles.
How many marbles in all?

$$45 + 23 = \underline{\ ?}$$

Here are some mental math
strategies you can use.

40 + 20 = 60
60 + 5 = 65
65 + 3 = 68

45 + 20 = 65
65 + 3 = 68

There are **68** marbles in all.

 Talk What are some other strategies you could use?

Working Together

Use mental math to solve.
Share your strategies with your partners.

1 Didi has 32 marbles.
Carl has 18 marbles.
How many do they have altogether?   _____ marbles

2 José has 21 marbles.
He buys 54 more.
Now how many marbles does he have?   _____ marbles

Try These!

 Use your head!

Solve. Use mental math.

1 Lara's game has 32 number cards.
It has 26 letter cards.
How many cards are in the game?   _____ cards

---

2 Sari has 19 colored pencils.
Ben has 33 colored pencils.
How many pencils do they have altogether?   _____ pencils

3 Explain how you solved problem 2. _____

_____

Add. Use mental math.

4 21 + 18 = ___   17 + 30 = ___   46 + 44 = ___

5 79 + 13 = ___   21 + 75 = ___   8 + 57 = ___

More to Explore   Number Sense

Cam used 3 packs of cards for a game.
There were 30 cards in each pack.
How many cards did she use?

_____ cards

Jonah used 4 bags of counters for a game.
There were 20 counters in each bag.
How many counters did he use?

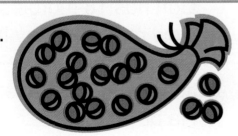

_____ counters

 At Home

We solved addition problems by using mental math
strategies. Have your child explain how to solve problem 1.

Name _____

There are 62 puzzle pieces.
13 pieces are from one puzzle.
How many pieces are from
another puzzle?

$62 - 13 = \underline{\ ?\ }$

62 – 10 = 52
52 – 3 = 49

62 – 10 = 52
Count back
51, 50, 49.

There are __49__ pieces from another puzzle.

 Talk What are some other strategies you could use?

Working Together

Use mental math to solve.
Share your strategies with your partners.

1 Jo had a puzzle with 59 pieces.
She lost 12 pieces.
How many pieces does she have now?   ____ pieces

2 Adam built a house with 78 blocks.
He built a wall with 34 blocks.
How many more blocks did he use
for the house?   ____ blocks

McGraw-Hill School Division

Try These!

Solve. Use mental math.

1 Jeanne has 27 dolls.
She has 16 dresses for the dolls.
How many more dolls than dresses
does she have?

_____ dolls

2 Lou had $46. He spent $42.
How much money does Lou have now?

_____

3 68 − 34 = _____   46 − 13 = _____   35 − 2 = _____

4 31 − 20 = _____   24 − 5 = _____   46 − 26 = _____

Cultural Connection

English Darts

Darts is an old English game
played around the world.
In the outside ring, points
are doubled. In the inside
ring, points are tripled.

Find the scores.
Then check with a calculator.

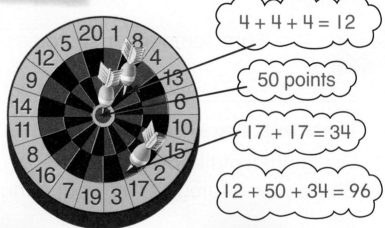

4 + 4 + 4 = 12

50 points

17 + 17 = 34

12 + 50 + 34 = 96

   _____

   _____

   _____

At Home

Have your child explain how to solve
problem 1 above.

Solve Multistep Problems

Mrs. Festa put 20 bows and 5 flowers on her new hat.
The wind blew off 3 bows and 2 flowers.
How many things are left on Mrs. Festa's hat?

Read
Plan
Solve
Look Back

 Talk What will you need to do to find the answer?

It helps to write each step.

Step 1
$20 + 5 = \underline{25}$

Step 2
$3 + 2 = \underline{5}$

Step 3
$25 - 5 = \underline{20}$

There are $\underline{20}$ things on Mrs. Festa's hat.

Solve. Show your work.

1 Isabel had 35 flowers. She bought 10 more. Then she gave away 3 of them. She just got 20 more flowers. How many flowers does Isabel have now?

____ flowers

_____

2 Sam bought 30 boxes.
He used 6 and gave away 9.
Then he used 5 more boxes.
How many boxes does Sam have left?

____ boxes

_____

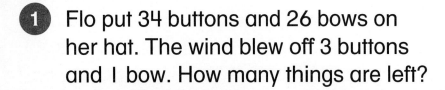

Try These!

Solve. Show your work.

1 Flo put 34 buttons and 26 bows on her hat. The wind blew off 3 buttons and 1 bow. How many things are left?

_____ things

2 What if the wind blew off 13 buttons and 11 bows. How many things are left?

_____ things

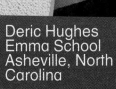

Write and Share

Deric wrote this problem.

I went to the store and got 30 grapes for my hat. Then I went to the plant store and got 10 roses. My mom gave me 10 buttons for my hat. My sister ate 20 grapes. My dad wanted 6 roses. How many things are still on my hat?

Deric Hughes
Emma School
Asheville, North Carolina

3 Show how to solve Deric's problem.

4 Write a word problem that uses addition and subtraction. Have a partner solve it.

Use your own paper.

 We solved problems with several steps. Ask about the problem your child wrote.

Chapter Review

Use mental math to add or subtract.

1 $68 + 3 =$ ___

2 $41 + 2 =$ ___

3 $40 + 30 =$ ___

4 $20 + 60 =$ ___

5 $16 - 3 =$ ___

6 $39 - 2 =$ ___

7 $50 - 20 =$ ___

8 $90 - 10 =$ ___

9 $86 - 30 =$ ___

10 $37 + 30 =$ ___

11 $43 + 10 =$ ___

12 $51 - 20 =$ ___

13 $75 - 10 =$ ___

14 $13 + 7 =$ ___

15 $22 + 38 =$ ___

16 $64 - 14 =$ ___

17 $87 - 45 =$ ___

18 $35 + 53 =$ ___

19 $21 + 10 =$ ___

20 $57 - 3 =$ ___

Solve.

21 Brad made 25 pictures. Then he made 30 more. How many pictures did he make in all?

___ pictures

22 Dora made 17 cards. She gave away 10. How many cards does she have left?

___ cards

Solve. Show how you found your answer.

23 Chim had 45 baseball cards.
He got 3 more.
Then he gave 10 cards to Pete.
How many cards does Chim have now? _____ cards

_____

24 Sherry had 38 points. She lost 2 points.
Then Sherry got 30 more points.
How many points does Sherry have now? _____ points

_____

25 Mr. Delano put 10 birdhouses and
15 bird feeders in a tree.
The wind blew down 2 birdhouses
and 2 bird feeders.
How many things are still in the tree? _____ things

_____

What Do You Think?

Which mental math strategy do you like best?

☑ Check one.

☐ Counting on by ones   ☐ Counting back by ones   ☐ Counting on by tens   ☐ Counting back by tens

Why? _____

Journal Show different ways to find 36 + 17.
Which do you like best?

Chapter Test

Use mental math to add or subtract.

1 $85 - 3 = $ ____

2 $51 + 3 = $ ____

3 $60 - 30 = $ ____

4 $38 + 10 = $ ____

5 $43 + 34 = $ ____

6 $52 - 12 = $ ____

7 $67 + 3 = $ ____

8 $96 - 23 = $ ____

Solve.

9 Ian made 56 cards.
He used 30 cards.
How many cards does
Ian have left?   ____ cards

Solve. Show how you found your answer.

10 Tina had 58 points in a game.
Then she lost 3 points.
On her next turn, she made
10 more points. How many
points does Tina have now?   ____ points

What Did You Learn?

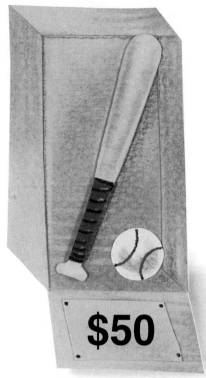 $50

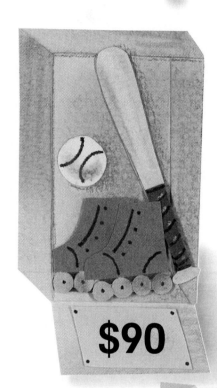 $90

 $60

Find out what each item costs.

1. The  cost _____.

2. The 🞟 costs _____.

3. The | costs _____.

4. Explain how you find the costs.

_____

_____

_____

 You may want to put this page in your portfolio.

Math Connection
Calculator

Name _____

Sums and Differences

Predict what your calculator will show.

Enter [+] [3].
What number will you get
after you press [=] [=] [=] [=]? _____

Try it. What number is in the display? _____

Predict these sums.
Then press the keys to check.

		Prediction	Display
1	[+] [4] [=] [=] [=] [=] [=]		
2	[+] [6] [=] [=] [=]		
3	[+] [3] [=] [=] [=] [=] [=]		
4	[+] [2] [=] [=] [=] [=] [=] [=] [=]		

Predict these differences.
Then press the keys to check.

		Prediction	Display
5	[4] [0] [–] [2] [=] [=]		
6	[3] [0] [–] [3] [=] [=] [=]		
7	[2] [8] [–] [2] [=] [=] [=] [=]		
8	[5] [7] [–] [1] [=] [=] [=] [=] [=]		

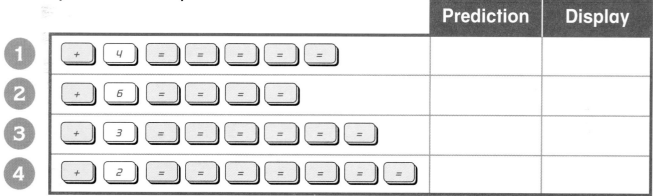

Jump-Rope Rhymes

 Listen to this poem.

Rope Rhyme

Get set, ready now, jump right in
Bounce and kick and giggle and spin
Listen to the rope when it hits the ground
Listen to the clappedy-slappedy sound
Jump right up when it tells you to
Come back down, whatever you do
Count to a hundred, count by ten
Start to count all over again
That's what jumping is all about
Get set, ready now

      jump
          right
             out!

—*Eloise Greenfield*

 Write your own jump-rope rhyme.
It can be long or short, but use some numbers.

_____

_____

_____

_____

Get a jump rope and some friends.
Try out your rhyme.

Cumulative Review

Choose the letter of the correct answer.

1

$8 - 5 = $ ___?___

- (a) 2
- (b) 3
- (c) 4
- (d) 13

6

$48 + 20 = $ ___?___

- (a) 28
- (b) 50
- (c) 68
- (d) 78

2

$\begin{array}{r} 8 \\ + 8 \\ \hline \end{array}$

- (a) 0
- (b) 8
- (c) 16
- (d) 18

7

$61 - 3 = $ ___?___

- (a) 64
- (b) 59
- (c) 58
- (d) 57

3

$\begin{array}{r} 17 \\ - 9 \\ \hline \end{array}$

- (a) 26
- (b) 12
- (c) 8
- (d) 7

8

$74 - 30 = $ ___?___

- (a) 34
- (b) 44
- (c) 71
- (d) not here

4

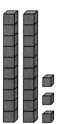

- (a) 23
- (b) 25
- (c) 28
- (d) 34

9

- (a) 2:00
- (b) 2:15
- (c) 2:30
- (d) 3:30

5

40, 45, 50, ___?___

- (a) 50
- (b) 55
- (c) 60
- (d) 65

10

- (a) 8:15
- (b) 8:30
- (c) 9:00
- (d) 9:15

11 Wes has 3 dimes and 2 nickels. How much money does Wes have?

(a) 5¢
(b) 32¢
(c) 40¢
(d) not here

16 Pam baked for 2 hours. She finished at 3:00. When did she start baking?

(a) 5:00
(b) 4:00
(c) 3:00
(d) 1:00

12 Rosa has 15 tapes. Mark has 8 tapes. How many more tapes does Rosa have?

(a) 10
(b) 9
(c) 8
(d) 7

17 Kim had 25 tickets. She got 20 more. How many does she have now?

(a) 55
(b) 45
(c) 20
(d) 5

13

(a) 36¢
(b) 45¢
(c) 46¢
(d) 61¢

18 Sara has 55 crayons. She gives away 20. How many does she have left?

(a) 35
(b) 45
(c) 53
(d) 75

14

(a) 59¢
(b) 63¢
(c) 68¢
(d) 77¢

19 John has 6 books. Jean has 6 books. How many books do they have in all?

(a) 0
(b) 6
(c) 11
(d) 12

15 The park had 47 trees. The club planted 10 more. Then 3 of the new trees died. How many trees does the park have now?

(a) 34
(b) 54
(c) 60
(d) 64

20

Number of Eggs Laid	
Day 1	⬭⬭⬭⬭⬭
Day 2	⬭⬭⬭⬭⬭
Day 3	⬭⬭⬭⬭⬭⬭⬭

Each ⬭ stands for 1 egg.

How many eggs were laid in all on Day 1 and Day 2?

(a) 5
(b) 6
(c) 10
(d) 11

Name

Number Card Game

PLAYERS   2 or more

MATERIALS   10 index cards, pencil

DIRECTIONS   Write a 2-digit number on each card.
Spread cards facedown on a table.
Take turns. Pick two cards. Use mental math to add.
If your answer is correct, keep the cards. The person
with the most cards at the end of the game is the winner.

As you play this game with your child, have your child
discuss what strategies he or she used to find the answer.

At Home

Dear Family,

We are beginning a new chapter in mathematics. During the next few weeks we will be learning to add 2-digit numbers such as:

$$38 + 19 \qquad 57 + 25$$

We will also be talking about how math is used at fairs. Please help me complete this interview.

Your child,

_____
Signature

Interview ....

Which of these have you attended?
(You may check more than one.)

❑ Fair (county, state, or other)

❑ Carnival

❑ Cinco de Mayo or other cultural celebration

❑ Amusement park

❑ Other _____

What are some of the things you can buy or win at these events? (List below ideas from family members.)

_____

_____

Fun at the Fair
Adding 2-Digit Numbers

 BEST IN SHOW

 Listen Listen to the story *Sam Johnson and the Blue Ribbon Quilt.*

 Talk Tell what you know about fairs.

What Do You Know?

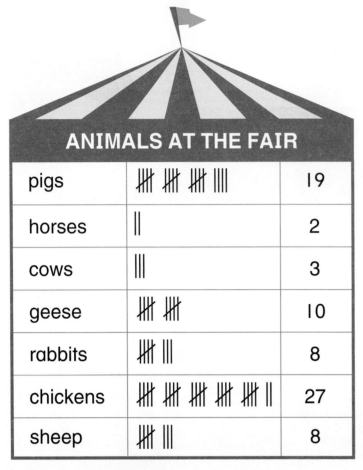

ANIMALS AT THE FAIR

pigs	卌 卌 卌 |||	19
horses	||	2
cows	|||	3
geese	卌 卌	10
rabbits	卌 |||	8
chickens	卌 卌 卌 卌 卌 ||	27
sheep	卌 |||	8

Jane counted the animals she saw at the fair.
Use the table. Find the total.

1 How many cows and sheep? _____

2 How many pigs and horses? _____

3 How many of the animals that Jane
   saw have feathers? _____

  Use the table.
Write pairs of numbers that are easy to add.
Do as many as you can.
Explain an interesting strategy that you used
to add.

Working Together

You and your partner need 2 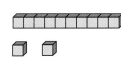 and 20 ▫.

▶ You show some ones.

▶ Your partner shows some ones.

▶ Make tens and ones.

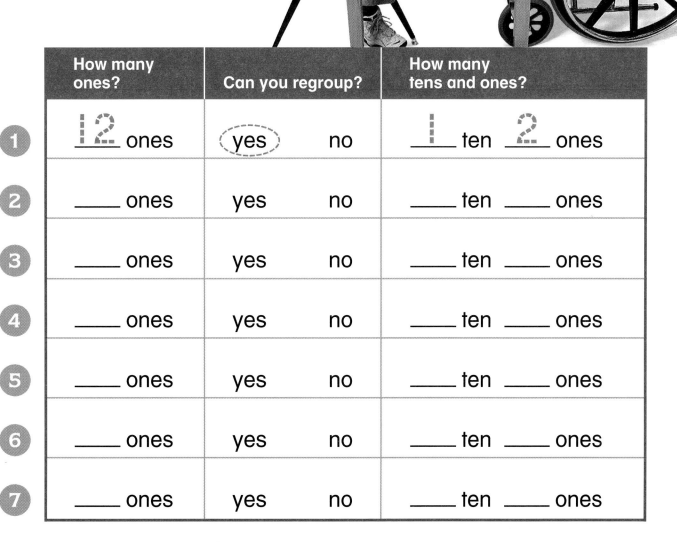

	How many ones?	Can you regroup?		How many tens and ones?
1	12 ones	(yes)	no	1 ten 2 ones
2	___ ones	yes	no	___ ten ___ ones
3	___ ones	yes	no	___ ten ___ ones
4	___ ones	yes	no	___ ten ___ ones
5	___ ones	yes	no	___ ten ___ ones
6	___ ones	yes	no	___ ten ___ ones
7	___ ones	yes	no	___ ten ___ ones

 Critical Thinking When can't you regroup?

Try These!

Use ▭ and ▫. Show the ones.
Regroup when you can.
Complete the chart.

		Can you regroup?		How many tens and ones?
1	16 ones	(yes)	no	_1_ ten _6_ ones
2	9 ones	yes	no	____ ten ____ ones
3	13 ones	yes	no	____ ten ____ ones
4	10 ones	yes	no	____ ten ____ ones
5	5 ones	yes	no	____ ten ____ ones
6	19 ones	yes	no	____ ten ____ ones

Mixed Review

7 Write each time in two ways.

____ o'clock

____ minutes after ____

____:____

____:____

At Home We regrouped when we had more than 10 ones. Ask your child how to regroup 15 ones.

Name _____

You need 5 ▭▭▭ and 20 ◻.

Show the numbers 16 and 8.

Regroup when you can.

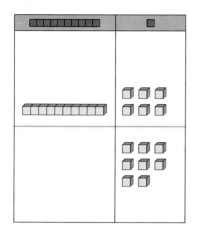 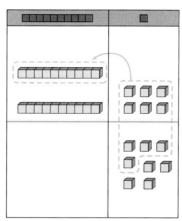

	Show	How many tens and ones?	Can you regroup?	How many tens and ones?
	16 8	__1__ tens __14__ ones	(yes) no	__2__ tens __4__ ones
	6 12	____ tens ____ ones	yes no	____ tens ____ ones
	23 9	____ tens ____ ones	yes no	____ tens ____ ones
	7 13	____ tens ____ ones	yes no	____ tens ____ ones
5	14 5	____ tens ____ ones	yes no	____ tens ____ ones

 Tell a partner how you regrouped.

Try These!

Use ⬚⬚⬚⬚⬚ and ⬚.

Show the tens and ones.
Regroup when you can.
Write the number.

1 1 ten 18 ones

tens	ones
2	8

2 2 tens 7 ones

tens	ones
2	7

3 1 ten 16 ones

tens	ones

4 3 tens 10 ones

tens	ones

5 15 ones

tens	ones

6 1 ten 6 ones

tens	ones

7 2 tens 14 ones

tens	ones

8 19 ones

tens	ones

9 4 tens 3 ones

tens	ones

10 1 ten 10 ones

tens	ones

 How do you know when to regroup?

At Home We regrouped greater numbers.
Have your child explain exercise 10.

Add 2-Digit Numbers

You need 9 ▭▭▭▭ and 20 ◻ .

You can use tens and ones models to add.

Show the numbers.	**Regroup ones when you can.**	**Count to find the sum.**
$\begin{array}{r} 39 \\ + \ 15 \\ \hline 54 \end{array}$	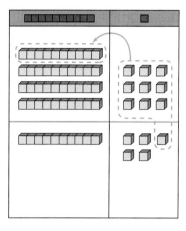	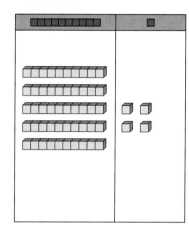

You can add without tens and ones models.

Add the ones.	**Regroup when you can.**	**Add all the tens.**

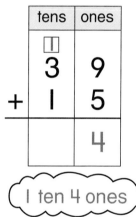

tens	ones
☐	
3	9
+ 1	5

(14 ones)

tens	ones
⊓	
3	9
+ 1	5
	4

(1 ten 4 ones)

tens	ones
⊓	
3	9
+ 1	5
5	4

(5 tens)

Add. Use tens and ones models to help.

1

tens	ones
⊓	
6	4
+	7
7	1

tens	ones
☐	
4	1
+ 2	3

tens	ones
☐	
3	6
+ 4	6

tens	ones
☐	
2	8
+ 3	5

 Critical Thinking How can you add without tens and ones models?

McGraw-Hill School Division

Try These!

Add. Use tens and ones models to help.

1

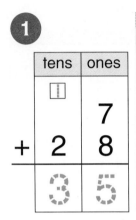

tens	ones
▮	7
+ 2	8
3	5

2

tens	ones
□	
3	3
+ 2	8

tens	ones
□	
1	2
+	9

tens	ones
□	
6	4
+ 1	6

tens	ones
□	
1	4
+ 5	3

3

tens	ones
□	
2	7
+ 1	8

tens	ones
□	
4	6
+ 4	7

tens	ones
□	
4	5
+ 1	6

tens	ones
□	
	8
+ 2	5

4

tens	ones
□	
3	5
+ 2	4

tens	ones
□	
	6
+ 2	1

tens	ones
□	
4	1
+ 2	9

tens	ones
□	
3	8
+ 1	9

At Home

We began adding with 2-digit numbers today. Ask your child to tell you about adding 7 + 28.

Use the table.
How many dolls did
Sam and Tama sell?

DOLLS SOLD	
Sam	23 dolls
Tama	25 dolls

Write the numbers.

23
+ 25

**Add the ones.
Do you need to regroup?**

☐
23
+ 25
8

(8 ones)

Add the tens.

☐
23
+ 25
48

(4 tens)

They sold __48__ dolls in all.

Add. Did you regroup?

1

☐
36   (yes)
+ 16   no
52

☐
45   yes
+ 22   no

☐
17   yes
+ 41   no

2

☐
58   yes
+ 34   no

☐
23   yes
+ 8   no

☐
63   yes
+ 16   no

Try These!

Add. Use tens and ones models to help.

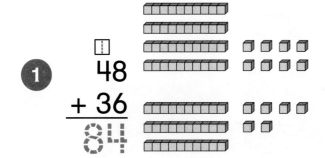

1
```
  □
 48
+36
 84
```

2
```
  □
 22
+37
 59
```

3
```
 □      □      □      □      □      □
 25     32     43     29     54     45
+46    +26    +45    +13    +19    +34
```

4
```
 □      □      □      □      □      □
 33     14     27     42     58     22
+28    +16    + 6    +24    +17    +43
```

5
```
 □      □      □      □      □      □
 65     13     37      7     35     52
+27    +44    +33    +66    +28    +26
```

More to Explore   Number Sense

Use each number once.

Write the numbers that equal the sum.

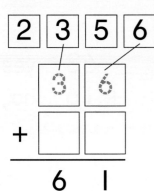

```
[2] [3] [5] [6]

  3   6

+ □   □
─────────
  6   1
```

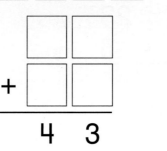

```
[1] [2] [5] [8]

  □   □

+ □   □
─────────
  4   3
```

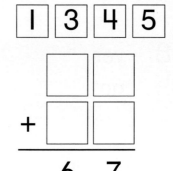

```
[1] [3] [4] [5]

  □   □

+ □   □
─────────
  6   7
```

 At Home

We continue to add with 2-digit numbers. Ask your child to explain how to add 35 + 28 and 52 + 26.

Add to Solve Problems

Carly made 24 large tacos to sell at the fair. She made 48 small tacos. How many tacos did Carly make?

Write the numbers.

$$24 \\ + 48$$

Add the ones. Regroup when you can.

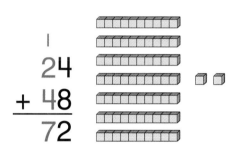

$$\begin{array}{r} 1 \\ 24 \\ + 48 \\ \hline 2 \end{array}$$

Add all the tens.

$$\begin{array}{r} 1 \\ 24 \\ + 48 \\ \hline 72 \end{array}$$

Carly made _72_ tacos.

Solve.

Workspace

1. Mr. Lewis bought 13 small tacos.
   He bought 8 large tacos.
   How many tacos did he buy? ____

2. Carly sold 46 tacos in the morning.
   She sold 24 tacos in the afternoon.
   How many tacos did she sell? ____

Critical Thinking Did Carly sell all the tacos she made? How do you know?

Workspace

1 The judges tasted 29 apple cakes.
They tasted 35 nut cakes.
How many cakes did the judges taste? __64__

$$\begin{array}{r} \overset{1}{29} \\ +\ 35 \\ \hline 64 \end{array}$$

2 Jamie's club won 8 yellow ribbons
and 11 blue ribbons.
How many ribbons did the club win? ____

3 Lee used 17 ride tickets.
Tito used 14 ride tickets.
How many tickets did the boys use? ____

4 Anna watched the sheep contest.
There were 38 black and 15 white sheep.
How many sheep did Anna see? ____

5 Nico scored 35 points in one game.
He scored 23 points in a second game.
How many points did Nico score? ____

Mixed Review

Use mental math to add or subtract.

6 $9 + 8 =$ ____ $12 - 3 =$ ____ $30 + 30 =$ ____

7 $50 - 20 =$ ____ $40 + 50 =$ ____ $16 - 7 =$ ____

At Home

We used addition to solve problems. Read problem 5 but use the numbers 26 and 49. Have your child find the answer.

Name _____

Use Estimation

Read   Tom played two games.
He scored a total of about 80 points.
Which two scores are his?

> Read
> Plan
> Solve
> Look Back

Plan   **Estimate** to find **about** 80 points.

Solve   Try 22 and 43 points.

> 22 is nearer to 20 than 30.

> 43 is nearer to 40 than 50.

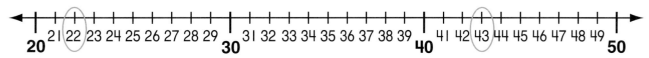

$$20 + 40 = \underline{60}$$ (22 and 43 are not the scores.)

Now try 38 and 43 points.

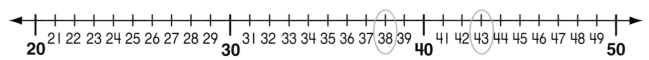

$$40 + 40 = \underline{80}$$

Tom's scores are 38 and 43.

Look Back   Do the scores of 38 and 43 make sense? _____

   Would scores of 48 and 22 make sense for a total of about 60 points? Explain.

McGraw-Hill School Division

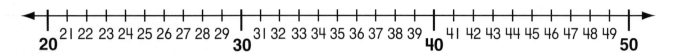

Try These!

Solve. Use estimation.

20 21 22 23 24 25 26 27 28 29 30 31 32 33 34 35 36 37 38 39 40 41 42 43 44 45 46 47 48 49 50

1 Joey played two games of ring toss.
He scored a total of about 60 points.
Which two scores are his? _____

2 Joyce sold tickets for two rides.
She sold about 80 tickets.
Which two groups of tickets did she sell? _____

   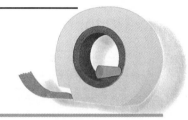

3 Tim played two games of ball toss.
He scored a total of about 50 points.
Which two scores are his? _____

4 Tiffany tried to ring the bell.
She took two swings with the hammer.
She scored a total of about 70 points.
Which two scores are Tiffany's? _____

At Home

We estimated to solve problems. Ask your child
to explain how to solve problem 4.

Name _____

Midchapter Review

Do your best!

Add. Use tens and ones
models if you want to.

1
tens	ones
□ 1	9
+ 5	4

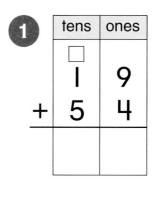

2
tens	ones
5	1
+ 3	6

3
tens	ones
□ 1	5
+	6

4   42
      + 36

5   53
      + 29

6   24
      + 45

7   47
      + 27

8   16
      + 66

Estimate to solve.

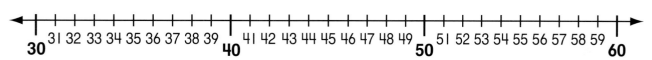

30 31 32 33 34 35 36 37 38 39 40 41 42 43 44 45 46 47 48 49 50 51 52 53 54 55 56 57 58 59 60

9 Rita sold about 70 tickets
for the school fair.
Which two groups of
tickets did she sell? _____

 52    33   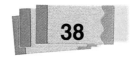 38

10 How did you estimate to solve problem 9?

_____

_____

Journal

How is estimating the sum of 33 and 38 different
from adding 33 and 38?

Get to the Fair!

You and your partner need 2 , 9 ▭, 20 ◻, and a ◉.

Take turns.

► Put your game marker on **Start.** Show 25 with tens and ones models.

► Spin for another number and show that many tens and ones.

► Combine the tens and ones.

► Move ahead one space if you regroup the ones. Stay in the space if you cannot regroup.

► For each turn, show the number in the space and the number you spin.

Name _____

Patch Patterns

 Listen to *Sam Johnson and the Blue Ribbon Quilt.*

Cultural Note
This is an Amish quilt called *Double Wedding Ring.*

A patch pattern can be a square like this. Squares are sewn together to make a patchwork quilt.

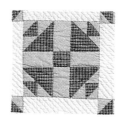

Working Together

You and your partner will make patchwork squares.

You each need crayons and 8 paper ◺ in two different colors.

▶ Use 8 ◺ to make a patchwork square.

▶ Draw your patch pattern and color it.

▶ Make 3 more patch patterns. Make all the patterns different. Draw and color them.

McGraw-Hill School Division

Decision Making

1 Use the price list.
What is the total
cost of this
patch pattern? _____

PRICE LIST		
Shape		**Cost**
red	■	12¢
yellow	■	9¢
green	■	8¢
red	◣	6¢
green	◤	4¢

2 Choose one of your patchwork squares.
Decide on a price for each color shape.
What is the total cost of your square? _____

Write a report.

3 Tell how you decided
on a price for each
color shape.

4 Tell how you found the
total cost of your
patchwork square.

More to Investigate

Tape or glue your patchwork pattern to a
square piece of paper.

PREDICT What if you make a class quilt.
Will the squares make a rectangle?

EXPLORE Try it. Make sure there are
no holes in the rectangle.

FIND Find the total cost of the class quilt.

Name _____

Jim's group made 18 signs for the fair.
Paul's group made 16 signs.
How many signs did they make in all?

Jim added this way to find out.	Paul added this way to find out.

$$\begin{array}{r} 1 \\ 18 \\ + 16 \\ \hline 34 \end{array}$$
$$\begin{array}{r} 1 \\ 16 \\ + 18 \\ \hline 34 \end{array}$$

 Talk Why did they get the same answer?

You can check your addition by adding
the numbers in a different order.

Add. Check your work.

1

$$\begin{array}{r} 23 \\ + 19 \end{array}$$
$$\begin{array}{r} 71 \\ + 4 \end{array}$$
$$\begin{array}{r} 37 \\ + 18 \end{array}$$
$$\begin{array}{r} 52 \\ + 29 \end{array}$$
$$\begin{array}{r} 63 \\ + 8 \end{array}$$
$$\begin{array}{r} 9 \\ + 19 \end{array}$$

2

$$\begin{array}{r} 81 \\ + 6 \end{array}$$
$$\begin{array}{r} 28 \\ + 62 \end{array}$$
$$\begin{array}{r} 14 \\ + 48 \end{array}$$
$$\begin{array}{r} 25 \\ + 14 \end{array}$$
$$\begin{array}{r} 46 \\ + 15 \end{array}$$
$$\begin{array}{r} 52 \\ + 7 \end{array}$$

3

$$\begin{array}{r} 47 \\ + 45 \end{array}$$
$$\begin{array}{r} 45 \\ + 43 \end{array}$$
$$\begin{array}{r} 24 \\ + 27 \end{array}$$
$$\begin{array}{r} 7 \\ + 36 \end{array}$$
$$\begin{array}{r} 55 \\ + 5 \end{array}$$
$$\begin{array}{r} 37 \\ + 19 \end{array}$$

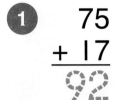

Try These!

Add. Check your work.

1

75	5	46	12	19	37
+ 17	+ 26	+ 50	+ 17	+ 7	+ 32
92					

2

42	18	3	33	19	45
+ 23	+ 19	+ 52	+ 27	+ 43	+ 16

3

39	56	27	7	16	68
+ 5	+ 17	+ 27	+ 41	+ 8	+ 22

Choose two of these numbers.
Write your own exercises.
Find the sums.

21   16   32   7   28   49   50

4

```
  49
+ 28
  77
```

5

6

7 Choose two more numbers.
Use them to write a word problem.
Then solve the problem.

Use your own paper.

At Home   We learned to check addition. Ask your child how he or she checks addition.

Score 10

You and your partner need 2  .

Take turns.

▶ Drop two counters on the squares.

▶ Write the addition and find the sum.

▶ Your partner checks your work.

▶ Score 10 points for each correct sum.

45
+ 29

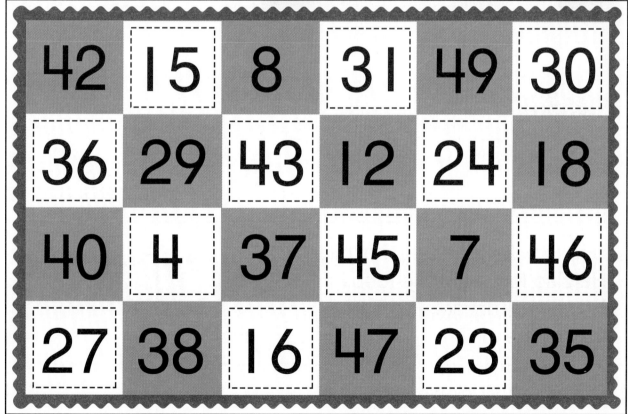

42	15	8	31	49	30
36	29	43	12	24	18
40	4	37	45	7	46
27	38	16	47	23	35

Color to show your score.

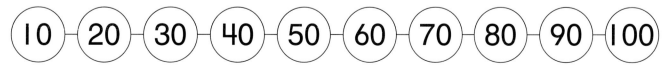

10 — 20 — 30 — 40 — 50 — 60 — 70 — 80 — 90 — 100

McGraw-Hill School Division

Add.

1
65	51	47	35	6	75
+ 27	+ 8	+ 34	+ 24	+ 14	+ 5
92					

2
23	12	42	53	18	31
+ 56	+ 41	+ 23	+ 24	+ 25	+ 36

3
19	52	34	27	79	3
+ 13	+ 39	+ 64	+ 26	+ 18	+ 85

4
8	45	63	35	59	21
+ 37	+ 12	+ 17	+ 23	+ 26	+ 48

Workspace

Solve.

5 Ben took 24 piglets to the fair. He also took 18 white rabbits. How many animals did Ben take to the fair? _____ animals

6 Rita made 37 clown dolls to sell. She made 26 baby dolls to sell. How many dolls did Rita make? _____ dolls

Name _____

Put price tags like these on things in your classroom.

Working Together

Take turns choosing two things to order. Fill out an order form. You and your partners find the total with , ▦ , and ✎ .

Compare totals. Write the total on the order form.

Order Form	
Item	**Price**

Order Form	
Item	**Price**

Order Form	
Item	**Price**

 Critical Thinking How is adding money like adding numbers?

McGraw-Hill School Division

Remember to write a ¢.

SCHOOL FAIR SNACK TENT

 yogurt 48¢   juice 34¢   peanuts 35¢   popcorn 47¢   milk 25¢   taco 59¢

Workspace

1 Cara buys yogurt and juice. How much does she spend?   82¢

$$\begin{array}{r} 48¢ \\ +\ 34¢ \\ \hline 82¢ \end{array}$$

2 Eric buys juice and peanuts. How much does he spend?   _____

3 Kim buys popcorn and milk. What is the total cost?   _____

4 Jon wants to buy milk and a taco. How much money does he need?   _____

More to Explore   Number Sense

Complete. Then make up another pattern.

$$\begin{array}{r} 8 \\ +7 \\ \hline 15 \end{array} \qquad \begin{array}{r} 8 \\ +17 \\ \hline \end{array} \qquad \begin{array}{r} 8 \\ +27 \\ \hline \end{array} \qquad \begin{array}{r} 8 \\ +37 \\ \hline \end{array} \qquad \begin{array}{r} 8 \\ +47 \\ \hline \end{array}$$

Ask your child to show you how to add 25¢ and 59¢. He or she may use pennies and dimes.

Name _____

Roger bought three toys at the crafts fair.
You can add to find how much he spent.

Add the ones.
Regroup when
you can.

$$\begin{array}{r} \overset{1}{1}6¢ \\ 23¢ \\ + 34¢ \\ \hline 3 \end{array}$$

Look for
a 10.

Add all the
tens.

$$\begin{array}{r} \overset{1}{1}6¢ \\ 23¢ \\ + 34¢ \\ \hline 73¢ \end{array}$$

Think
of doubles.

How much did Roger spend? __73¢__

Add.

1

42¢	32¢	20¢	13¢	3¢
13¢	21¢	2¢	16¢	64¢
+ 28¢	+ 15¢	+ 29¢	+ 33¢	+ 12¢

2

28¢	24¢	44¢	27¢	9¢
+ 54¢	+ 1¢	+ 21¢	+ 19¢	+ 22¢

Critical Thinking What strategies did you use to add?

Add.

1

16¢	60¢	42¢	8¢	16¢
+ 25¢	+ 22¢	+ 19¢	+ 41¢	+ 24¢
41¢				

2

13¢	24¢	29¢	18¢	15¢
+ 42¢	+ 18¢	+ 31¢	+ 33¢	+ 8¢

3

7¢	55¢	19¢	35¢	14¢
22¢	16¢	20¢	3¢	13¢
+ 11¢	+ 14¢	+ 22¢	+ 29¢	+ 24¢

 ## Cultural Connection — **Indian Addition**

In ancient India, Bhaskara invented this method of adding.

$$2 + 5 + 23 + 48$$

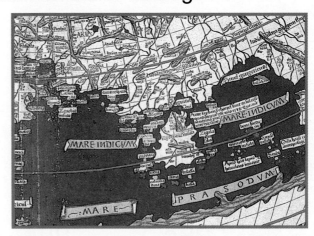

sum of ones	2	5	3	8	18
sum of tens			2	4	+ 6
					78

Add these numbers.
Use the same method.

$$6 + 8 + 34 + 51$$

sum of ones ____ ____ ____ ____

sum of tens   ____ ____ + ____

At Home — Ask your child to show you how to add three numbers.

Choose the Method

Lulu sells her crafts at the market.
The chart shows what she sold.

Read
Plan
Solve
Look Back

SALES	
Item	**Number Sold**
jar	32
small bowl	47
large bowl	24
giant bowl	10
mug	38

Solve. Choose the best method for you.

Mental Math

1 How many bowls did Lulu sell?   ____

 How did you solve the problem?

_____

2 How many jars and mugs did
Lulu sell?   ____

_____

3 Which two items did Lulu sell the most of?

_____

How many of these items
did she sell in all?   ____

1 What if Lulu sold 18 jars and 16 mugs on Tuesday. What would be the total number sold? ____

2 What if she sold 10 more jars and 10 more mugs on Wednesday. What would be the total for both days? ____

Talk Did you use different methods for problems 1 and 2? Explain.

Write and Share

Turrelle wrote this problem.
How many large bowls, small bowls, and jars did Lulu sell in all?

Turrelle Sims
Snowden School
Memphis, Tennessee

3 Solve Turrelle's problem. ____

What method did you choose? _____

_____

4 **Write** Write a problem using information from the chart. Have a partner solve it.

Use your own paper.

What method did your partner use? _____

What method would you use? _____

At Home Ask your child to tell you how to solve the problem he or she wrote.

Chapter Review

Add. Did you regroup? Mark *yes* or *no*.

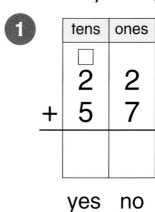

1

tens	ones
☐	
2	2
+ 5	7

yes   no

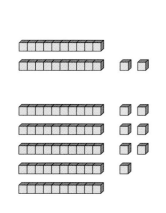

2

tens	ones
☐	
3	6
+ 1	8

yes   no

Add.

3

tens	ones
☐	
5	9
+ 1	3

4

tens	ones
☐	
4	5
+ 2	2

5

tens	ones
☐	
8	4
+	6

6

tens	ones
☐	
6	3
+ 2	7

7

tens	ones
☐	
	8
+ 3	4

8

tens	ones
☐	
5	6
+ 3	3

9
```
  76
+ 14
```

10
```
  72
+ 26
```

11
```
  69¢
+  8¢
```

12
```
  27¢
+ 38¢
```

13
```
  34
+ 25
```

14
```
  17
+ 16
```

15
```
  43
+  4
```

16
```
  28¢
+ 18¢
```

Estimate to solve.

```
◄──┼──┼──┼──┼──┼──┼──┼──┼──┼──┼──┼──┼──┼──┼──┼──┼──┼──┼──┼──┼──┼──┼──┼──┼──┼──┼──┼──┼──┼──┼──►
   30  31 32 33 34 35 36 37 38 39  40  41 42 43 44 45 46 47 48 49  50  51 52 53 54 55 56 57 58 59  60
```

17 Liz bowled two games. She scored a total of about 90. Which two scores are hers?

_____

18 Sam collects sports cards. He has a total of about 80 cards. Which two groups of cards are Sam's?

_____

19 On Monday 52 chicks hatched. On Tuesday 19 more hatched. How many chicks hatched in all?

_____ chicks

20 Sara used 27 pounds of feed in May. In June she used 38 pounds. How many pounds of feed did she use?

_____ pounds

What Do You Think?

Which is the quickest way to add 15 and 45?
☑ Check one.

    ☐   ☐   Mental Math   ☐

Why? _____

 Write these exercises in your journal. Find the sums. Explain which is easier to add.

```
  18      79
+ 25    + 10
```

Name _____

Add.

1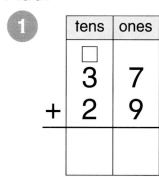

tens	ones
☐	
3	7
+ 2	9

2
```
   53
 + 37
```

3
```
   31
 + 18
```

4
```
   75
 +  9
```

5
```
   24
 + 18
```

6
```
    8¢
 + 73¢
```

7
```
   13¢
 + 84¢
```

Solve.

8 José made 26 small cakes.
He made 38 large cakes.
How many cakes did José make?   _____ cakes

Estimate to solve.

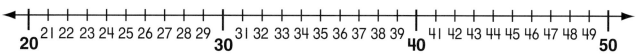

20 21 22 23 24 25 26 27 28 29 30 31 32 33 34 35 36 37 38 39 40 41 42 43 44 45 46 47 48 49 50

9 Tina sold tickets at the fair.
She sold about 40 tickets.
Which two groups of tickets did she sell?   _____

18   12   23

10 Kim plays two games at the fair.
He scores a total of about 30 points.
Which two game scores are Kim's?   _____

 29   8   19

McGraw-Hill School Division

What Did You Learn?

$$3\blacksquare + \blacksquare7 = 91$$

What is $\blacksquare$ (gray) ? ____

How do you know? _____

_____

_____

_____

What is $\blacksquare$ (blue) ? ____

How do you know? _____

_____

_____

_____

 You may want to put this page in your portfolio.

Math Connection
Patterns and Functions

Name

Addition Tables

Look at the numbers. What patterns do you see?

6
16
26
36

Add 2. What patterns do you see?

	+ 2
6	
16	
26	
36	

Complete each table.

	+ 6
32	
42	
52	
62	

	+ 8
24	
34	
44	
54	

	+ 15
5	
15	
25	
35	

	+ 29
3	
13	
23	
	62

Make your own table. Your partner tells you what sums to write. Talk about the patterns.

Show a number pattern in this column.

	+

Write a number to add here.

McGraw-Hill School Division

Technology Connection
Computer

Make a Bar Graph

Talk What is your favorite ride at the fair? This computer spreadsheet shows what some people chose.

FAVORITE RIDES				
Rides	**Children**	**Teachers**	**Parents**	**Total**
Ferris Wheel	35	2	27	
Roller Coaster	13	1	25	
Carousel	26	1	44	

At the Computer

1 Complete the spreadsheet.

How many people chose the Ferris wheel?

_____ people

2 Use the data in the spreadsheet to make a bar graph.

What does the bar graph tell you about people's favorite rides?

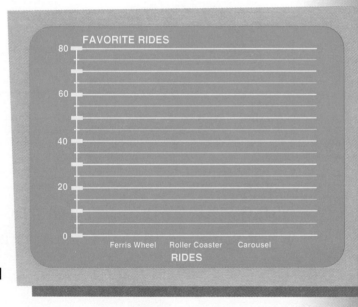

_____

_____

_____

Name

Game of the Century!

PLAYERS	2 or more
MATERIALS	pencil and paper

DIRECTIONS The first player writes any number between 1 and 5 on a sheet of paper. Then each player in turn adds another number between 1 and 15 and writes the sum.

The winner is the player who adds to get a sum of exactly 100.

 Play this game with your child. Note that as the sum reaches 70, players must plan ahead to increase their chance of being able to be the last player able to add to get exactly 100.

At
Home

Dear Family,

We are beginning a new chapter in mathematics. During the next few weeks we will be learning to subtract 2-digit numbers such as:

$$\begin{array}{r} 47 \\ -\ 29 \\ \hline \end{array} \quad \text{and} \quad \begin{array}{r} 30 \\ -\ 12 \\ \hline \end{array}$$

We will also be talking about animals that migrate from one place to another. Please help me complete this interview.

Your child,

_____
Signature

Interview ···

These are some animals that migrate. Which of these animals have you seen?

❑ Geese ❑ Whales ❑ Monarch butterflies

❑ Seals ❑ Sea turtles ❑ Hummingbirds

Do you know any other animals that migrate to or from your neighborhood? _____

If so, what are they? _____

_____

_____

Animals on the Move
Subtracting 2-Digit Numbers

 Listen Listen to the story *the Great Monarch Butterfly Chase.*

 Talk Tell about butterflies or other animals that you know migrate.

What Do You Know

There are 18 cards in each set of animal cards.

Find the number of cards you need to complete each set.

ANIMALS-ON-THE-GO COLLECTION

Set of Cards	Cards You Have	Cards You Need
Insects	17	
Birds	10	
Fish	9	
Mammals	5	
Reptiles/Amphibians	3	

Tell how you found the number of cards needed to complete each set. What strategies did you use? Explain.

Name _____

Working Together

You and your partner need
5 ▭▭ and 20 ◻.

Regroup
1 ten as 10 ones.
Now there are
12 ones.

Take turns.

▶ You show tens and ones.

▶ Your partner regroups if needed.
Then your partner takes away ones.

▶ Write how many tens and ones are left.

	Show.	Take away.	Did you regroup?	How many tens and ones are left?
1	1 ten 2 ones	4 ones	yes no	_0_ tens _8_ ones
2	1 ten 8 ones	6 ones	yes no	___ tens ___ ones
3	1 ten 3 ones	8 ones	yes no	___ tens ___ ones
4	1 ten 6 ones	9 ones	yes no	___ tens ___ ones
5	1 ten 5 ones	1 one	yes no	___ tens ___ ones

Critical Thinking When don't you need to regroup?

Regroup when you need to.

Use ▭ and ▪.
Complete the chart.

	Show.	Take away.	Did you regroup?	How many tens and ones are left?
1	2 tens 6 ones	8 ones	(yes) no	__1__ tens __8__ ones
2	1 ten 6 ones	5 ones	yes no	____ tens ____ ones
3	4 tens 3 ones	7 ones	yes no	____ tens ____ ones
4	1 ten 4 ones	6 ones	yes no	____ tens ____ ones
5	3 tens 9 ones	8 ones	yes no	____ tens ____ ones

Mixed Review

Write the number.

6 _____

7 _____

8 _____

9 _____

At Home — We explored regrouping for subtraction. Ask your child how to regroup 1 ten 4 ones.

Name _____

Working Together

You and your partner need
5  and 20 ▫.
Take turns.

▶ Your partner shows
tens and ones.

▶ You regroup if needed.
Take away tens and ones.

▶ Write the number that is left.

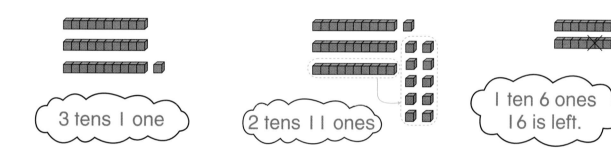

3 tens 1 one

2 tens 11 ones

1 ten 6 ones
16 is left.

	Show.	Take away.	Did you regroup?		Number left.
1	31	15	(yes)	no	16
2	26	19	yes	no	___
3	55	21	yes	no	___
4	41	6	yes	no	___
5	37	12	yes	no	___
6	28	9	yes	no	___

Try These!

Regroup when you need to.

Use ▭▭▭ and ▪.
Complete the chart.

	Show.	Take away.	Did you regroup?		Number left.
1	45	26	(yes)	no	19
2	29	13	yes	no	
3	31	24	yes	no	
4	25	6	yes	no	
5	56	30	yes	no	
6	50	16	yes	no	
7	28	7	yes	no	
8	47	38	yes	no	
9	16	11	yes	no	
10	20	19	yes	no	

At Home

We regrouped with greater numbers. Ask your child to explain exercise 10 above.

You need 9 ▭ and 20 ◻.
You can use tens and ones models
to subtract.

Show 43.	Look at the ones. Regroup 1 ten as 10 ones if you need to.	Take away ones. Take away tens.

43
– 15
28

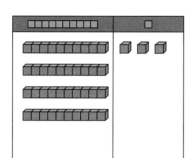 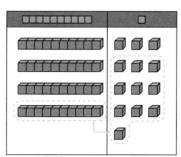 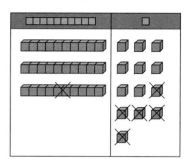

You can subtract without tens and ones models.

Look at the ones.	Regroup if you need to.	Subtract the ones.	Subtract the tens.

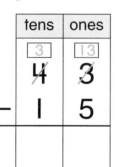 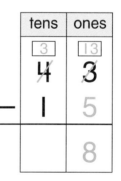 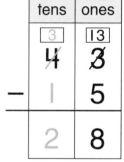

3 ones are not enough.	3 tens 13 ones	8 ones are left.	2 tens are left.

Subtract. Use tens and ones models to help.

 1

tens	ones
5̸ 6̸	1̸3̸ 3
– 2	7
3	6

tens	ones
☐	☐
3	8
–	9

tens	ones
☐	☐
8	6
– 4	2

tens	ones
☐	☐
2	1
– 1	8

 Critical Thinking Do you get the same answer with and without tens and ones models? Explain.

Try These!

Subtract. Use tens and ones models to help.

1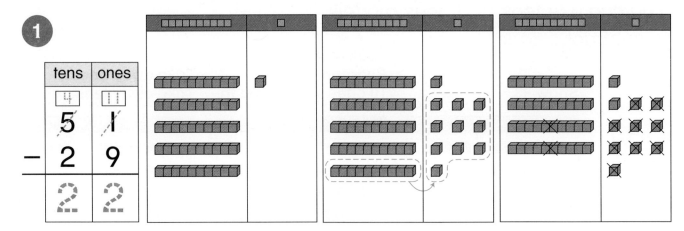

tens	ones
~~5~~ 4	~~1~~ 11
5	1
− 2	9
2	*2*

2

tens	ones
☐	☐
3	6
− 1	9

tens	ones
☐	☐
4	2
−	7

tens	ones
☐	☐
9	1
− 4	3

tens	ones
☐	☐
3	8
− 2	2

3

tens	ones
☐	☐
4	5
− 2	5

tens	ones
☐	☐
2	4
− 1	5

tens	ones
☐	☐
5	9
− 3	1

tens	ones
☐	☐
7	3
− 3	4

4

tens	ones
☐	☐
2	7
−	6

tens	ones
☐	☐
6	2
− 1	5

tens	ones
☐	☐
8	0
− 4	6

tens	ones
☐	☐
5	4
− 1	8

Journal Write a subtraction rule that tells you when you need to regroup.

At Home We subtracted with and without tens and ones models. Ask your child to explain how to subtract 54 − 18.

Use the table.
How many more swallowtails are there than painted lady butterflies?

Swallowtail

BUTTERFLY WATCH	
Swallowtail	26
Painted lady	14

Painted Lady

Write the numbers.

☐☐
26
− 14

Regroup if you need to. Subtract the ones.

☐☐
26
− 14
2

(2 ones)

Subtract the tens.

☐☐
26
− 14
12

(1 ten)

There are __12__ more swallowtails.

Subtract. Did you regroup?

1. 34
    − 25
    9   (yes)   no

    ☐☐
    98
    − 40   yes   no

    ☐☐
    60
    − 31   yes   no

2. ☐☐
    36
    − 23   yes   no

    ☐☐
    57
    − 9   yes   no

    ☐☐
    82
    − 27   yes   no

Try These!

Subtract. Use tens and ones models if you want to.

1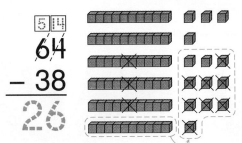
```
  5 14
  6̶ 4̶
- 3 8
─────
  2 6
```

2
```
  □□
  5 7
- 4 3
─────
  1 4
```

3
```
  □□        □□        □□        □□        □□        □□
  4 5       6 8       2 0       3 1       9 6       5 9
- 1 7     - 3 3     -   4     - 2 1     - 5 9     - 5 1
```

4
```
  □□        □□        □□        □□        □□        □□
  8 2       2 9       3 4       7 3       8 6       4 1
-   8     - 1 5     - 2 9     - 3 7     - 4 0     - 1 6
```

5
```
  □□        □□        □□        □□        □□        □□
  4 8       9 4       8 3       5 0       3 7       7 5
-   5     - 6 5     - 4 6     - 3 0     - 1 2     - 2 9
```

Solve.

6 How many more zebra butterflies than monarchs are there?

Monarch

Zebra

BUTTERFLY WATCH	
Monarch	18
Zebra	30

Workspace

There are _____ more zebra butterflies.

 At Home

We continue to subtract 2-digit numbers. Ask your child to explain how to subtract 37 – 12 and 75 – 29.

Name

A bird spreads its wings to fly.
This measure is called *wingspan.*

Osprey
54 inches

Wood Duck
28 inches

Prairie Falcon
40 inches

Bald Eagle
80 inches

How much larger is the wingspan of the
falcon than the wingspan of the duck?

**Regroup if you need to.
Subtract the ones.**

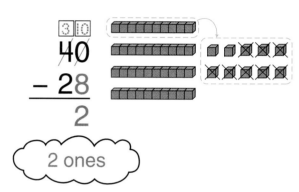

2 ones

Subtract the tens.

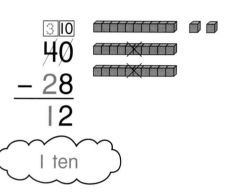

1 ten

The wingspan of the falcon is  inches larger.

Solve.

Workspace

1 How much larger is the wingspan
of the osprey than of the duck?

_____ inches

2 How much larger is the wingspan
of the eagle than of the osprey?

_____ inches

Critical Thinking Why do you subtract to compare?

McGraw-Hill School Division

Try These!

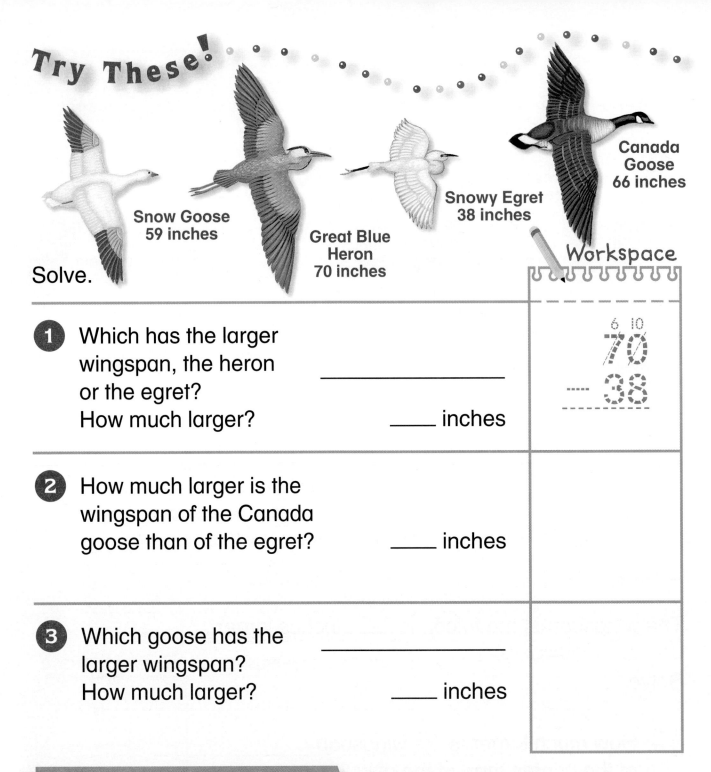

Snow Goose
59 inches

Great Blue
Heron
70 inches

Snowy Egret
38 inches

Canada
Goose
66 inches

Solve.

Workspace

6 10
7̶0̶
− 38

1. Which has the larger wingspan, the heron or the egret? How much larger?

_____

____ inches

2. How much larger is the wingspan of the Canada goose than of the egret?

____ inches

3. Which goose has the larger wingspan? How much larger?

_____

____ inches

More to Explore   Number Sense

 Calculator

Solve.

Each van can hold 8 people. 56 people will ride in the vans to the birdwatch. How many vans are needed?

____ vans

 At Home

We used subtraction to solve problems. Have your child explain how to solve problem 3 above.

Blackbird, Fly!

You and your partner need a 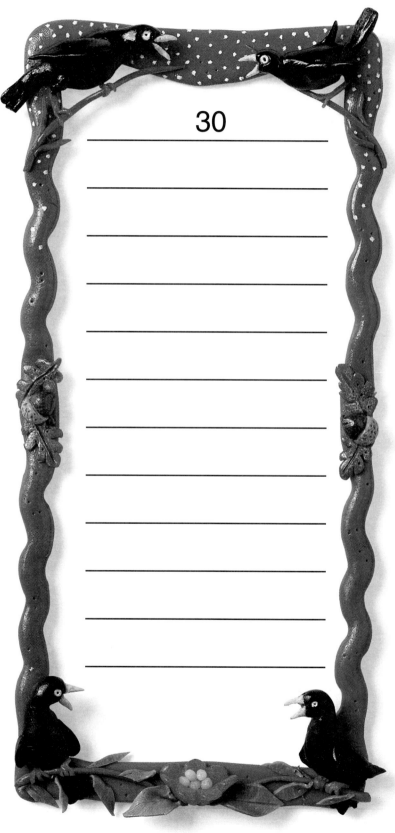,
6 ▨▨▨▨ , and 20 ▫.

Take turns.

▶ Each of you starts with
  3 ▨▨▨▨ .These are your
  "blackbirds."

▶ Each of you spins for the
  number of "blackbirds"
  that fly south for the
  winter.

▶ Subtract that number.
  Regroup if you need to.

▶ Write each new total.

▶ Play until all of one
  player's "blackbirds"
  are gone.

30

Subtract.

1

$$\begin{array}{r} \overset{7\ 16}{\cancel{8}\cancel{6}} \\ -\ 17 \\ \hline 69 \end{array}$$
$$\begin{array}{r} 67 \\ -\ 46 \\ \hline \end{array}$$
$$\begin{array}{r} 32 \\ -\ 28 \\ \hline \end{array}$$
$$\begin{array}{r} 44 \\ -\ 39 \\ \hline \end{array}$$
$$\begin{array}{r} 68 \\ -\ 47 \\ \hline \end{array}$$
$$\begin{array}{r} 96 \\ -\ 47 \\ \hline \end{array}$$

2

$$\begin{array}{r} 60 \\ -\ 48 \\ \hline \end{array}$$
$$\begin{array}{r} 30 \\ -\ 16 \\ \hline \end{array}$$
$$\begin{array}{r} 27 \\ -\ 19 \\ \hline \end{array}$$
$$\begin{array}{r} 62 \\ -\ 48 \\ \hline \end{array}$$
$$\begin{array}{r} 93 \\ -\ 60 \\ \hline \end{array}$$
$$\begin{array}{r} 88 \\ -\ 72 \\ \hline \end{array}$$

3

$$\begin{array}{r} 23 \\ -\ 19 \\ \hline \end{array}$$
$$\begin{array}{r} 44 \\ -\ 26 \\ \hline \end{array}$$
$$\begin{array}{r} 51 \\ -\ 29 \\ \hline \end{array}$$
$$\begin{array}{r} 88 \\ -\ 46 \\ \hline \end{array}$$
$$\begin{array}{r} 72 \\ -\ 44 \\ \hline \end{array}$$
$$\begin{array}{r} 63 \\ -\ 18 \\ \hline \end{array}$$

4

$$\begin{array}{r} 45 \\ -\ 23 \\ \hline \end{array}$$
$$\begin{array}{r} 75 \\ -\ 68 \\ \hline \end{array}$$
$$\begin{array}{r} 37 \\ -\ 29 \\ \hline \end{array}$$
$$\begin{array}{r} 71 \\ -\ 18 \\ \hline \end{array}$$
$$\begin{array}{r} 39 \\ -\ 21 \\ \hline \end{array}$$
$$\begin{array}{r} 80 \\ -\ 65 \\ \hline \end{array}$$

Solve.

Workspace

5 Bob says he counted 76 blackbirds in a flock. Marie says she counted 59 blackbirds in another flock. How many more birds did Bob count?

_____ birds

Name _____

Make a List

Scientists tag some animals to help keep track of them.

Read   Dr. Ross puts tags on butterflies. She uses the numbers 2, 4, and 5 to make 2-digit tag numbers with different digits. How many different tag numbers can Dr. Ross make?

Plan   You can **make a list** to organize this information.

Solve   The list shows the 6 possible tag numbers.

Start with	Tag Numbers
2	24, 25
4	42, 45
5	52, 54

Look Back   Have you answered the question?

Make a list to solve.

1   Dr. Soto tags geese. He uses the numbers 1, 3, and 7 to make 2-digit tag numbers with different digits. How many tag numbers can Dr. Soto make?

Start with	Tag Numbers
1	
3	
7	

_____ tag numbers

McGraw-Hill School Division

Make a list to show all the 2-digit numbers.

1 Dr. Johnson tags ducks.
She uses the numbers 3, 5, and 9
to make 2-digit tag numbers.
What numbers can she make?

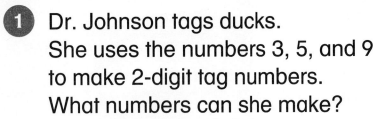

35 39

She can make _____.

2 A group of scientists has to tag seals.
The scientists use the numbers 4, 6,
and 8 to make 2-digit tag numbers.
What numbers can they make?

They can make _____.

3 Dr. Sanchez made tags for
crabs. Then he lost his list.
What 2-digit numbers did he
make with 3, 4, and 7?

He made _____.

4 Two scientists tag geese.
The scientists use the numbers
1, 2, 3, and 4 to make 2-digit tag
numbers. What numbers
can they make?

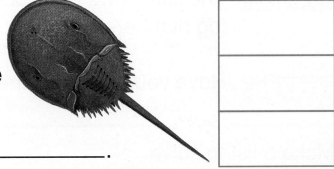

They can make _____

_____.

Talk How many more 2-digit numbers can you
make with 4 numbers than with 3 numbers?

Name _____

Subtract. Use tens and ones models if you want to.

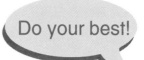

Do your best!

1

tens	ones
☐	☐
3	3
− 1	7

2

tens	ones
☐	☐
5	2
− 3	0

3

tens	ones
☐	☐
2	6
− 1	9

4
$$52 - 5$$

5
$$73 - 48$$

6
$$41 - 12$$

7
$$39 - 24$$

8
$$45 - 36$$

Solve.
Make a list to find all the 2-digit numbers.

9 Dr. Beck made tags for some birds. He used the numbers 5, 7, and 9 to make 2-digit tag numbers. What numbers did he make?

He made _____.

10 How did you solve problem 9? _____

_____

For 2-digit numbers, how is regrouping in subtraction different from regrouping in addition?

Fly South to Mexico!

Listen to *the Great Monarch Butterfly Chase*.

You and your partner need 2 , a , and a .

Take turns. Pretend you are both butterflies on your way to Mexico.

▶ Put your counter on **Garden**.

▶ Spin the spinner twice. Subtract the lesser number from the greater number.

▶ Your partner checks your work.

▶ Move ahead one space if you are correct. If not, go back one space.

The winner is the first player to reach **Mexico**.

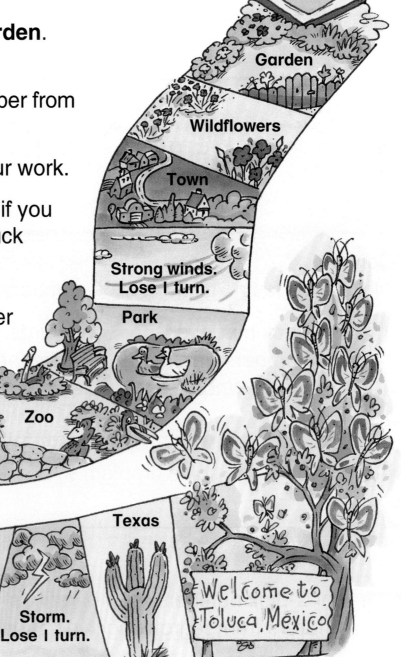

Start

Garden

Wildflowers

Town

Strong winds. Lose 1 turn.

Park

Ride the wind. Move ahead 2 spaces.

Zoo

New York City

Washington, D.C.

Gulf of Mexico

Storm. Lose 1 turn.

Texas

Welcome to Toluca, Mexico

Name _____

Bird Count

You can learn a lot about birds by watching and counting them.

Talk   Tell the class about the kinds of birds that live near you.

Working Together

▶ Make a feeder like this one.

▶ Hang the feeder on a tree or on a pole.

▶ Find out the kinds of birds that visit the feeder before you start to count.

▶ Each group member decides which kind of bird he or she will count.

▶ Count the birds for a half hour. Use tally marks to show each bird.

▶ Find the total for each kind of bird.

Bird	Number	Total
Sparrow	⊬⊬⊬ ⊬⊬⊬ ⊬⊬⊬ || 17

Decision Making

1 Decide how to show what your group found. You can make a picture, a graph, or another kind of display.

2 How many birds did your group count in all?_____

3 How many more or fewer birds did you count than each of your group members? _____

_____

4 What do you think you learned about the kind of bird that you counted? _____

_____

Write a report.

5 Tell what your group learned about the numbers and kinds of birds counted.

6 Tell how your group decided to show what they found.

More to Investigate

PREDICT Will the numbers and kinds of birds be different at another time of the day?

EXPLORE Choose a different time of the day. Count and record the new information.

FIND Find the total for each kind of bird. Compare the totals with what you found before.

Working Together

Take turns.

▶ Choose an amount of money and an item to buy.

▶ You and your partners use , and 📱 to find how much money is left.

▶ Compare your differences.

▶ Write the subtraction.

60¢ 43¢ 94¢ 81¢ 32¢ 50¢ 55¢ 88¢

 Critical Thinking How is subtracting money like subtracting numbers?

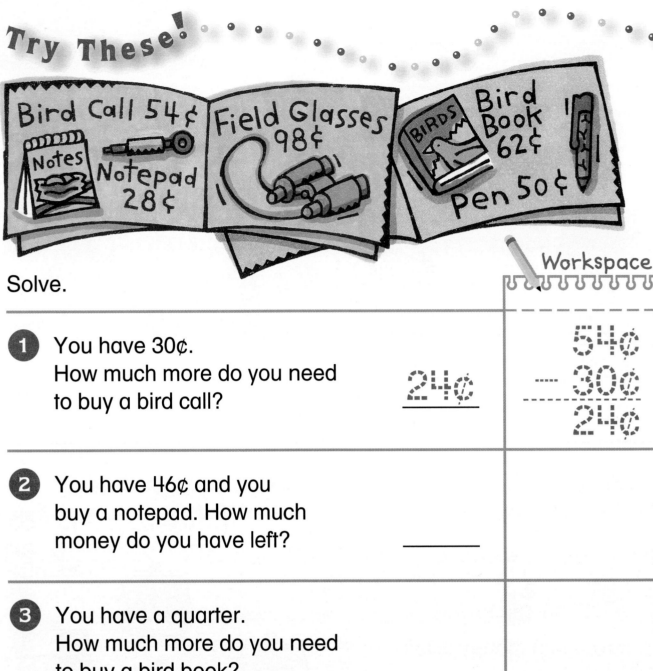

Bird Call 54¢

Notes Notepad 28¢

Field Glasses 98¢

BIRDS Bird Book 62¢

Pen 50¢

Workspace

Solve.

---

1 You have 30¢.
How much more do you need
to buy a bird call?

24¢

54¢
— 30¢
24¢

---

2 You have 46¢ and you
buy a notepad. How much
money do you have left?

_____

---

3 You have a quarter.
How much more do you need
to buy a bird book?

_____

---

4 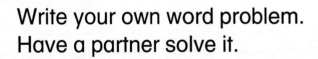 Write your own word problem.
Have a partner solve it.

Use your own paper.

More to Explore   **Estimate**

Ring the estimate you think is best.

51¢ – 29¢	90¢ – 31¢	82¢ – 38¢
more than 50¢	more than 50¢	more than 50¢
less than 50¢	less than 50¢	less than 50¢

 At Home

We subtracted money amounts. Ask your child
to tell you about the problem he or she wrote.

Catch the Salmon!

Salmon return each year to the same rivers where they were hatched.

You and your partner need a  red and orange.
Choose your color crayon.
Take turns.

▶ Choose a salmon. Subtract.

▶ Your partner checks your work.

▶ If correct, color the fish with your crayon.
   If not correct, color the fish with your partner's crayon.

The winner is the one with more salmon colored.

$$52 - 45$$

$$50 - 31$$

$$85 - 58$$

$$55 - 30$$

$$33 - 18$$

$$44 - 25$$

$$67 - 49$$

$$99 - 50$$

$$66 - 47$$

$$23 - 17$$

$$76 - 28$$

$$71 - 36$$

Subtract.

1.
$\begin{array}{r} ^{6}\,^{18}\!\!\!\not{7}\not{8} \\ -\ 49 \\ \hline 29 \end{array}$
$\begin{array}{r} 44 \\ -\ 38 \\ \hline \end{array}$
$\begin{array}{r} 95 \\ -\ 73 \\ \hline \end{array}$
$\begin{array}{r} 25 \\ -\ \ 7 \\ \hline \end{array}$
$\begin{array}{r} 53 \\ -\ 14 \\ \hline \end{array}$
$\begin{array}{r} 30 \\ -\ 19 \\ \hline \end{array}$

2.
$\begin{array}{r} 43 \\ -\ 15 \\ \hline \end{array}$
$\begin{array}{r} 17 \\ -\ 15 \\ \hline \end{array}$
$\begin{array}{r} 82 \\ -\ 48 \\ \hline \end{array}$
$\begin{array}{r} 63 \\ -\ 36 \\ \hline \end{array}$
$\begin{array}{r} 74 \\ -\ 56 \\ \hline \end{array}$
$\begin{array}{r} 87 \\ -\ 44 \\ \hline \end{array}$

3.
$\begin{array}{r} 90 \\ -\ 37 \\ \hline \end{array}$
$\begin{array}{r} 55 \\ -\ \ 9 \\ \hline \end{array}$
$\begin{array}{r} 51 \\ -\ 23 \\ \hline \end{array}$

4.
$\begin{array}{r} 64 \\ -\ 45 \\ \hline \end{array}$
$\begin{array}{r} 96 \\ -\ 56 \\ \hline \end{array}$
$\begin{array}{r} 38 \\ -\ 38 \\ \hline \end{array}$

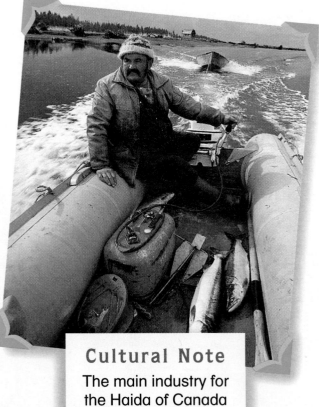

Cultural Note
The main industry for the Haida of Canada is salmon fishing.

Mixed Review

Add.

5.
$\begin{array}{r} 23 \\ +\ 26 \\ \hline \end{array}$
$\begin{array}{r} 46 \\ +\ 38 \\ \hline \end{array}$
$\begin{array}{r} 14¢ \\ +\ 27¢ \\ \hline \end{array}$
$\begin{array}{r} 27 \\ +\ 57 \\ \hline \end{array}$
$\begin{array}{r} 36¢ \\ +\ 10¢ \\ \hline \end{array}$

6.
$\begin{array}{r} 16¢ \\ +\ 18¢ \\ \hline \end{array}$
$\begin{array}{r} 80¢ \\ +\ 19¢ \\ \hline \end{array}$
$\begin{array}{r} 35 \\ +\ 35 \\ \hline \end{array}$
$\begin{array}{r} 17 \\ +\ 43 \\ \hline \end{array}$
$\begin{array}{r} 48 \\ +\ 13 \\ \hline \end{array}$

Name _____

Dr. Dell buys field glasses
for the whale watch.
The glasses cost $43.
She gives the clerk $60.
The clerk gives her $17
change. Is her change correct?

Subtract.

$$\begin{array}{r} \overset{5\ 10}{\$6\cancel{0}} \\ -\ 43 \\ \hline \$17 \end{array}$$

Add to check.

$$\begin{array}{r} \overset{1}{\$17} \\ +\ 43 \\ \hline \$60 \end{array}$$

 What do you notice about the numbers?

Dr. Dell's change is correct.

Subtract. Then add to check the difference.

1
$$\begin{array}{r} \overset{3\ 15}{\cancel{45}} \\ -\ 18 \\ \hline 27 \end{array} \quad \begin{array}{r} \overset{1}{27} \\ +\ 18 \\ \hline 45 \end{array} \qquad \begin{array}{r} 80¢ \\ -\ 65¢ \\ \hline \end{array}$$

2
$$\begin{array}{r} 52 \\ -\ 29 \\ \hline \end{array} \qquad \begin{array}{r} 75¢ \\ -\ 18¢ \\ \hline \end{array}$$

 Critical Thinking What does it mean if the sum is not the same
as the number you subtract from?

Try These!

Subtract. Then add to check the difference.

1
$$\begin{array}{r}58\\-23\\\hline 35\end{array}\qquad\begin{array}{r}35\\+23\\\hline\end{array}\qquad\begin{array}{r}71\\-22\\\hline\end{array}\qquad\begin{array}{r}35¢\\-\ 7¢\\\hline\end{array}$$

2
$$\begin{array}{r}81\\-43\\\hline\end{array}\qquad\qquad\begin{array}{r}45\\-18\\\hline\end{array}\qquad\begin{array}{r}60¢\\-44¢\\\hline\end{array}$$

3
$$\begin{array}{r}55\\-32\\\hline\end{array}\qquad\qquad\begin{array}{r}\$76\\-\ 69\\\hline\end{array}\qquad\begin{array}{r}93\\-15\\\hline\end{array}$$

Solve. Then add to check your answer.

Workspace

4 The team counted 47 sea lions in the morning. They counted 29 in the afternoon. How many more sea lions did they count in the morning? _____ sea lions

5 Jorge counted 18 of the 47 sea lions. How many of the sea lions did Jorge *not* count? _____ sea lions

At Home

We added to check subtraction. Ask your child to explain how to check subtraction.

Name _____

There were 56 seals on the rocks.
Then 48 seals jumped in the water.
How many seals are still on the rocks?

 How do you decide if you
should add or subtract?

$$
\begin{array}{r}
\overset{4\ \ 16}{\cancel{5}\cancel{6}} \\
-\ 48 \\
\hline
8
\end{array}
$$

__8__ seals are still on the rocks.

Add or subtract to solve.

Workspace

1 Lydia sees 33 seals.
15 of the seals are sleeping.
How many seals are awake? ____ seals

2 38 seals are born on Monday.
25 seals are born on Tuesday.
How many seals are born? ____ seals

3 Mr. Yoshi spends $56 for tickets
to see the seals and $14 for film.
How much does he spend in all? _____

 When might you decide to use mental math
to solve a problem?

McGraw-Hill School Division

Try These!

Add or subtract to solve.

Workspace

1 There are 86 seals on land. There are 42 seals in the water. How many more seals are on land? _____

2 A ticket to the seal show costs $14. How much will it cost to buy 2 tickets? _____

3 Tony has $37 for 3 tickets. Three tickets cost $42. How much more money does he need? _____

4 Write Use the numbers 53 and 29. Write your own word problem. Have a partner solve it.

Use your own paper.

Cultural Connection

Guatemala

People in Guatemala like to shop at outdoor markets. The money they use is *quetzales*.

Margarita bought a case of candies at a market. One case costs 20 quetzales.

Margarita gave the seller 50 quetzales.

How much money does Margarita have left? _____ quetzales

At Home We solved addition and subtraction problems. Ask your child to explain problems 1 to 3 above.

Identify Extra Information

Once a year, sea turtles return
to land to lay eggs.

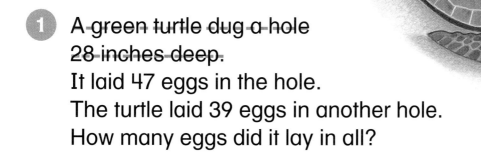

1. A ~~green turtle dug a hole~~
~~28 inches deep.~~
It laid 47 eggs in the hole.
The turtle laid 39 eggs in another hole.
How many eggs did it lay in all?

This problem has **extra information.**
You can cross out the extra information.
Then add to solve the problem.

The turtle laid **86** eggs in all.

$$\begin{array}{r} 47 \\ + 39 \\ \hline 86 \end{array}$$

Cross out any extra information. Then solve.

Workspace

2. A green turtle is 60 inches long.
A leatherback turtle is 96 inches long.
A hawksbill turtle is 36 inches long.
How much longer is the green
turtle than the hawksbill turtle? ____ inches

3. A snapping turtle lays up to 30 eggs.
It lays eggs 14 inches underground.
A green turtle lays eggs 28 inches
underground.
How much deeper does the
green turtle lay its eggs? ____ inches

1 One softshell turtle lays 33 eggs. Another softshell turtle lays 18 eggs. 26 of the eggs hatch. How many eggs were laid altogether?

_77_ eggs

What should the answer be?

_____ eggs

2 How could someone get 77 as the answer?

Write about it. _____

_____

Write and Share

Rothanna wrote this problem.

A black cat has 2 kittens.
A brown cat has 4 kittens.
The white dog has
5 puppies.
How many kittens are there?

Rothanna Sarath
Shaughnessy School
Lowell, Massachusetts

3 Solve Rothanna's problem. _____

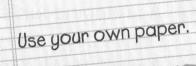
Use your own paper.

4 Write a problem with extra information. Have a partner solve it.

What method did your partner use? _____

  Ask your child how to solve the problem he or she wrote.

Chapter Review

Subtract. Did you regroup? Mark *yes* or *no*.

1

tens	ones
☐	☐
5	6
− 2	7

yes   no

2

tens	ones
☐	☐
3	1
−	9

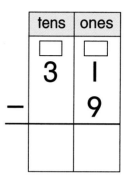

yes   no

Subtract.

3

tens	ones
☐	☐
4	8
− 1	9

4

tens	ones
☐	☐
9	0
− 2	1

5

tens	ones
☐	☐
6	8
− 6	3

6

tens	ones
☐	☐
2	5
− 1	5

7

tens	ones
☐	☐
5	3
− 1	6

8

tens	ones
☐	☐
9	3
− 5	8

9
```
  74
− 66
```

10
```
  88¢
− 40¢
```

11
```
  52
−  5
```

12
```
  61
− 37
```

13
```
  77
− 11
```

14
```
  37¢
− 29¢
```

15
```
  $84
−  62
```

16
```
  40
− 25
```

Solve.

17 Ann bought a book for 55¢ and a pencil for 36¢. How much did she spend?

_____

18 There are 45 ducks on the pond. 23 of them fly away. How many ducks are left?

_____ ducks

19 Gerry made tags. She used the numbers 3, 5, and 9. What 2-digit numbers did she make? Make a list.

She made _____.

Cross out the extra information. Then solve.

20 One turtle laid 21 eggs.
Another turtle laid 34 eggs.
46 eggs hatch.
How many eggs did the two turtles lay?   _____ eggs

What Do You Think?

Which is the easiest way to subtract 40 – 15?

☑ Check one.

☐ ▨▨▨▨▨▨▨ ▪   ☐ Write   ☐ Mental Math   ☐ 🖩

Why? _____

Journal   Write 35 – 6. Show the subtraction by drawing models.

Chapter Test

Subtract. Did you regroup? Mark *yes* or *no*.

1

tens	ones
□	□
4	3
− 2	6

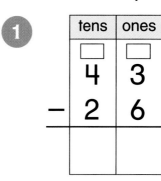

yes   no

2

tens	ones
□	□
5	2
− 3	8

yes   no

Subtract.

3   91
      − 23

4   36
      − 21

5 $72
      − 65

6   25¢
      − 10¢

7   54
      − 26

---

8 There are 35 seals on the rocks. 15 more seals climb on the rocks. How many seals are there?

_____ seals

9 There are 43 crabs on the beach. 25 crawl away. How many crabs are on the beach now?

_____ crabs

Make a list to solve.

10 Sarah tags some ducks. She uses the numbers 2, 4, and 8. What 2-digit numbers does she make?

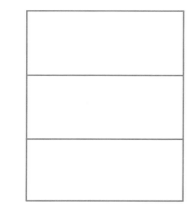

She makes _____.

What Did You Learn?

The second-grade class took a survey to find out their favorite bird. Use the clues to tell how the class voted.

FAVORITE BIRDS	
Birds	Votes
	8
	24
	14
	38
	27

Birds we saw
blue jays
robins
crows
wrens
eagles

1. The blue jay was voted the favorite.

2. The crow got 19 votes fewer than the robin.

3. The eagle got 3 votes fewer than the robin.

4. The wren got 10 votes fewer than the eagle.

 Explain how you decided where to place each bird in the survey.

 You may want to put this page in your portfolio.

Name _____

Missing Number

What is the number?

Take turns.

▶ Subtract to find the missing number. Shh! Do not tell your partner the answer.

▶ Your partner guesses the missing number and checks it on the calculator.

▶ Your partner has four guesses.

▶ After each guess, give your partner a clue such as "Go higher" or "Go lower."

▶ Then write the missing number.

1 $57 - \boxed{} = 39$

2 $65 - \boxed{} = 28$

3 $24 - \boxed{} = 18$

4 $36 - \boxed{} = 17$

5 $46 - \boxed{} = 12$

6 $70 - \boxed{} = 54$

7 $32 - \boxed{} = 23$

8 $81 - \boxed{} = 56$

Critical Thinking How could you use addition to find the missing numbers?

Compare Animal Speeds

giraffe

wildebeest   zebra

elephant

antelope

Use the table to solve.

1 How much faster is a zebra than an elephant?

_____ miles per hour

2 How much faster is an antelope than an elephant?

_____ miles per hour

3 Which animal is slower, an elephant or a giraffe?

_____

How much slower?   _____ miles per hour

ANIMAL SPEEDS	
Animal	**Average Speed (Miles per Hour)**
elephant	25
zebra	39
antelope	61
wildebeest	50
giraffe	28

Write your own subtraction problem about these animals. Then solve it.

Use your own paper.

Name

Get to Zero First!

PLAYERS   2 or more

MATERIALS   pencil and paper

DIRECTIONS   The first player writes a starting number between 87 and 93 on a sheet of paper. Then each player in turn chooses a number between 1 and 15 for his or her partner to subtract and write the difference.

The winner is the player who reaches 0 first.

As you play this game, note that as the difference reaches 15, players must plan ahead to increase their chance of being the player to get to 0 first.

Dear Family,

We are beginning a new chapter in mathematics. During the next few weeks we will be learning about geometry and fractions.

We will also be talking about how shapes and patterns are used in art. Please help me complete this interview.

Your child,

_____
Signature

Interview ....

Which of these shapes do we have in our home? If possible, list some items for each shape.

☐ square _____

△ triangle _____

◯ circle _____

◼ cube _____

⬭ cylinder _____

Shapes in Art
Geometry and Fractions

Listen Listen to the book *Jamaica Louise James.* Look at the pictures.

Talk What shapes do you see in Jamaica's drawings?

311

What Do You Know?

Look at the shapes.
Choose a way to sort them into two groups.

Write a name for each group inside a circle.

Draw a line from each shape to the group
where it belongs.

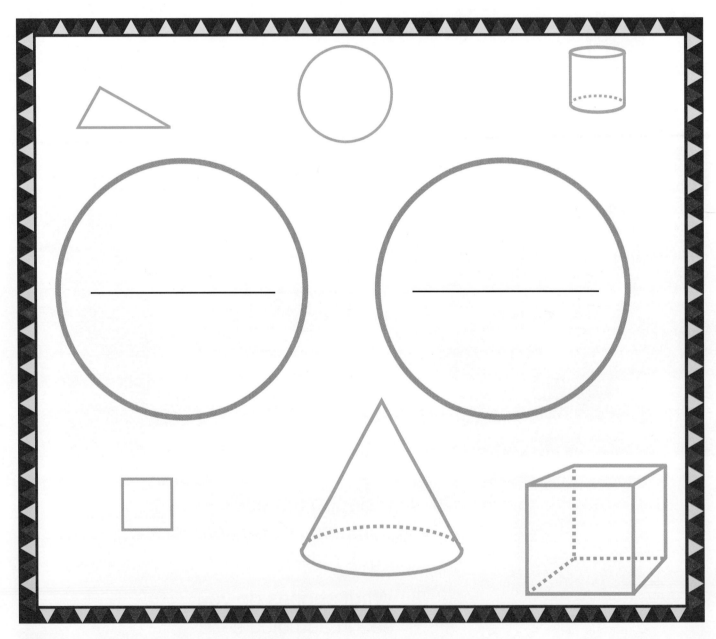

 Explain how you sorted.
Then tell about a different way to sort the
shapes into two groups.

Working Together

You and your partner need 40 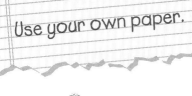.

▶ Use 4 cubes. Build different shapes.

▶ Your partner builds the **same shapes** you built.

▶ Draw the shapes.

How many different shapes did you make? _____

▶ Use 6 cubes. Your partner builds different shapes.

▶ You build the same shapes your partner built.

▶ Draw the shapes.

Use your own paper.

 Can you make more shapes with 4 cubes or with 6 cubes? Why?

Try These!

Write the number of cubes in each shape.

Use cubes to build each shape.

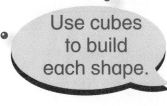

1

6
___

2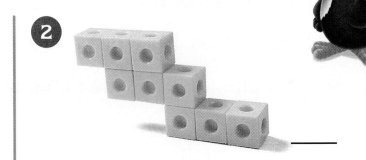
___

3
___

4
___

5
___

6
___

More to Explore   Spatial Sense

You can look at a shape from different sides.
Each time the shape looks different.

Build your own shape.
Try to draw it from different sides.

Use your own paper.

 At Home

Ask your child to tell how to find the number of cubes in one of the pictures above.

Name

3-Dimensional Shapes

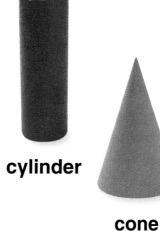

corner

edge

face

cube

sphere

cylinder

cone

rectangular prism

▶ Find classroom objects with these shapes.

▶ Complete the chart.

object	shape	faces	corners	edges
1	rectangular prism	6	8	12
2				
3				
4				
5				

 Critical Thinking How are the cube and rectangular prism the same? How are they different?

McGraw-Hill School Division

Try These!

Find objects with these shapes.
Write or draw a picture of them.

1 sphere

2 rectangular prism

3 cone

4 cylinder

5 cube

 Talk with a partner. Which of these shapes
can you roll? Which can you stack?

Mixed Review

Write the number.

6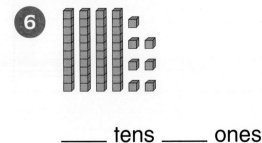

_____ tens _____ ones

_____

7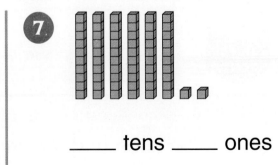

_____ tens _____ ones

_____

At Home — We learned about 3-dimensional shapes. Ask your child to name an object shaped like a sphere.

Name _____

square	**circle**	**triangle**	**rectangle**

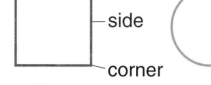—side
—corner

4 sides
4 corners

0 sides
0 corners

3 sides
3 corners

4 sides
4 corners

You can make shapes from other shapes.

► Cut out and fold some , △, and  .

► Draw lines to show the folds.

► Write the name of the shapes made by the folds.

triangles _____ _____ _____

_____ _____ _____

_____ _____ _____

McGraw-Hill School Division

How many triangles are in these squares?

1  ___

2 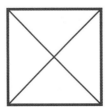 ___

3 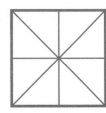 ___

4 How many rectangles are in this square? ___

5 How many triangles? ___

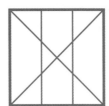

More to Explore   Spatial Sense

Here is a large square made up of 4 smaller squares.

Draw the largest possible square you can make on the grid. How many smaller squares is it made of? Color it.

4

At Home   Ask your child to fold a sheet of paper and name the shapes made by the folds.

Name _____

The two shapes in each pair are **congruent.**

The shapes in these pairs are **not congruent.**

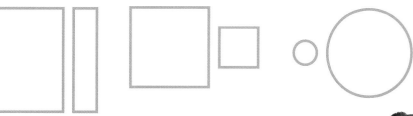

 What makes two shapes congruent?

Working Together

You and your partner need scissors, glue, and paper shapes.

▶ Cut out 4 different shapes.

▶ Fold each shape to make two shapes that are congruent. Cut on the fold.

▶ Match a cut-out shape to a congruent shape below. Glue the shape onto the shape it matches.

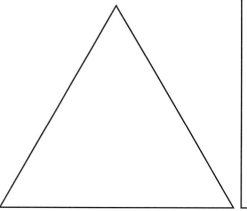

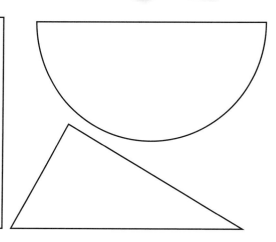

McGraw-Hill School Division

Draw a triangle that is congruent.

1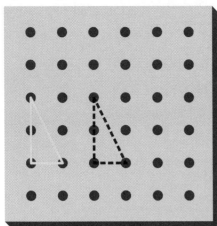

2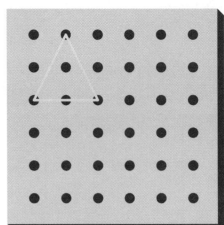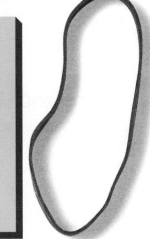

Draw a square that is congruent.

3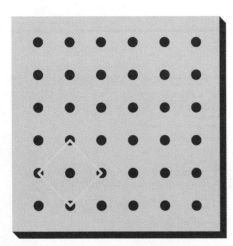

4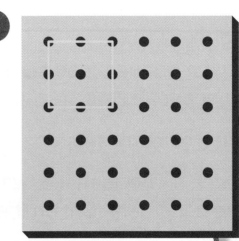

Draw a rectangle that is congruent.

5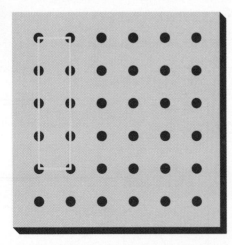

6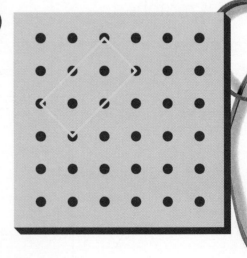

 Draw two shapes that are congruent.
Write how you know they are congruent.

 We learned about congruent shapes. Ask your child to explain what two congruent shapes are.

These shapes show a
line of symmetry.

These shapes do **not** show
a line of symmetry.

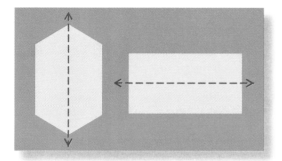

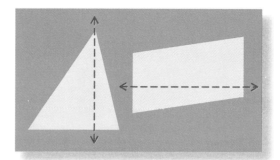

 What do you notice about shapes that have
a line of symmetry?

Working Together

▶ Cut out paper shapes.

▶ Fold each shape to make a line of symmetry.

▶ Draw the line in the fold.

 How do your lines compare with your
partner's?

 1

 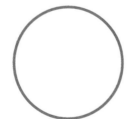 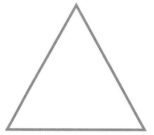

2

CHAPTER 9 *Lesson 3*

Try These!

Make a shape with a line of symmetry. Draw the matching part.

1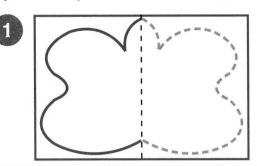

"Another Silence"
by Jimmy Ernst

2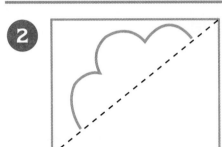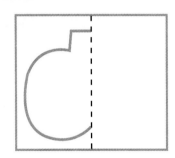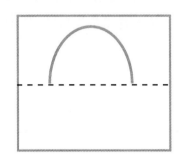

3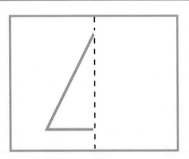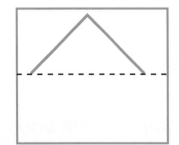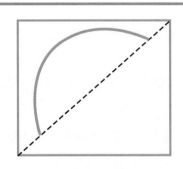

More to Explore — Spatial Sense

Color inside the closed figures.

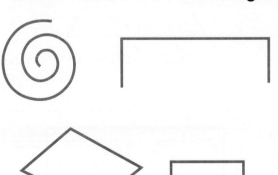   

 open closed

We learned about lines of symmetry. Ask your child to show you how to fold a shape to find a line of symmetry.

Name _____

Use a Pattern

| **Read** | Winnie is making a picture with 15 shapes in a pattern. How many triangles does she need? |

| **Plan** | You can **use a pattern** to solve. |

| **Solve** | Draw to complete the pattern. Then count the triangles. |

Winnie needs _____.

| **Look Back** | Have you answered the question? Explain. |

Use a pattern to solve.

1 Luke paints pictures of shapes.
He will paint 20 shapes in a row.
How many squares will he paint? _____

How many circles will he paint? _____

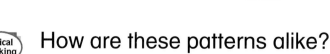

Critical Thinking How are these patterns alike?
How are they different?

Try These!

1 Luke paints patterns on clay pots.
He will paint 17 triangles in a row.
How many triangles will have dots inside? _____

2 Laura makes a beaded bracelet.
How many red rectangles will she need
to finish this bracelet? _____

3 George's necklace will have 30 beads.
How many red beads does he use? _____

How many green beads does he use? _____

Cultural Connection

Ashanti Fabric Patterns

The Ashanti of Africa stamp patterns onto cloth. They mix and repeat designs to make patterns.

Draw to complete the pattern. How many of each are in the completed pattern?

 _____ _____ _____

At Home — We used a pattern to solve problems. Ask your child to explain how he or she solved problem 2 above.

Midchapter Review

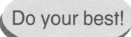

Do your best!

How many faces are on each shape?

_____   _____   _____   _____   _____

Match.

| 3 sides | 4 sides | 0 sides |
| 3 corners | 4 corners | 0 corners |

Color inside the shapes that are congruent.

 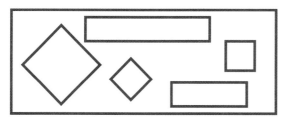   

9 How do you know which shapes are congruent? _____

Use a pattern to solve.

10 Rolanda makes a bracelet 18 beads long. How many square beads does she use? _____

 Draw these shapes in your journal. Explain why they are all triangles.

Tangram Shapes

You and your partner need a 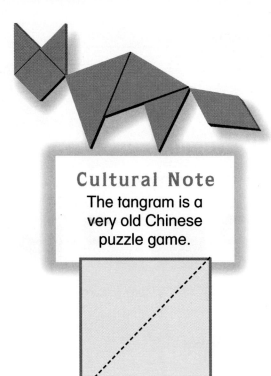.

Take turns.

▶ Choose a shape below.

▶ Use more than one tangram piece to make that shape.

▶ Draw lines to show the pieces you used.

Cultural Note

The tangram is a very old Chinese puzzle game.

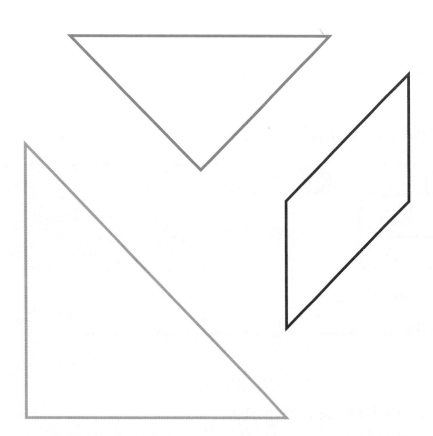

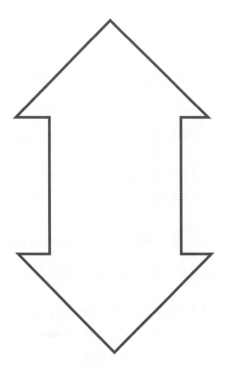

1 How many triangles did you make in the four shapes?

_____ triangles

How many squares did you make in the four shapes?

_____ squares

Name

Cover-Up Game

Working Together

You and your partners need 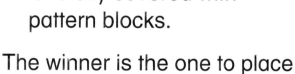.

▶ Take turns. Each player covers part of the shape below with one of the blocks.

▶ Each color must be used at least once. Each block must touch another on at least one side.

▶ Continue until the shape is totally covered with pattern blocks.

The winner is the one to place the last block.

Decision Making

1 Decide on a way to show your covered shape.

2 Compare your shape with those of other groups.

What was the greatest number of blocks used? _____

What was the fewest number of blocks used? _____

3 Using the same colors and rules, what would be the most blocks needed to cover the shape? _____

Explain how you found your answer.

_____

Write a report.

4 Write about any strategies you used, or might use, to place the last block.

5 Write about the shapes you used. How are they different? How are they alike?

More to Investigate

PREDICT What if you could change the shape you cover up?

EXPLORE Decide on a shape to cover up. Test your game to see if it works.

Use your own paper.

FIND Trade your cover-up game with another group. Play it.

Chapter Review

Write the name of the shape.

1

2

3

_____   _____   _____

Write the number of sides each shape has.

4

5

6

7

___   ___   ___   ___

Draw a line of symmetry.

8

9

10

Write the fraction for the shaded part.

11

12

13

14

___   ___   ___   ___

Write the fraction for the part that is green.

15    ___

16   ___

Use a pattern to solve.

17 Kathy makes a picture with 18 shapes.
How many blue shapes will the picture have? _____

18 Craig's picture will have 16 shapes on it.
How many squares will it have? _____

Draw a picture to solve.

Use your own paper.

19 Tyrell bought a pack of 6 cards. He shares them equally with Gus. How many cards does each child get?

_____

20 Lisa and 3 friends share a pie equally. The pie has 8 slices. How many slices does each child get?

_____

What Do You Think?

What do you like best about geometry?
☑ Check one.

☐ 2-dimensional shapes

☐ 3-dimensional shapes

☐ Patterns with shapes

Why? _____

Journal Write your name. Use capital letters. Draw arrows to show which letters have lines of symmetry.

Chapter Test

1 Write the name of the shape.

 _____

2 Write the number of sides on the shape.

 _____

Draw a line of symmetry.

3

4

5

Write the fraction for the shaded part.

6 ____

7 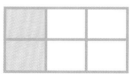 ____

Write a fraction for the part that is orange.

8

____

9

____

Use a pattern to solve.

10 Mandy's picture will have 15 shapes. ○○△○○△○○△○○

How many circles will it have? _____

Performance Assessment

What Did You Learn?

Look at each shape.
Tell what you know about it.

1 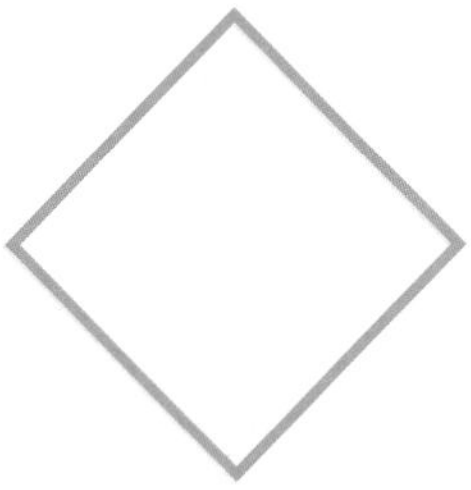

____

____

____

2 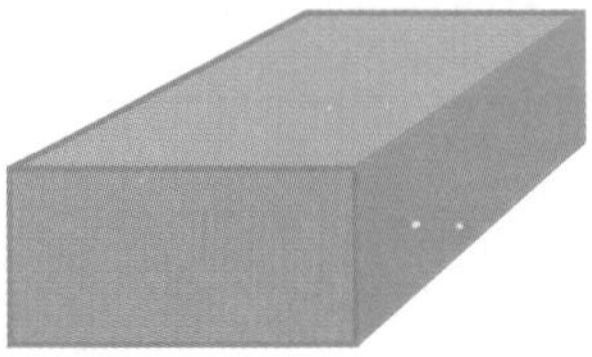

____

____

____

3 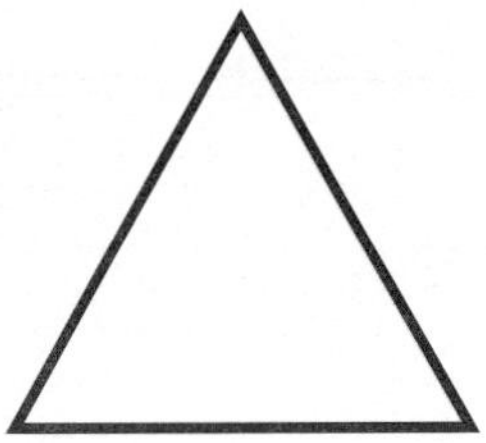

____

____

____

4 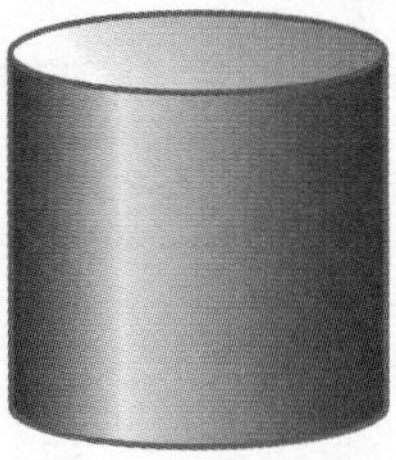

____

____

____

You may want to put this page in your portfolio.

Name

Experiment

You and your partner need I  blue ,

I red , I , 3 , and a paper bag.

▶ Put the cubes in the bag and shake.

▶ Take turns. Pick I cube from the bag.

▶ Color I box the same color as the cube you pick.

▶ Put the cube back in the bag.

▶ Do this 20 times.

I	2	3	4	5	6	7	8	9	10	11	12	13	14	15	16	17	18	19	20

1 How many times did you pick blue? _____ times out of 20, or $\frac{}{20}$

2 How many times did you pick red? _____ times out of 20, or $\frac{}{20}$

3 What if you picked cubes another 20 times. Are you more likely to pick more blue cubes or red cubes? _____

4 Repeat the experiment. Compare the results.

Make a Pattern

You can use a computer to make a pattern.

Continue the pattern until there are 12 shapes.

How many triangles? _____

What fraction of the pattern are the triangles? _____

How many circles? _____

What fraction of the pattern are the circles? _____

How many squares? _____

What fraction of the pattern are the squares? _____

At the Computer

1 Draw your own shapes.
Copy them to make a pattern.

2 Record how many of each shape you use.
Write the fraction of the pattern for each shape.

Name

Pick a Fraction

PLAYERS   2

MATERIALS   4 red buttons, 4 blue buttons, paper bag, pencils

Player 1

$\frac{1}{4}$	$\frac{2}{4}$
$\frac{3}{4}$	$\frac{4}{4}$

Player 2

$\frac{1}{4}$	$\frac{2}{4}$
$\frac{3}{4}$	$\frac{4}{4}$

DIRECTIONS   Put the buttons in the bag. Take turns. Pull out 4 buttons. Name a fraction that tells about the buttons you picked. Ring the fraction you named on your chart below. If the fraction is already marked, skip a turn. Put the buttons back in the bag.

Play until one player marks off all the fractions on his or her chart.

Player 1

$\frac{1}{4}$	$\frac{2}{4}$
$\frac{3}{4}$	$\frac{4}{4}$

Player 2

$\frac{1}{4}$	$\frac{2}{4}$
$\frac{3}{4}$	$\frac{4}{4}$

$\frac{1}{4}$ are red.

At Home   This game will help your child practice naming fractions that show part of a group.

McGraw-Hill School Division

Dear Family,

We are beginning a new chapter in mathematics. During the next few weeks we will be learning to measure length, weight, capacity, and temperature.

We will also be talking about making and using maps. Please help me complete this interview.

Your child,

_____
Signature

Interview ....

How do maps help people?

_____

_____

When do you use maps?
(You may check more than one.)

❑ Vacation trips

❑ Family visits

❑ Business trips

❑ Other _____

_____

Mapping Adventures
Measurement

 Listen to the story
As the Crow Flies.

 What maps have you
seen or used?

What Do You Know?

Use ⊂▭⊃ to measure each path.

		Estimate	**Measure**
1	🦓 to 🦁	about ____ ⊂▭⊃	about ____ ⊂▭⊃
2	🐘 to 🦓	about ____ ⊂▭⊃	about ____ ⊂▭⊃
3	🦁 to 🐘	about ____ ⊂▭⊃	about ____ ⊂▭⊃
4	🦓 to 🦛	about ____ ⊂▭⊃	about ____ ⊂▭⊃

 What else could you use to measure? How do you think the measurements would change?

 Choose another way to measure. Record.

Trace around your foot.
Cut out 2 paper footprints.

How **long** is your classroom?

Estimate ____

Measure ____

How **wide** is your classroom?

Estimate ____

Measure ____

I foot, 2 feet, 3 feet

Working Together

▶ You and your partner each use your own footprints to measure.

▶ Complete the chart.

	Length of chalkboard	Width of hall	Height of door
Estimate	____	____	____
Measure	____	____	____

Critical Thinking Why might your measurements be different from your partner's?

Try These!

You need 10 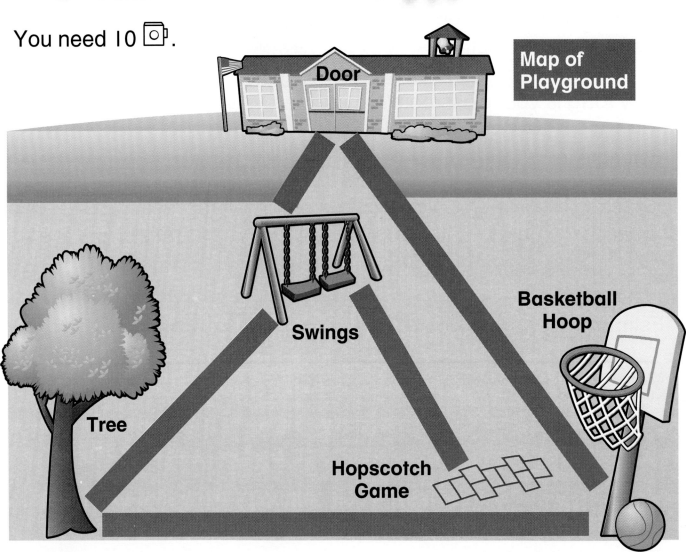.

Map of Playground

Door

Basketball Hoop

Swings

Tree

Hopscotch Game

Use 🔲 to measure each path.

1. tree to basketball hoop   about ____ 🔲

2. swings to tree   about ____ 🔲

3. swings to hopscotch game   about ____ 🔲

4. door to swings   about ____ 🔲

5. door to basketball hoop   about ____ 🔲

Journal How is measuring with cubes different from measuring with footprints?

At Home Have your child use a pair of shoes to measure the length of a room.

Name _____

TICKET

I **inch** or I in.

|———————|
0   1   2

about 2 **inches**

12 **inches** equal I **foot.**

You need a  .

▶ Find these objects.

▶ Estimate. Then measure and record.

▶ Write how many *inches* or *feet.*

Remember to start from 0 to measure.

		Estimate	Measure
1	|———————|	about _____	about _____
2	APRIL	about _____	about _____
3	MATH BOOK EMMA GORDON MISS WATSON 28-22	about _____	about _____
4		about _____	about _____

McGraw-Hill School Division

Try These!

Use a  to measure each path.

1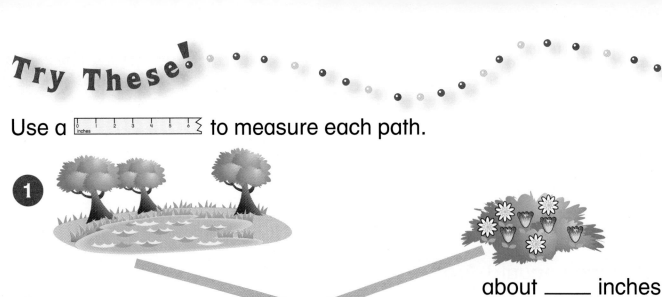

about ____ inches

2

about ____ inches

3

about ____ inches

More to Explore — Measurement Sense

Use a 🧵 or a 📏
to measure your classroom.
Write how many yards.

> 3 feet
> equal 1 **yard.**

My Classroom

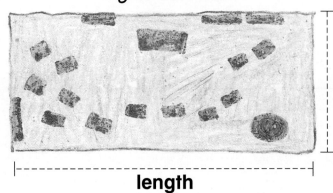

about ____ yards wide

width

length

about ____ yards long

At Home

We measured in inches, feet, and yards. Have your child show you how to measure with a ruler.

Name _____

├---┤

├----------------┤

I centimeter   about 4 **centimeters**
   I cm

You need a 〔0 1 2 3 4 5 6 7 8 9 10 11 12 13 14 15 16〕 centimeters.

▶ Find these objects.

▶ Estimate. Then measure and record.

▶ Write how many *centimeters*.

		Estimate	Measure
1	MARKS-A-LOT ├----------------┤	about _____ cm	about _____ cm
2	├----------┤	about _____ cm	about _____ cm
3	MATH BOOK EMMA GORDON	about _____ cm	about _____ cm
4		about _____ cm	about _____ cm

Critical Thinking How is measuring with a centimeter ruler the same as or different from measuring with an inch ruler?

Use a ▱ to measure the bug's path.

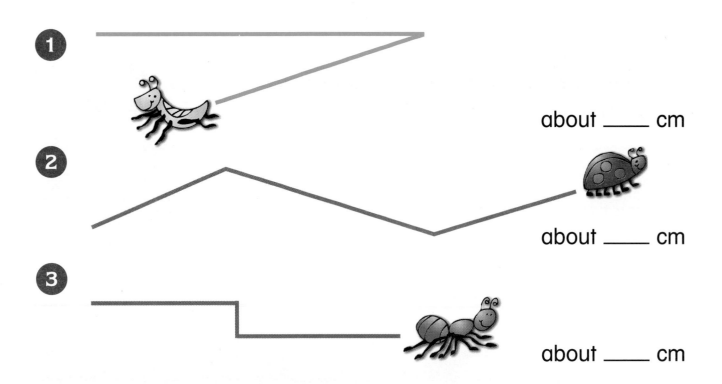

1

about _____ cm

2

about _____ cm

3

about _____ cm

More to Explore   Measurement Sense

Use a ▱ or a  .

100 **centimeters** equal 1 **meter.**

How many meters long is the chalkboard?

about _____ meters

Choose something to measure in meters.

I measured the _____.

It is about _____ meters long.

It is about _____ meters wide.

My bat is about 1 meter long.

At Home

We measured in centimeters and meters. Ask your child to explain how he or she measured in exercise 2 above.

Name _____

The distance around
a shape is called
the **perimeter.**

Working Together

You and your partner need a .

▶ Find these objects.

▶ Measure each side and record.

▶ Add the sides to find the
perimeter.

1

_____ + _____ + _____ + _____

The perimeter is about _____ cm.

2

_____ + _____ + _____ + _____

The perimeter is about _____ cm.

3

_____ + _____ + _____ + _____

The perimeter is about _____ cm.

 Talk Tell your partner what you notice
about the measures of some sides.

McGraw-Hill School Division

Try These!

Measure. Add to find the perimeter.

1

_4_ cm

_2_ cm   _2_ cm

_4_ cm   _12_ cm

2

____ cm

____ cm   ____ cm

____ cm   ____ cm

3

____ cm

____ cm   ____ cm

____ cm

____ cm

4

____ cm

____ cm   ____ cm

____ cm

____ cm

More to Explore   Measurement Sense

Trace paths that are about the same length.
Use a different color for each length.

We explored finding perimeters. Ask your child how he or she solved exercise 3 above.

Area is measured in square units.

I **square unit**

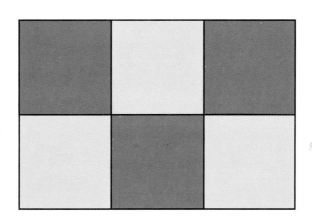

6 square units

The area is 36 square units.

Working Together

You and your partner need 40 paper squares.

▶ Find these objects.

▶ Cover each object with squares.

▶ Count the squares to find the area. Record.

1

about ____ square units

2

about ____ square units

3

about ____ square units

4

about ____ square units

 Critical Thinking How are perimeter and area different?

McGraw-Hill School Division

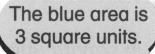
The blue area is 3 square units.

Color to show the number of square units.

 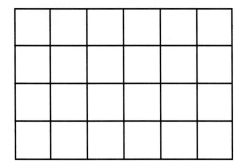

12 square units

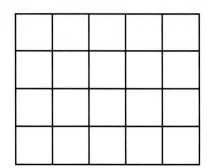

9 square units

 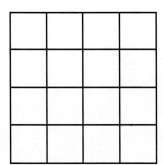

11 square units

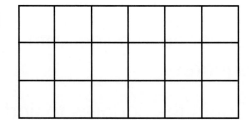

13 square units

Color an area.
Write how many square units you colored.

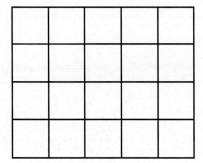

_____ square units

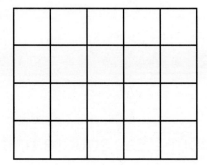

_____ square units

At Home

We explored finding area. Have your child explain the area shown in exercise 6 above.

Draw a Diagram

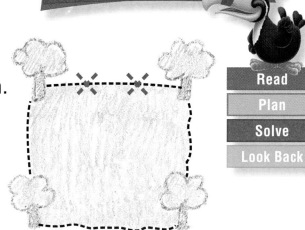

| Read | Joe planted a tree in each corner of his square garden. He planted 2 bushes between each tree. How many bushes did Joe plant? |

Read
Plan
Solve
Look Back

| Plan | What strategy could you use to solve the problem? |

| Solve | Joe drew a **diagram.** Finish it. How many bushes did Joe plant? _____ bushes |

| Look Back | Did you answer the question? Explain. |

Draw a diagram to solve.

1 Lu made a map of her street. There is a large house on each corner. There are 5 more houses on each side of the street. How many houses are on Lu's street?

_____ houses

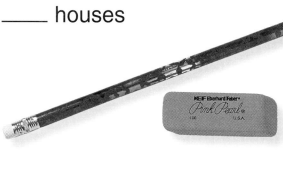

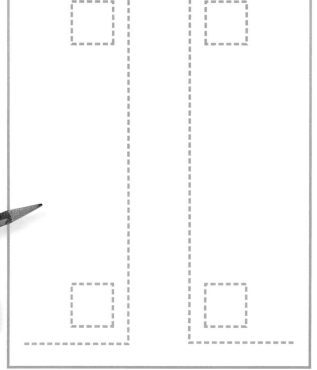

Try These!

Draw a diagram to solve.

1 Sal's garden is shaped like a triangle. There are 6 plants on each side of the garden. How many plants are in Sal's garden?

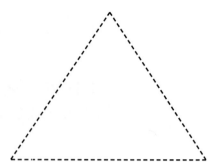

_____ plants

2 Mi made a fence around a pigpen. She used 6 pieces of fence on 2 sides of the pen and 3 pieces of fence on the other two sides. How many pieces of fence did Mi use?

_____ pieces

3 Juan's map shows each student's desk. He drew 5 rows of desks. Each row has 6 desks. How many desks are on Juan's map?

_____ desks

Mixed Review

Subtract.

4

$$
\begin{array}{r} 21 \\ -\ 19 \\ \hline \end{array}
\qquad
\begin{array}{r} 76 \\ -\ 34 \\ \hline \end{array}
\qquad
\begin{array}{r} 68 \\ -\ 27 \\ \hline \end{array}
\qquad
\begin{array}{r} 57 \\ -\ 49 \\ \hline \end{array}
\qquad
\begin{array}{r} 45 \\ -\ 16 \\ \hline \end{array}
\qquad
\begin{array}{r} 87 \\ -\ 22 \\ \hline \end{array}
$$

At Home — We drew diagrams to solve problems. Ask your child to explain how to solve problem 3 above.

Midchapter Review

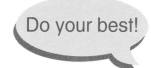
Do your best!

Estimate. Then measure.

	Estimate	**Measure**

1 ▬▬▬▬▬▬▬ about ____ inches about ____ inches

2 ▬▬▬▬ about ____ inches about ____ inches

3 ▬▬▬▬▬▬ about ____ cm about ____ cm

4 ▬▬▬▬▬ about ____ cm about ____ cm

Measure each path.

5 about ____ inches

6 about ____ cm

Measure. Add to find the perimeter.

7 ____ cm

8 ____ cm

Draw a diagram to solve.

Use your own paper.

9 A map shows a square garden.
There is a big tree in each corner.
There are 2 small trees between each
big tree. How many trees are in the garden? ____ trees

10 How did you solve problem 9? _____

Journal

How do you estimate the length of an object?

Scavenger Hunt

You and your partners each need a  and a .

▶ Play with other groups.

▶ Your group must find one object for each measure in the chart.

▶ Write the name or draw the object on the chart.

The first group to complete the chart wins!

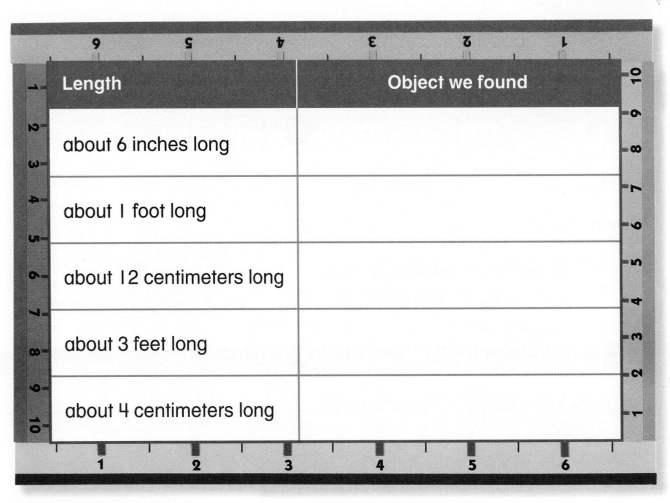

Length	Object we found
about 6 inches long	
about 1 foot long	
about 12 centimeters long	
about 3 feet long	
about 4 centimeters long	

Name _____

Make a Map

 Listen to *As the Crow Flies*.

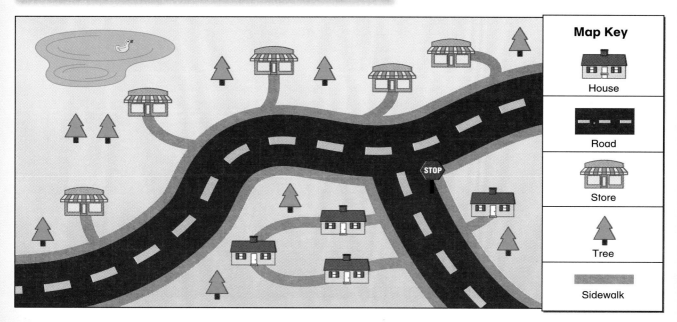

Map Key

| House |
| Road |
| Store |
| Tree |
| Sidewalk |

Tell how the **map key** helps you to read the map of this neighborhood.

Working Together

Your group will make a map of your school neighborhood.

▶ Take a walk around your neighborhood. Talk about what you want to show on your map.

▶ Make notes about the buildings, streets, and other things that you see.

CHAPTER 10 *Real-Life Investigation*

Decision Making

1 What do you want to show on your map and how will you show it?

2 Choose the materials that you want to use, and make your map.

Write a report.

3 Tell what you decided to show on your map.

4 How did you make your map?

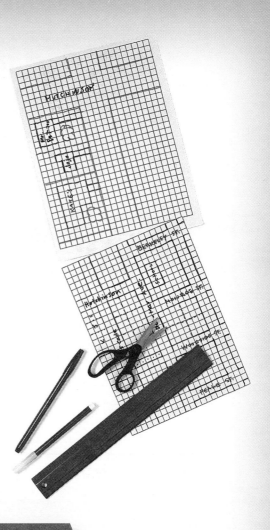

More to Investigate

PREDICT What if you made your school neighborhood map part of a bigger community map. Where does your neighborhood fit?

EXPLORE Try it. Make a new map. Show more of the community where you live.

FIND Compare the maps. How are they alike? How are they different?

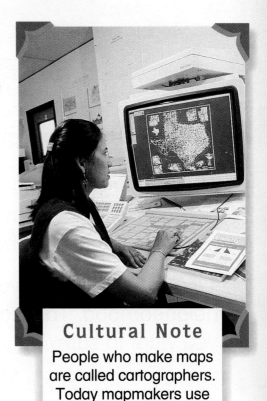

Cultural Note
People who make maps are called cartographers. Today mapmakers use computers to sort and arrange the data.

Name _____

less than 1 **pound**

1 pound

3 pounds

 Talk What would the balance look like if you put two oranges on each pan?

Working Together

You and your partner need a 🖾 and a 🖾.
Take turns.

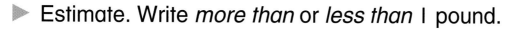

▶ Find these objects.

▶ Hold the 🖾 in one hand and the object in your other hand.

▶ Estimate. Write *more than* or *less than* 1 pound.

▶ Measure and record.

	Estimate *more than* or *less than* 1 pound	Measure
MATH BOOK		about _____ pounds
lunch box		about _____ pounds
backpack		about _____ pounds

 Critical Thinking Do big objects always weigh more than small objects? Explain.

Write *more than* or *less than*.

1

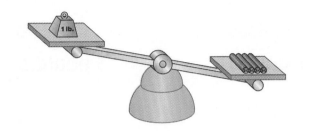

more than I pound

2

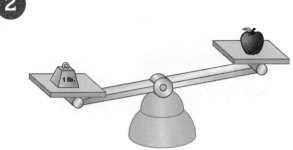

_____ I pound

3

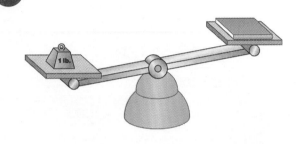

_____ I pound

4

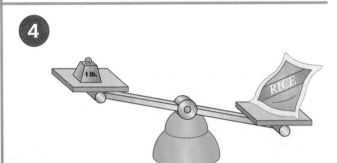

_____ I pound

How many pounds?

5

about ____ pounds

6

about ____ pounds

Write or draw to show how to find the number of pounds.

At Home

Have your child estimate the weight of several objects as *more than* or *less than* I pound.

less than I **kilogram**   I kilogram   2 kilograms

Talk What would the balance look like if you put 2 kilograms of apples on it?

Working Together

You and your partner need a 📷 and a 🔩.

▶ Find these objects.

▶ Hold the 🔩 in one hand and the object in your other hand.

▶ Estimate. Write *more than* or *less than* I kilogram.

▶ Measure and record.

	Estimate *more than* or *less than* I kilogram	Measure
Dictionary		about ____ kilograms
Finger Paints		about ____ kilograms
Shoes		about ____ kilograms

Critical Thinking Which is heavier: I kilogram of rocks or I kilogram of feathers? Explain.

Try These!

Write *more than* or *less than*.

1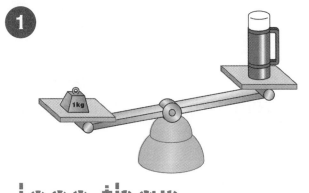

___less than___ I kilogram

2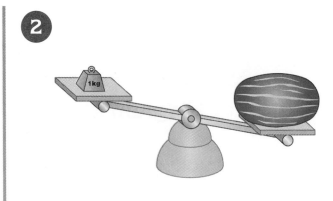

_____ I kilogram

3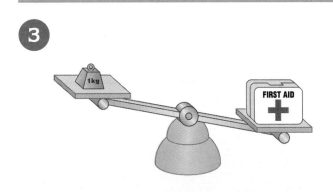

_____ I kilogram

4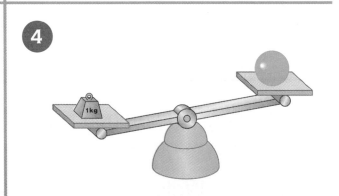

_____ I kilogram

How many kilograms?

5

about ____ kilograms

6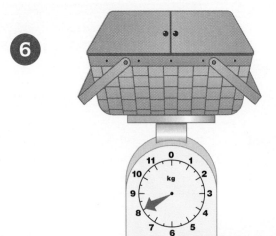

about ____ kilograms

At Home

Have your child estimate the measure of several objects as *more than* or *less than* I kilogram.

I **cup**   I **pint**   I **quart**

Talk How can you find how many cups will fill a
pint? a quart?

Working Together

You and your partner need I cup,
I pint, and I quart containers.

Take turns.

▶ Fill and pour to measure.

▶ Complete the table.

_____ cups = I pint

_____ pints = I quart

_____ cups = I quart

▶ Choose a container.

▶ Estimate how much it will hold.   about _____

▶ Measure to find out.   about _____

Try These!

Choose the better estimate.

1 I cup

more than I cup

less than I cup

2 I pint

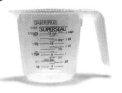

more than I pint

less than I pint

3 I quart

more than I quart

less than I quart

More to Explore

Number Sense

Fractions are used to show parts of a cup.

$\frac{1}{3}$ **cup**

Which cup has more?

$\frac{1}{2}$ cup

$\frac{1}{4}$ cup

Which cup has less?

$\frac{1}{2}$ cup

$\frac{1}{3}$ cup

At Home

We measured in cups, pints, and quarts.
Ask your child to show you how much $\frac{1}{2}$ cup is.

Name _____

This bottle holds
I **liter.**

Talk

How can you find out if other containers
hold more or less than I liter?

Working Together

You and your partner need a
I-liter container.

▶ Choose some containers.

▶ Estimate if the container
holds more or less than
I liter. Record your estimate.

▶ Fill and pour to measure.
Record the measure.

The mug holds
less than I liter.

1 Container _____

  Estimate _____

  Measure _____

2 Container _____

  Estimate _____

  Measure _____

3 Container _____

  Estimate _____

  Measure _____

4 Container _____

  Estimate _____

  Measure _____

McGraw-Hill School Division

Try These!

Choose the better estimate.

1

more than 1 liter

less than 1 liter

2

more than 1 liter

less than 1 liter

3

more than 1 liter

less than 1 liter

4

more than 1 liter

less than 1 liter

Mixed Review

5 Write the fraction for the shaded part.

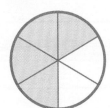 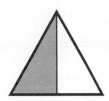  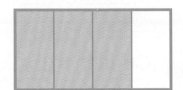

_____   _____   _____   _____

At Home Ask your child to find containers in your home that hold about 1 liter.

Temperature

Temperature can be measured in **degrees Fahrenheit** (°F).

This thermometer shows ___24___ °F.

Talk What kind of day is it when the temperature is 24°F?

Write the temperature. Write *hot, warm,* or *cold.*

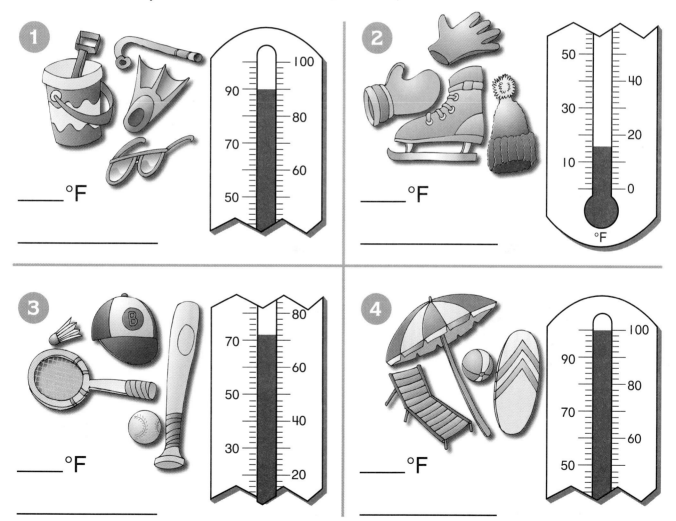

1 ____°F
_____

2 ____°F
_____

3 ____°F
_____

4 ____°F
_____

 Critical Thinking What might the temperature be on a hot day? a cold day? a warm day?

McGraw-Hill School Division

Try These!

Temperature can also be measured in **degrees Celsius** (°C).

1 This thermometer shows ___°C.

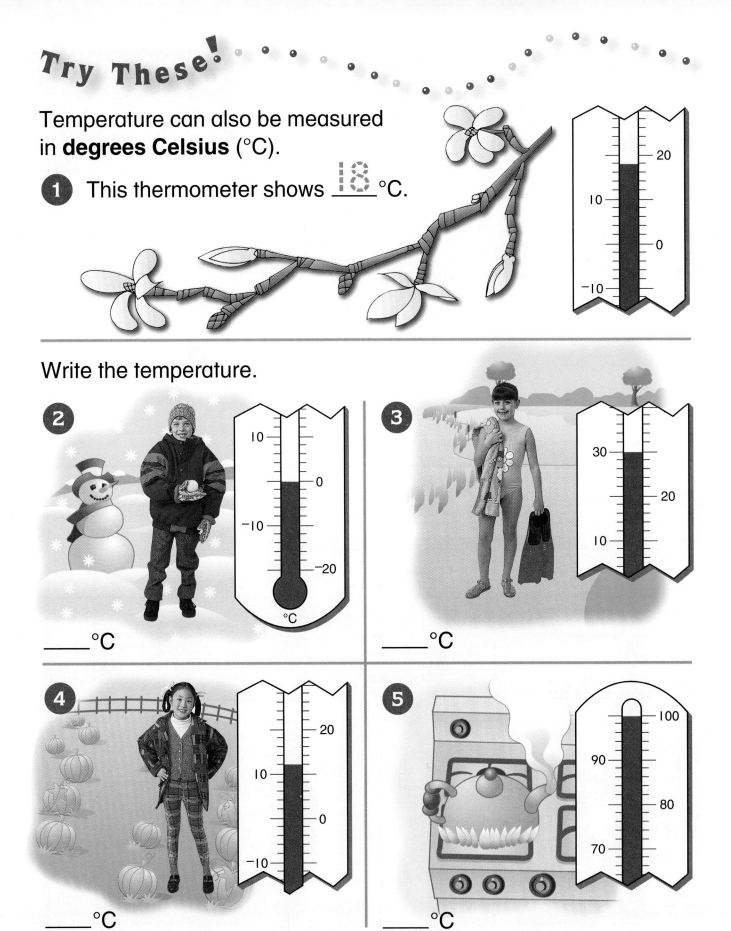

Write the temperature.

2 ___°C

3 ___°C

4 ___°C

5 ___°C

Journal Write about or draw a picture of today's weather. Find out the temperature.

At Home Ask your child what you might wear if the weather were 20°F.

Name _____

Jenna wants to check how much cereal is left in the box.

Which tool should she use to measure?

Ruler?   Scale?   Thermometer?

Jenna should use a _____scale_____ .

Choose the tool you would use to measure:

1 how much water is in a fish tank.

2 how warm it is outside.

3 how heavy a rock is.

4 how long a lunchbox is.

 Critical Thinking How many ways can you measure a book? Which tools would you use to measure?

Try These!

Match to show which tool you would use to measure:

1 how much it holds.

2 how long it is.

3 how heavy it is.

4 how cold it is.

Cultural Connection

African Clay Beads

Make some clay beads.
Mix the ingredients.
Cook until thick.
Let clay cool.

Shape the beads.

Make a hole in each.
Bake 45 minutes at 300°F.

List the measurement tools
you need to make the beads. _____

Ingredients

1 cup cornstarch

$2\frac{1}{2}$ cups baking soda

$1\frac{1}{2}$ cups cold water

At Home Ask your child to explain which measurement tools he or she would use to measure various household items.

Reasonable Answers

Tori and Jan put a rug
in their tree house.
About how long is the rug?

5 inches   5 feet   15 feet

Which answer makes sense?
Think.

> A tree house is
> smaller than a
> room in a house.

> 5 inches is too small.
> 15 feet is too big.
> 5 feet makes sense.

Choose the answer that makes sense.

1. Jack reads a thermometer on
   a warm, sunny day.
   About what temperature is it?

   8°F   48°F   84°F

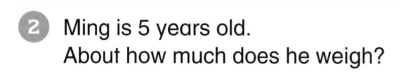

2. Ming is 5 years old.
   About how much does he weigh?

   4 pounds   40 pounds   400 pounds

Try These!

Choose the answer that makes sense.

1 Kelly makes a container of lemonade for her three friends. About how much does she make?

     I cup   I pint   I quart

2 Zach measures the length of his room. About how long is his room?

     10 inches   10 feet   100 feet

Write and Share

Dara wrote this problem.

I have a puppy named Lucky. He is small. About how much does he weigh?

5 pounds   50 pounds   100 pounds

Dara Chhin
Shaughnessy School
Lowell, Massachusetts

STUDENT TO STUDENT

3 Solve Dara's problem. _____

     How did you decide on your answer? _____

_____

4 Write a measurement problem for your partner to solve. Write three answers to choose from.

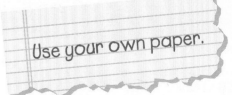
Use your own paper.

At Home

Ask your child to explain how to solve the problem that he or she wrote.

Chapter Review

Estimate. Then measure. Use a or a .

		Estimate	**Measure**
1	————	about ___ inches	about ___ inches
2	—————	about ___ inches	about ___ inches
3	—————	about ___ cm	about ___ cm
4	———	about ___ cm	about ___ cm

Measure. Add to find the perimeter.

5 ___ cm

6 ___ cm

Choose the better estimate.

7
more than I pound

less than I pound

8
more than I kilogram

less than I kilogram

9
more than I cup

less than I cup

10
more than I pint

less than I pint

11
more than I quart

less than I quart

12
more than I liter

less than I liter

How many pounds?

13 about ____ pounds

How many kilograms?

14 about ____ kilograms

Write the temperature.

15 ____°F

16 ____°C

17 ____°F

18 ____°C

Draw a diagram to solve.

19 Amy's garden is a triangle.
There is 1 tree in each corner.
There are 3 flowers between each tree.
How many flowers are in Amy's garden?

Use your own paper.

____ flowers

Choose the answer that makes sense.

20 Diana measured her desk.
About how long was it?   2 inches   20 feet   2 feet

What Do You Think?

Which is easier to measure?

☑ Check one.   ☐ Inches   ☐ Feet   ☐ Pounds

Why? _____

Journal Draw a 1-inch line. Tell what you know about inches.

Chapter Test

Estimate. Then measure.

	Estimate	**Measure**

1 ▬▬▬▬▬▬▬▬ about ____ inches about ____ inches

2 ▬▬▬▬▬▬▬▬ about ____ cm about ____ cm

3 Measure. Add to find the perimeter.  ____ cm

Ring the better estimate.

4  more than 1 pint

less than 1 pint

5 more than 1 liter

less than 1 liter

Write the temperature.

6 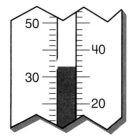 ____ °F

7 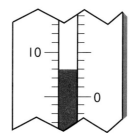 ____ °C

8 How many pounds?

about ____ pounds

9 How many kilograms?

about ____ kilograms

Draw a diagram to solve.

10 Pat used 5 pieces of fence on each of 2 sides of his garden. He used 3 pieces on each of the other 2 sides of his garden. How many pieces of fence did Pat use?

Use your own paper.

____ pieces

What Did You Learn?

Work with a partner.

Choose two different kinds of objects to measure. Measure each object as many ways as you can. Record the measure and the tool you used.

Object 1:	Object 2:
measure: tool:	measure: tool:
measure: tool:	measure: tool:
measure: tool:	measure: tool:
measure: tool:	measure: tool:

Write about how you measured and why you chose the tools and units you did.

Use your own paper.

 You may want to put this page in your portfolio.

Name

Coordinate Grids

This grid shows where things are at a campground. How can you find the tent?

► Always start at 0.

► First count across →.

► Then count up ↑.

> To find the tent, go across 3 and up 1.

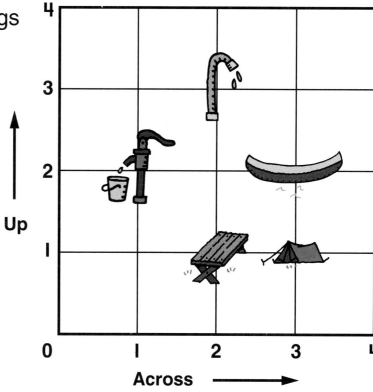

Which things will you find?

	Across →	Up ↑			
1	3	1			
2	2	1			
3	1	2			
4	2	3			
5	3	2			

Perimeter

Talk How can different shapes have the same perimeter?

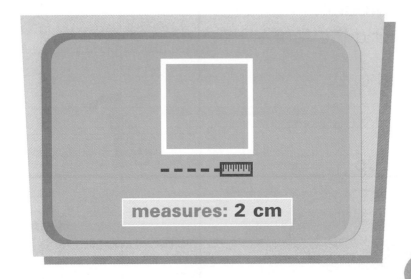

measures: 2 cm

What is the perimeter of this square? _____

At the Computer

1. Draw a rectangle with the same perimeter as the square above.

2. Draw a square with a perimeter of 12 cm. Then draw a rectangle with the same perimeter. Compare your rectangle to those of others.

3. Choose a perimeter. Draw a square with that perimeter. Draw as many rectangles with that perimeter as you can.

4. Draw a triangle with the same perimeter as one of the squares above.

Name

MATERIALS hanger, 2 identical metal clips, 2 identical clothespins

DIRECTIONS Make a balance like this. Find the real objects listed on the chart. Balance them with other objects.

Write the objects you find on the chart.

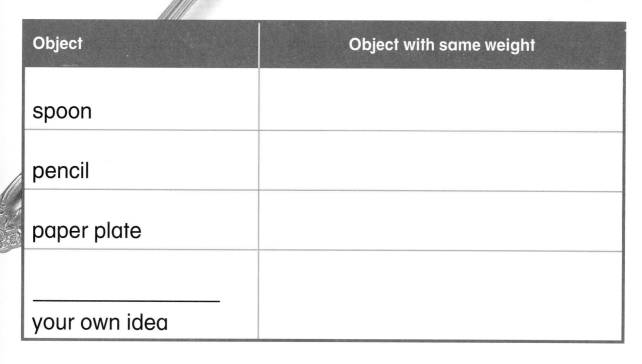

Object	Object with same weight
spoon	
pencil	
paper plate	
_____ your own idea	

At Home

This activity will help to develop your child's ability to estimate weight. Point out to your child that on this balance, when neither side of the hanger tips, the objects have the same weight.

At Home

Dear Family,

We are beginning a new chapter in mathematics. During the next few weeks we will be learning about comparing, ordering, adding, and subtracting 3-digit numbers.

We will also be talking about music, concerts, bands, and instruments. Please help me complete this interview.

Your child,

_____
Signature

Interview ···

What kind of music do you like? _____

Have you ever attended a concert or
listened to a concert on tape, TV, or radio? _____
What kind of music did you hear?

❑ Jazz ❑ Folk ❑ Rock ❑ Country

❑ Classical ❑ Other _____

About how many people do
you think were at the concert? _____

Math and Music
Numbers to 1,000
Adding and Subtracting

 Listen to the story *The Philharmonic Gets Dressed.*

 What numbers does the author use in the story?

Name _____

What Do You Know?

The orchestra wants to play a concert for the school. The gym will hold only 155 students at a time.

SMITHTOWN SCHOOL	
Grade	**Number of Students**
Kindergarten	85
First	67
Second	78
Third	73
Fourth	59
Fifth	68

1. Can the kindergarten and the first grade go to the concert at the same time? _____

   Explain. _____

2. Which two grades cannot go to the concert

   at the same time? _____

   Explain. _____

   _____

 Which grades could go together to the concert? How many students could attend each concert?

 You may want to put this page in your portfolio.

Working Together

You and your partner need 9 ,

9 ⬛⬛⬛⬛, and 9 ▫.

Take turns.

▶ Pick up some of each model.

▶ Estimate what number
the models show.
Then count.

▶ Your partner writes
how many hundreds,
tens, and ones and
writes the number.

1 __3__ hundreds __8__ tens __2__ ones __382__

2 _____ hundreds _____ tens _____ ones _____

3 _____ hundreds _____ tens _____ ones _____

4 _____ hundreds _____ tens _____ ones _____

5 _____ hundreds _____ tens _____ ones _____

6 _____ hundreds _____ tens _____ ones _____

7 _____ hundreds _____ tens _____ ones _____

8 _____ hundreds _____ tens _____ ones _____

Critical Thinking What number has 1 ten more than 465?
How do you know?

Try These!

Write how many hundreds,
tens, and ones.
Write the number.

1  __1__ hundred __4__ tens __6__ ones

__146__

2  _____ hundreds _____ tens _____ ones

_____

3  _____ hundreds _____ tens _____ ones

_____

4 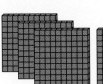 _____ hundreds _____ tens _____ ones

_____

5 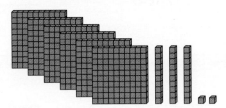 _____ hundreds _____ tens _____ ones

_____

 At Home Have your child tell you the number of hundreds, tens, and ones for this page number.

Two hundred six students
play in the Parkview High
School band.

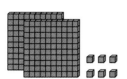

hundreds	tens	ones
2	0	6

206

Talk

Tell why there is a 0 in the tens place.

Write how many hundreds, tens, and ones.
Write the number.

  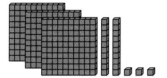

hundreds	tens	ones

_____

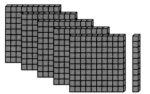

hundreds	tens	ones

_____

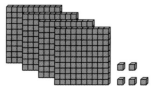

hundreds	tens	ones

_____

Critical
Thinking

What is the greatest 3-digit number you
can write with the digits 0, 2, and 8?

Try These!

Write how many hundreds, tens, and ones.
Write the number.

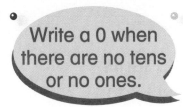 

Write a 0 when there are no tens or no ones.

1

hundreds	tens	ones
2	2	4

224

2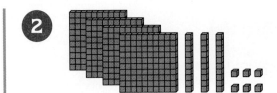

hundreds	tens	ones

_____

3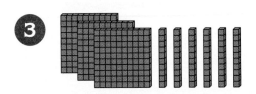

hundreds	tens	ones

_____

4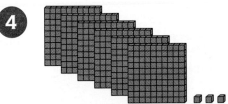

hundreds	tens	ones

_____

More to Explore   Number Sense

Here is another way to write numbers.

5 hundreds 2 tens 1 one

500 + 20 + 1   521

1 hundred 8 tens 6 ones

_____ + ___ + ___   _____

9 hundreds 0 tens 4 ones

_____ + ___ + ___   _____

2 hundreds 7 tens 0 ones

_____ + ___ + ___   _____

 At Home

We continue to work with 3-digit numbers. Ask your child to write the number for 9 hundreds 9 tens 9 ones.

Name _____

There were 452 tickets sold for the
school concert.

hundreds	tens	ones
4	5	2

The **value** of 4 is 400.
The value of 5 is 50.
The value of 2 is 2.

 Talk In the number 162, how do you know
if the 6 means 600, 60, or 6?

Working Together
Take turns.

▶ Write a 3-digit number.

▶ Circle one of the digits.

▶ Your partner writes the
value of the circled digit.

	3-digit number	value of circled digit
1	⃝138	100
2		
3		
4		
5		

	3-digit number	value of circled digit
6		
7		
8		
9		
10		

 Critical Thinking What is the same about 432 and 234?
What is different?

Try These!

Circle to show the value of the underlined digit.

1. 3<u>8</u>7   800   (80)   8
2. <u>6</u>92   600   60   6
3. 5<u>4</u>   400   40   4
4. 8<u>1</u>6   100   10   1
5. 14<u>3</u>   300   30   3
6. <u>8</u>0   800   80   8
7. <u>7</u>77   700   70   7

Cultural Connection   Early Arabic Numbers

Early Arabic numbers did not use a zero.
Instead, dots showed what a digit meant.
One dot above a digit meant *tens*.
Two dots above a digit meant *hundreds*.

$$\dot{7}2 = 72 \qquad \ddot{7}2 = 720$$
$$\ddot{7}2 = 702 \qquad \ddot{7}2\dot{2} = 722$$

Write the number.

$\ddot{2}6 =$ __206__ $\ddot{8}7 =$ _____ $\ddot{2}\dot{1} =$ _____

$\ddot{1}\dot{7}4 =$ _____ $\ddot{1}\dot{2} =$ _____ $\ddot{6}\dot{1}8 =$ _____

At Home

We learned the value of digits in 3-digit numbers.
Have your child tell you what the 2 means in 523.

What's My Number?

Play in a large group. Sit in a circle.

▶ The leader thinks of a secret 3-digit number.

▶ Each person in turn asks a question about the number.

▶ The leader answers *yes* or *no*.

▶ As you hear clues, write them down.

Winner: the player who guesses the number
The winner becomes the new leader.

Yes.

Is the number greater than 100?

Write clues here or use your own paper.

hundreds	tens	ones

Write how many hundreds, tens, and ones.
Write the number.

1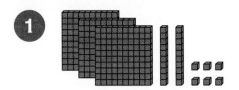

hundreds	tens	ones

_____

2

hundreds	tens	ones

_____

3

hundreds	tens	ones

_____

4

hundreds	tens	ones

_____

5

hundreds	tens	ones

_____

Circle to show the value of the
underlined digit.

6 9<u>7</u>0   700   70   7

7 <u>4</u>62   400   40   4

8 80<u>4</u>   400   40   4

9 <u>1</u>53   100   10   1

Write the numbers
in order.

101	102	103							110
111				115					120
						127			
		133							
				145					
151									
								169	
	172								
							188		
									200

Critical
Thinking

What is the number pattern going across?
What is the number pattern going down?
What is the number pattern going from right to left?

Try These!

Remember the patterns in the chart.

Write the missing numbers.

1 412, 413, __414__, __415__, 416, __417__, __418__

2 994, 995, 996, ____, ____, 999, ____

3 279, 280, 281, ____, ____, ____, ____

4 888, 889, ____, ____, ____, ____, ____

5 327, 326, __325__, __324__, __323__, 322, ____

6 683, 682, 681, ____, ____, ____, ____

7 748, 747, ____, 745, ____, ____, ____

8 560, 559, ____, ____, ____, ____, ____

9 ____, 263, ____, 265, ____, ____, ____

More to Explore   Patterns

Skip-count to connect the dots.

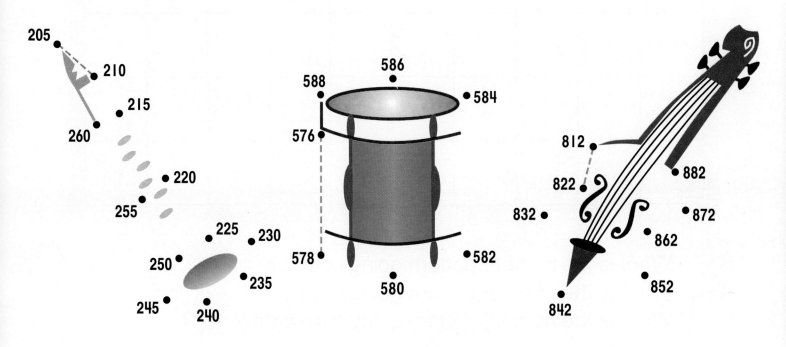

402 • four hundred two

At Home

Name _____

Peter put his numbered sheets of music in order from least to greatest.

284 is just before 285.

285 is between 284 and 286.

286 is just after 285.

Write the number that is just after.

1  697 | 698   202   439

2  755   170   999

Write the number that is just before.

3 562 | 563   888   390

4 941   427   775

Write the number that is between.

5  816 | 817 | 818   188   190

6 633   635   945   947

Write the number just after, just before,
or between.

1 421 | 422   806 | ___   ___ | 799

2 158 | ___ | 160   806 | ___   ___ | 637

3 339 | ___   951 | ___ | 953   ___ | 400

4 674 | ___ | 676   289 | ___ | 291

5 554 | ___   831 | ___ | 833   ___ | 262

Mixed Review

Add or subtract.

6
$$59 + 37$$ $$34 - 8$$ $$83 + 6$$ $$24 + 24$$ $$52 - 19$$ $$67 - 36$$

7
$$42 - 25$$ $$9 + 57$$ $$80 - 46$$ $$49 + 41$$ $$65 + 16$$ $$23 - 19$$

At Home — We learned more about ordering numbers to 1,000. Ask your child to tell you the number that comes just after 600.

A music store has 118 opera CDs. It has 135 jazz CDs. Which kind of CDs does the store have more of?

Compare 118 and 135 to find out.

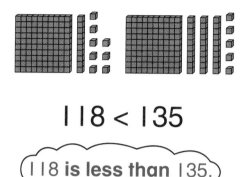

118 < 135

(118 **is less than** 135.)

135 > 118

(135 **is greater than** 118.)

The store has more jazz CDs.

Working Together

You and your partner need 10 ☐,

18 , and 18 ▪.

Take turns.

▶ You show a 3-digit number with models.

▶ Your partner shows a different 3-digit number.

▶ Write the numbers below.

▶ Compare. Write > or <.

365 ⊃ 345		___ ◯ ___		___ ◯ ___	
___ ◯ ___		___ ◯ ___		___ ◯ ___	
___ ◯ ___		___ ◯ ___		___ ◯ ___	

McGraw-Hill School Division

Try These!

Compare. Write > or <.

Remember:
> means *is greater than*.
< means *is less than*.

1 341 ⊳ 241   194 ◯ 199   673 ◯ 623

2 556 ◯ 159   978 ◯ 987   480 ◯ 380

3 179 ◯ 279   747 ◯ 737   255 ◯ 329

4 908 ◯ 897   499 ◯ 498   84 ◯ 174

5 470 ◯ 475   283 ◯ 224   636 ◯ 549

6 264 ◯ 363   219 ◯ 608   933 ◯ 930

7 838 ◯ 818   147 ◯ 347

8 335 ◯ 330   421 ◯ 428

Solve.

9 Mimi's family has 139 CDs.
Keith's family has 160 CDs.
Whose family has more CDs? _____

10 Choose two 3-digit numbers.
Use them to write a word problem
about comparing. Then solve it.

 Use your own paper.

 Write how to put these numbers in order from least to greatest.

| 347 | 385 |
| 147 | 305 |

 At Home   We used the symbols > and < to compare numbers. Ask your child to tell whether 987 is greater than or less than 798.

Name _____

Extra Practice
Game !

Get to the Concert!

You and your partner need 2 ⬤, a 🧭, and a 🎲.

▶ Put your game marker on **Start.**
Spin. Move that many spaces.

▶ Roll the cube three times for
hundreds, tens, and ones.

▶ Tell the number that is *just before*
or *just after* the number you rolled.

▶ Stay in the space if correct.
Move back one space if not correct.

Winner: the first player to reach the **Concert.**

CHAPTER 11 *Extra Practice*

four hundred seven • **407**

McGraw-Hill School Division

Write the missing numbers.

1. 140, 141, ____, ____, ____, 145
2. 736, ____, 738, ____, ____, 741
3. 420, 419, ____, 417, ____, ____

Write the number just after, just before, or between.

4. 416, ____   523, ____   ____, 640
5. 111, ____, 113   ____, 612   899, ____
6. 912, ____, 914   335, ____, 337

Compare. Write > or <.

7. 306 ◯ 206   510 ◯ 501   729 ◯ 792
8. 246 ◯ 256   631 ◯ 635   537 ◯ 457
9. 832 ◯ 732   136 ◯ 132   900 ◯ 898

Solve.

10. 245 people sang in the concert. 250 people played instruments in the concert. Were there more singers or instrument players?

_____

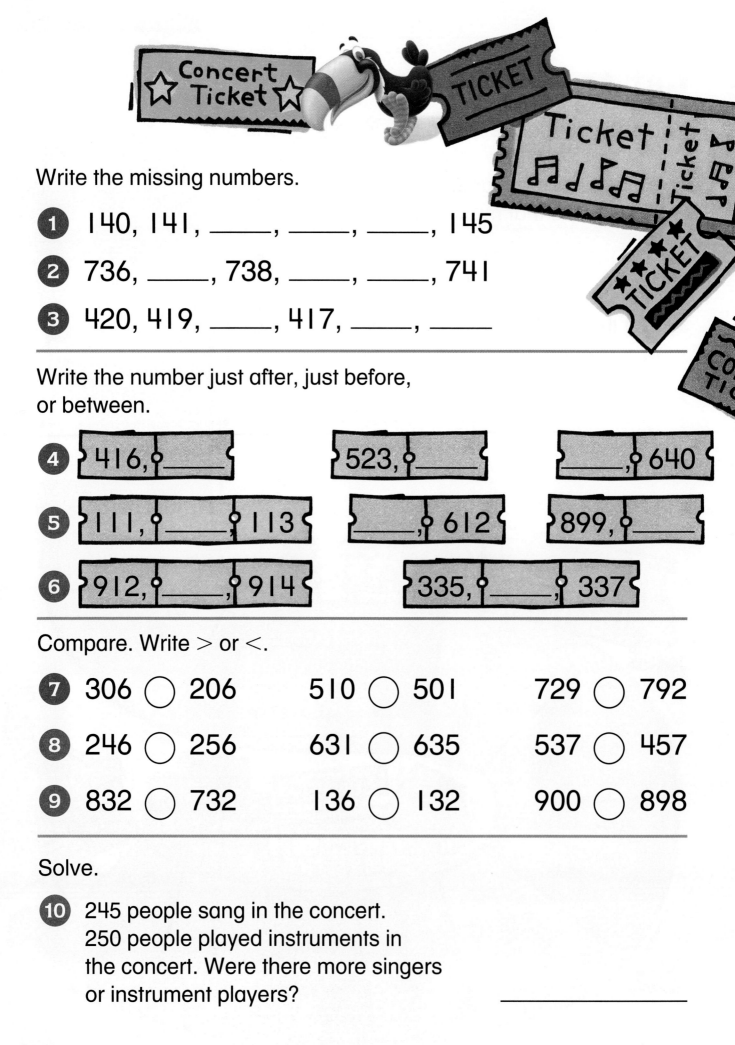

Midchapter Review

Write how many hundreds, tens, and ones. Write the number.

 Do your best!

1  _____ hundreds _____ tens _____ ones

_____

2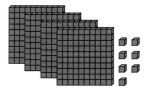

hundreds	tens	ones

_____

3 What does the digit 7 mean in 6<u>7</u>4?

How do you know? _____

Write the missing numbers.

4 937, 938, 939, _____, _____, _____

5 603, _____, 605, _____, _____, _____

Write the number just after, just before, or between.

6 198, _____, 200   **7** 575, _____   **8** _____, 611

Compare. Write > or <.

9 329 ◯ 368   **10** 897 ◯ 743

 Tell how you compare 3-digit numbers.

Comparing Cards

You and your partner need number cards.
Each player gets half the cards.

▶ You and your partner each show
  the top three cards in your pile.

▶ Make the greatest 3-digit number that
  you can. Compare your numbers.

▶ The player with the greater number
  wins all six cards.

Talk — Talk to your partner about how to make the
greatest possible number.

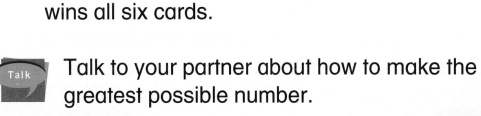

Play until one player has all the cards.

Play again. Make the least possible number.

Name

A Music Tour

 Listen to *The Philharmonic Gets Dressed.*

Each year the New York Philharmonic tours for 1 month.

The tour director is planning a short tour. The orchestra will visit six cities.

Working Together

▶ Your group will make a tour schedule for the orchestra.

▶ Look at the map. Choose six cities.

▶ Decide on the order of cities to visit. Find the shortest route.

▶ Make notes for what you decide.

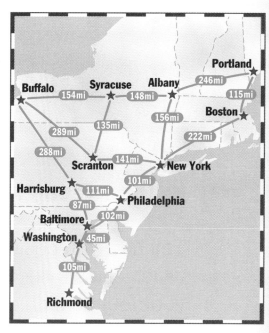

mi stands for miles.

McGraw-Hill School Division

Decision Making

1 Decide what to include on your schedule. Think about what the orchestra needs to know.

2 Make a schedule.

 Write a report.

3 Tell how you decided which cities to include on your tour schedule.

4 Explain how you found the shortest route for the tour.

More to Investigate

PREDICT What if the tour director only wants to travel 1,000 miles on the tour. Would you have to change your schedule?

EXPLORE Try different methods for finding the total miles.

FIND Compare your total miles to 1,000. Show how you could change your schedule.

Name _____

Working Together

You and your partner need 6
and 20 ▭.

► You show some tens.

► Your partner shows some tens.

► Complete the table.

Regroup
10 tens as
1 hundred.

(14 tens)

(1 hundred) (4 tens)

	How many tens?	Can you regroup?		How many hundreds and tens?	
1	14 tens	(yes)	no	1 hundreds	4 tens
2	_____ tens	yes	no	_____ hundreds	_____ tens
3	_____ tens	yes	no	_____ hundreds	_____ tens
4	_____ tens	yes	no	_____ hundreds	_____ tens
5	_____ tens	yes	no	_____ hundreds	_____ tens
6	_____ tens	yes	no	_____ hundreds	_____ tens
7	_____ tens	yes	no	_____ hundreds	_____ tens

 Critical Thinking When can't you regroup?

Try These!

Use models. Show the hundreds, tens, and
ones. Regroup when you can.
Write the number.

1 3 hundreds 11 tens 6 ones

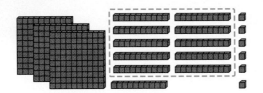

hundreds	tens	ones
4	1	6

2 6 hundreds 2 tens 9 ones

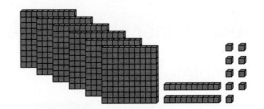

hundreds	tens	ones

3 5 hundreds 15 tens

hundreds	tens	ones

4 1 hundred 18 tens 3 ones

hundreds	tens	ones

5 2 hundreds 9 tens 1 one

hundreds	tens	ones

6 4 hundreds 16 tens 2 ones

hundreds	tens	ones

More to Explore — Number Sense

Without adding, which sums will be greater
than 100? Ring them.

49	27	68	43	38	40
+ 83	+ 21	+ 78	+ 33	+ 72	+ 53

At Home   We regrouped 10 tens for 1 hundred. Ask
your child how to regroup 15 tens.

Name _____

You need 9 ▦, 20 ▭, and 20 ▫.
Add 156 + 273.

Add the ones. Regroup when you can.

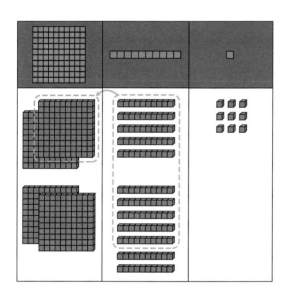

hundreds	tens	ones
☐	☐	
1	5	6
+ 2	7	3
		9

(9 ones)

Add all the tens. Regroup when you can.

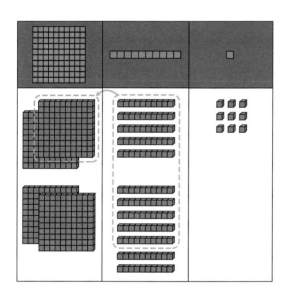

hundreds	tens	ones
☐	☐	
1	5	6
+ 2	7	3
	2	9

(12 tens
1 hundred 2 tens)

Add all the hundreds.

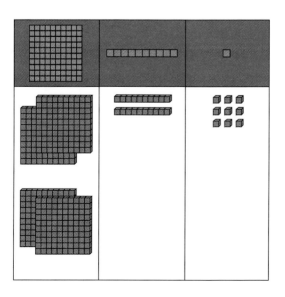

hundreds	tens	ones
☐	☐	
1	5	6
+ 2	7	3
4	2	9

(4 hundreds)

Try These!

Add. Use hundreds, tens, and ones models to help.

1

hundreds	tens	ones
☐ 3	⦂ 2	9
+ 1	3	8
4	6	7

hundreds	tens	ones
☐	☐ 7	5
+ 6	7	1

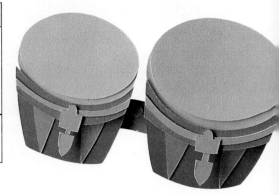

2

hundreds	tens	ones
☐	☐ 5	2
+ 5	6	3

hundreds	tens	ones
☐ 4	☐ 2	8
+ 1	3	4

hundreds	tens	ones
☐ 2	☐ 0	4
+ 3	7	5

3

hundreds	tens	ones
☐ 4	☐ 3	1
+		9

hundreds	tens	ones
☐ 1	☐ 4	9
+ 2	7	0

hundreds	tens	ones
☐ 6	☐ 4	6
+	5	2

4

hundreds	tens	ones
☐ 3	☐ 8	7
+ 4	9	0

hundreds	tens	ones
☐ 5	☐ 3	7
+ 1	3	9

hundreds	tens	ones
☐ 6	☐ 1	2
+ 1	9	4

At Home We began adding with 3-digit numbers. Ask your child to tell you about adding 329 + 138.

Name _____

The band sold 368 CDs last year.
This year they have sold 185 CDs.
How many CDs has the band sold?

Add the ones. Regroup when you can.	**Add all the tens. Regroup when you can.**	**Add all the hundreds.**

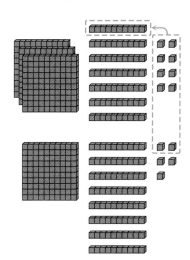 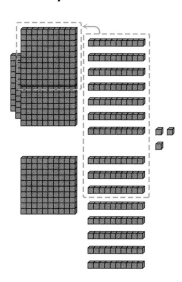 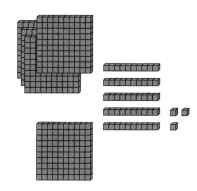

```
  □ |           □ |           □ |
  368           368           368
+ 185         + 185         + 185
————          ————          ————
    3            53           553
```

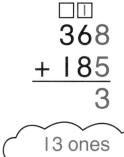

13 ones 1 ten 3 ones	15 tens 1 hundred 5 tens	5 hundreds

The band sold ___553___ CDs.

Add.

1
```
   349        195        427        564         79
 +  63      + 606      + 231      +   8      + 312
 —————      —————      —————      —————      —————
   412
```

McGraw-Hill School Division

Try These!

Add.

1
297	48	670
+ 315	+ 468	+ 126
612		

2
175	847	325
+ 473	+ 151	+ 85

3
533	488	172	394	406
+ 90	+ 286	+ 69	+ 7	+ 422

Solve.

 Workspace

4 There are 379 rock-and-roll cassettes.
There are 452 classical cassettes.
How many cassettes
are there? _____ cassettes

5 One bin in the music store had 68 CDs.
Another bin had 256 CDs. How many
CDs are in both bins?

_____ CDs

6 Write a word problem.
Use the numbers 273 and 685.
Then solve the problem.

 Use your own paper.

At Home

We continue to add with 3-digit numbers. Ask
your child to explain how to add 394 + 27.

Reach 999!

Each team needs 9 ▦,
20 ▬, 20 ▪, and a ⬛.

Teams take turns.

▶ Start with 8 ▬ and 6 ▪.
Write 86 in the chart.

▶ Throw the cube three times
to get hundreds, tens, and
ones. Write the number in the
chart. Show the number with
models.

▶ Combine the new and old
models. Regroup when you
can. Write the new number.

Winner: the first team to reach
or pass 999

hundreds	tens	ones
	8	6
+		
+		
+		
+		
+		
+		
+		

Add.

1
```
  430        257        375          6        347
+  84      + 686      + 149      + 508      + 383
─────
 514
```

2
```
  291        711         38        425        268
+ 456      +   4      + 338      + 172      + 693
```

3
```
   24        432          8        304        257
+ 580      + 389      + 146      +  76      + 256
```

Solve.

Workspace

4 There were 128 band members from Westen School. There were 97 band members from Travers School. How many band members is that altogether?

_____ band members

5 There were 46 drummers and 138 bugle players in the drum and bugle band. How many band members is that altogether?

_____ band members

Name _____

Regrouping for Subtraction

Working Together

You and your partner need 7 ,
20 ▱▱▱▱▱, and 9 ▫.

Take turns.

▶ Your partner shows hundreds, tens, and ones.

▶ You regroup if needed.
Take away hundreds, tens, and ones.

▶ Write the number that is left.

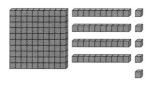

Regroup I hundred as 10 tens.

Take away 82.

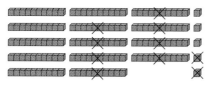

6 tens 3 ones left

	Show.	Take away.	Did you regroup?		Number left.
1	145	82	(yes)	no	63
2	284	144	yes	no	
3	205	184	yes	no	
4	132	51	yes	no	
5	507	95	yes	no	
6	328	217	yes	no	
7	459	166	yes	no	

Try These!

Use ▦, ▭, and ▪ to show the number. Complete the chart.

Remember: 1 hundred = 10 tens

	Show.	Take away.	Did you regroup?		Number left.
1	641	250	(yes)	no	391
2	397	172	yes	no	
3	436	63	yes	no	
4	308	154	yes	no	
5	122	71	yes	no	
6	659	447	yes	no	
7	275	65	yes	no	
8	504	372	yes	no	
9	766	534	yes	no	

Mixed Review

Choose the tool you would use to measure:

10 how tall a bottle is.

11 how heavy a bottle is.

12 how much a bottle holds.

 At Home

We regrouped 1 hundred as 10 tens. Ask your child how to subtract 60 from 429.

Name _____

You need 9 ▦, 20 ▭, and 20 ▫.
Subtract 318 − 165.

**Look at the ones.
Regroup if you
need to.
Subtract the ones.**

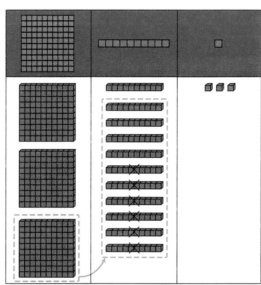

hundreds	tens	ones
□	□	□
3	1	8
− 1	6	5
		3

(3 ones left)

**Look at the tens.
Regroup if you
need to.
Subtract the tens.**

hundreds	tens	ones
2	11	□
3̷	1̷	8
− 1	6	5
	5	3

(5 tens left)

**Subtract
the
hundreds.**

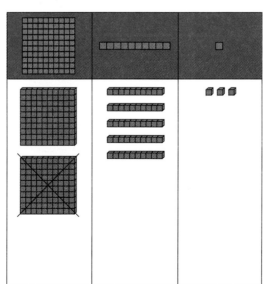

hundreds	tens	ones
2	11	□
3̷	1̷	8
− 1	6	5
1	5	3

(1 hundred left)

Try These!

Subtract. Use hundreds, tens, and ones models to help.

1

hundreds	tens	ones
3	10	☐
4	0	5
− 2	9	3
1	1	2

hundreds	tens	ones
☐	☐	☐
8	6	4
− 3	7	1

2

hundreds	tens	ones
☐	☐	☐
5	4	6
−	8	3

hundreds	tens	ones
☐	☐	☐
8	7	7
− 6	0	4

hundreds	tens	ones
☐	☐	☐
4	1	7
− 1	3	5

3

hundreds	tens	ones
☐	☐	☐
3	2	1
− 2	6	0

hundreds	tens	ones
☐	☐	☐
6	6	4
− 1	7	2

hundreds	tens	ones
☐	☐	☐
2	0	9
−	1	8

4

hundreds	tens	ones
☐	☐	☐
9	2	9
− 4	3	7

hundreds	tens	ones
☐	☐	☐
7	3	8
−		6

hundreds	tens	ones
☐	☐	☐
6	3	1
− 3	7	0

At Home

We began subtracting with 3-digit numbers. Ask your child to tell you about subtracting 293 from 405.

Name _____

The drama club had 143
students try out for parts
in a musical.
109 students did not get parts.
How many students got parts?

Look at the ones. Regroup if you need to. Subtract the ones.	Look at the tens. Regroup if you need to. Subtract the tens.	Subtract the hundreds.

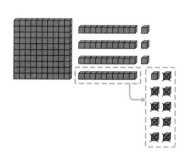 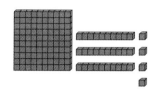 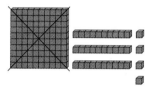

☐ 3 13	☐ 3 13	☐ 3 13
1 4̷3̷	1 4̷3̷	1 4̷3̷
− 1 0 9	− 1 0 9	− 1 0 9
4	3 4	3 4

 4 ones   3 tens    0 hundreds

 __34__ students got parts.

Subtract.

1
☐ 8 15				
8 9̷5̷	462	531	227	739
− 407	− 138	− 325	− 164	− 6
488				

Try These!

Subtract.

1)
$$\begin{array}{r} \square\square12 \\ 742 \\ -\ 528 \\ \hline 214 \end{array}$$

$$\begin{array}{r} 528 \\ -\ 383 \\ \hline \end{array}$$

$$\begin{array}{r} 254 \\ -\ 32 \\ \hline \end{array}$$

2)
$$\begin{array}{r} 416 \\ -\ 173 \\ \hline \end{array}$$

$$\begin{array}{r} 399 \\ -\ 268 \\ \hline \end{array}$$

$$\begin{array}{r} 860 \\ -\ 435 \\ \hline \end{array}$$

3)
$$\begin{array}{r} 657 \\ -\ 234 \\ \hline \end{array}$$

$$\begin{array}{r} 270 \\ -\ 180 \\ \hline \end{array}$$

$$\begin{array}{r} 768 \\ -\ 475 \\ \hline \end{array}$$

$$\begin{array}{r} 444 \\ -\ 313 \\ \hline \end{array}$$

$$\begin{array}{r} 993 \\ -\ 567 \\ \hline \end{array}$$

Solve.

Workspace

4) The auditorium has 328 seats.
53 seats are empty during the play.
How many seats are filled?

_____ seats

5) 390 people went to the musical on Monday.
287 people went on Tuesday. How many
more people went to the musical on
Monday than Tuesday?

_____ people

6) *Write* — Use the numbers 527 and 182
to write a word problem.
Then solve the problem.

Use your own paper.

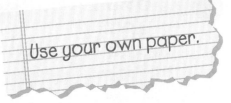

At Home — We continue to subtract with 3-digit numbers. Ask your child to explain how to subtract 993 − 567.

Subtraction Action

You and your partner need 2 .

Take turns.

▶ Drop a counter on each sheet of music. Write the subtraction.

▶ Subtract.

Starting number

382	967	439	553	875
545	694	833	729	387
929	736	689	418	896

Number to subtract

307	191	5	204	60
91	129	215	13	382
8	353	82	271	160

Subtraction exercises

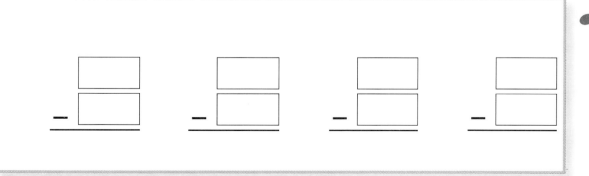

Subtract.

1 ⁴¹²
   528   851   374   643   967
 − 463   − 339   −   7   − 220   − 685
   6̶5̶

2   230   589   438   724   152
  − 28   − 412   − 293   − 13   − 136

3   987   360   138   827   577
  − 656   − 112   − 98   − 384   − 268

Solve.

4 Chaz practiced piano for 147 minutes.
   Jo practiced piano for 109 minutes.
   How many more minutes did Chaz practice?

                            _____ minutes

5 The band room has 219 brass instruments.
   There are 56 fewer stringed instruments.
   How many stringed instruments are
   there?
                    _____ stringed instruments

Name _____

Solve a Simpler Problem

Read
Plan
Solve
Look Back

Read A rock band traveled 336 miles on Monday. They traveled 428 miles on Tuesday. How many miles did the band travel during the 2 days?

Plan You can make the problem **simpler.**

Solve Think: 3 miles and 4 miles
How many miles?

You can add.

Add: 336
     + 428
     ‾‾‾‾‾
      764   The band traveled _____ miles.

Look Back Does the answer make sense? Explain.

Solve.

Workspace

1 The band sold 120 T-shirts. They also sold 239 posters and 385 tapes. How many more posters than T-shirts did the band sell?

_____

Critical Thinking What numbers did you think of to make problem 1 simpler?

Try These!

Solve.

1 Cheri travels 85 miles for her singing lesson. Then she travels 85 miles back home. She does this 2 times a week. How many miles does Cheri travel each week?

_____

2 Sid played the song on page 327 of his songbook. He turned back 109 pages and played a second song. On what page was the second song?

_____

3 A piano has 52 white keys and 36 black keys. How many more keys are white than black?

_____

Cultural Note
Jazz is a mix of African, Latin, and American music. It began in New Orleans.

At Home

We solved problems by thinking of simpler or easier numbers. Have your child explain how to solve problem 2 above.

Name _____

$0.36 **pick**

$2.85 **cymbals**

$1.26 **bells**

maraca

music

$1.35

$1.95 **triangle**

$3.51 **sticks**

$2.17

tambourine

recorder

$4.04

$3.29

You have $5.50 to spend.

▶ Choose two different items to buy.

▶ Find the total cost.

▶ Find how much money you have left.

Items	Total Cost	Money Left
1 maraca bells	$2.17 + 1.26 $3.43	$5.50 − 3.43 $2.07
2 _____ _____		
3 _____ _____		

Critical Thinking Which two items can't you buy? Explain.

McGraw-Hill School Division

Try These!

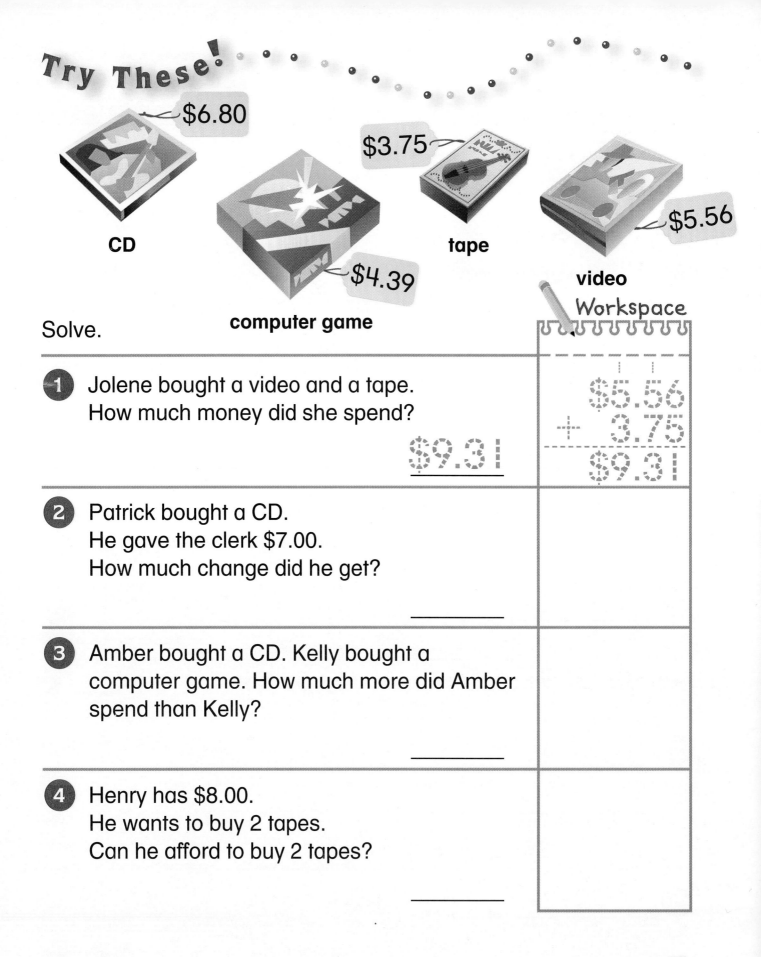

$6.80

CD

$3.75

$4.39

computer game

tape

$5.56

video

Workspace

Solve.

1 Jolene bought a video and a tape.
How much money did she spend?

$9.31

$5.56
+ 3.75
$9.31

2 Patrick bought a CD.
He gave the clerk $7.00.
How much change did he get?

_____

3 Amber bought a CD. Kelly bought a
computer game. How much more did Amber
spend than Kelly?

_____

4 Henry has $8.00.
He wants to buy 2 tapes.
Can he afford to buy 2 tapes?

_____

5 Write your own money problem.
Have a partner solve it.

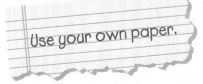
Use your own paper.

At Home

We added and subtracted money amounts. Have your child
find the total price of two items from a supermarket flyer.

Choose the Method

When an orchestra travels, so do many instruments. The chart shows how much the instruments weigh.

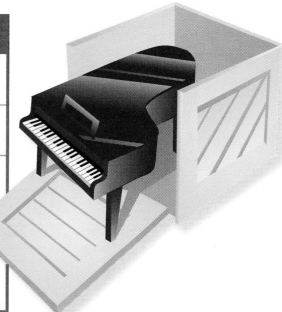

Instrument	Weight
drum set	124 pounds
tuba	45 pounds
harp	239 pounds
double bass	52 pounds
piano	648 pounds

Solve. Choose the best method for you.

1 How much do the tuba and harp weigh together? _____ pounds

 Critical Thinking How did you solve the problem? Which method did you choose?

2 How much more does the piano weigh than the harp? _____ pounds

3 Which two instruments are the heaviest? _____

4 How much do the two heaviest instruments weigh altogether? _____ pounds

1 A truck can hold 600 pounds more. How many harps can fit?

_____ harps

How many more pounds can the truck hold now?

_____ pounds

drum set	124 pounds
tuba	45 pounds
harp	239 pounds
double bass	52 pounds
piano	648 pounds

2 Which instruments would you put in a truck that could fit 600 pounds more? _____

_____

Talk Explain how you solved problem 2.

Write and Share

Meghan wrote this problem.

How much do the heaviest instrument and the lightest instrument weigh together?

Meghan Petchell
Northwest School
Howell, Michigan

3 Solve Meghan's problem. _____

What method did you choose? _____

4 Write a problem using information from the chart. Have a partner solve it.

Use your own paper.

What method did your partner use? _____

What method would you use? _____

At Home Ask your child to tell you how to solve the problem he or she wrote.

Chapter Review

Write how many hundreds, tens, and ones.
Write the number.

1

hundreds	tens	ones

_____

2 508 _____ hundreds _____ tens _____ ones

3 9 hundreds 3 tens 7 ones _____

Write the number just after, just before, or between.

4 287, _____   454, _____, 456   _____, 800

Compare. Write > or < .

5 734 ◯ 750   387 ◯ 378

Add or subtract.

6

hundreds	tens	ones
□	□	
6	7	7
+	4	3

$$426 + 391$$ $$\$5.50 + 2.87$$ $$\$1.95 + 4.76$$

7

hundreds	tens	ones
□	□	□
9	3	4
− 4	2	9

$$442 - 18$$ $$681 - 190$$ $$\$8.76 - 5.47$$

Solve.

8 A songbook has 173 folk songs, 46 marches, and 126 jazz songs. How many more folk songs than jazz songs are there?

_____ folk songs

9 Dino bought popcorn for $1.75 and juice for $2.15. What should his change be from $5.00?

_____

10 Meg had 217 tapes. She bought 36 more. How many tapes does she have now?

_____ tapes

What Do You Think?

Which is the quickest way to subtract 261 from 523?
☑ Check one.

Why? _____

 Write these exercises in your journal. Find the sums. Explain which is easier to add.

$1.04   369
+ 5.86   + 255

Name _____

Chapter Test

Write how many hundreds, tens, and ones.
Write the number.

1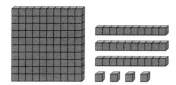

hundreds	tens	ones

_____

2 620 _____ hundreds _____ tens _____ ones

3 8 hundreds 6 tens 5 ones _____

4 Write the number just after, just before, or between.

408, _____, 410   _____, 700   365, _____

5 Compare. Write > or <.

> means *is greater than.*
< means *is less than.*

831 ◯ 854   762 ◯ 759

Add or subtract.

6 561
    + 372

7 $382
    − 167

8 $292
    + 365

9 893
    − 268

Solve.

10 The band sold 225 tapes.
They also sold 109 CDs and 352 posters.
How many more tapes than CDs did the
band sell?   _____ tapes

McGraw-Hill School Division

What Did You Learn?

$5.05 — piano

$3.95 — harmonica

$6.42 — drum

$4.63 — trumpet

$3.63 — flute

$6.88 — xylophone

$2.57 — violin

$4.90 — music book

You have $9.00 to spend.

Which two toys could you buy?

Show as many combinations as you can.

_____

_____

_____

_____

You may want to put this page in your portfolio.

Name

Compute with Greater Numbers

You can use a calculator to add and subtract greater numbers.

$$\begin{array}{r} 1,987 \\ + 4,530 \\ \hline 6,517 \end{array}$$

Press these keys.

ON/C 1 9 8 7 + 4 5 3 0 =

To add or subtract dollars and cents, you need to use the ⌐·⌐.

$$\begin{array}{r} \$5.53 \\ - \ 2.89 \\ \hline \$2.64 \end{array}$$

Press these keys.

ON/C 5 . 5 3 − 2 . 8 9 =

Use a calculator to add or subtract.

1.
$$\begin{array}{r} 5,241 \\ - 3,875 \\ \hline 1,366 \end{array}$$
$$\begin{array}{r} \$69.23 \\ + \ 89.67 \end{array}$$
$$\begin{array}{r} \$17.30 \\ - \ 6.82 \end{array}$$
$$\begin{array}{r} 2,348 \\ + 5,629 \end{array}$$

2.
$$\begin{array}{r} 848 \\ + 929 \end{array}$$
$$\begin{array}{r} \$52.18 \\ - \ 24.75 \end{array}$$
$$\begin{array}{r} 9,200 \\ - 4,867 \end{array}$$
$$\begin{array}{r} \$3.86 \\ + \ 9.59 \end{array}$$

3.
$$\begin{array}{r} 700 \\ - 433 \end{array}$$
$$\begin{array}{r} 6,009 \\ - 3,667 \end{array}$$
$$\begin{array}{r} \$35.46 \\ + \ 3.95 \end{array}$$
$$\begin{array}{r} 658 \\ + 885 \end{array}$$

Curriculum Connection
Social Studies

Roman Numerals

The Romans of long ago used letters to name numbers.

To read Roman numerals, you need to add or subtract.

Roman Numeral	Our Numeral
I	1
V	5
X	10
C	100

XXX — Add letter values together. $10 + 10 + 10 = 30$

XVII — Add letter values together. $10 + 5 + 1 + 1 = 17$

IV — Subtract when a letter with less value comes just before a letter with greater value. $5 - 1 = 4$

Write the number for each Roman numeral.

1. XC =  90

2. CCC = _____

3. IX = _____

Subtract. $100 - 10 = 90$

4. VII = _____

5. CX = _____

6. XXII = _____

Write Roman numerals for each number.

7. 105 = CV

Add. $100 + 5 = 105$

8. 33 = _____

9. 200 = _____

10. 101 = _____

Name

High Number, Low Number

PLAYERS 2

MATERIALS 3 sets of cards for 0 to 9

DIRECTIONS Each player picks 3 cards. Lay the cards faceup to show a 3-digit number. Compare the numbers. The player with the greater number takes all 6 cards. Play until all the cards are picked.

The winner is the player with the most cards.

 This card game will help your child practice comparing two 3-digit numbers. Make 3 sets of cards for 0 to 9 from construction paper. A variation of the game would be to play rounds where the lesser number wins.

At
Home

Dear Family,

We are beginning the last chapter in our mathematics book. We will be learning about multiplication and how to find how many groups and how many in each group.

3 groups of 2
$3 \times 2 = 6$

We will also be talking about food, especially vegetables. Please help me complete this interview.

Your child,

_____
Signature

Interview ....

What vegetable do
you eat the most of? _____

What vegetable do
you like the most? _____

Have you ever seen a
really gigantic vegetable? _____

What was it? _____

What vegetables, if any, do you grow? _____

_____

Vegetables

Exploring Multiplication and Division

 Listen Listen to the story *June 29, 1999.*

 Talk Tell about your favorite vegetable.

Name _____

What Do You Know?

You and your friends are having a picnic.

This is what is in the basket.

Find out how many in all for each item. Show your work.

1 4 bags with 2 sandwiches in each _____

_____

2 2 bags with 8 carrots in each _____

_____

3 2 packages with 5 plates in each _____

_____

4 4 bags with 3 cookies in each _____

_____

5 3 packages with 2 juice boxes in each _____

_____

Portfolio
Add something else to the basket. Show how many in all.

Name _____

Working Together

You and your partner need 25 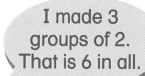, a ⊗,

and [○○○].

Take turns.

▶ You spin to find how many groups to make.

▶ Your partner spins to find how many ◐ in each group.

▶ Show the groups of ◐ on your workmat. Complete the chart.

I made 3 groups of 2. That is 6 in all.

Talk How many different ways can you and your partner find the total number of ◐?

	Number of groups	Number in each group	Number in all
1	3	2	6
2			
3			
4			
5			

Try These!

Use counters and . Complete the chart.

	Number of groups	Number in each group	Number in all
1	5	3	15
2	2	4	
3	3	1	
4	3	4	
5	4	5	
6	1	2	

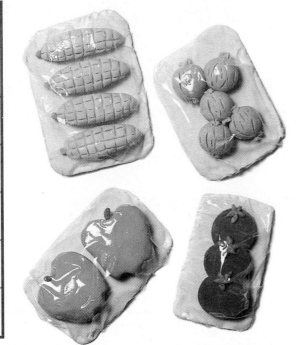

Cultural Connection   India

In Bombay, India, some merchants use fingers to show numbers.

Each finger of the right hand stands for a group of 5.

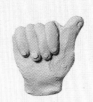 I group of 5

 ____ groups of 5

 ____ groups of 5

 ____ groups of 5

At Home We explored making equal groups. Ask your child to find the total for 5 groups of 4.

Name _____

You can **multiply** to find
how many ears of corn in all.

4 groups of 2 __8__

$4 \times 2 = $ __8__

(4 times 2 equals 8.)

There are __8__ ears of corn.

Cultural Note
Hopis grow blue corn,
which is used to make
blue *piki* bread.

Working Together

You and your partner need 15 and .

▶ Use counters to make the groups.

▶ Draw dots to show the groups you made.

▶ Write how many in all.

1 4 groups of 3 __12__

$4 \times 3 = $ ___

2 5 groups of 1 ___

$5 \times 1 = $ ___

 Critical Thinking What does 5×3 mean?
How do you find how many in all?

Try These!

Use counters if you want to.

Multiply.

 1

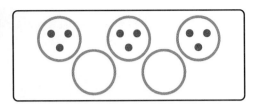

3 groups of 3 ___9

$3 \times 3 =$ ___

2

5 groups of 2 ___

$5 \times 2 =$ ___

3

3 groups of I ___

$3 \times 1 =$ ___

4

2 groups of 3 ___

$2 \times 3 =$ ___

Mixed Review

Write the fraction for the shaded part.

 5

 ___

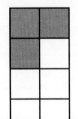 ___

 ___

 6

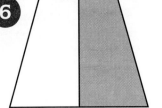 ___

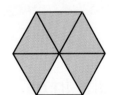 ___

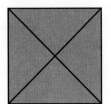 ___

At Home

We multiplied by I, 2, and 3. Ask your child to show 4 groups of 3 and find how many in all.

Write a **multiplication sentence.**
Find how many jars of salsa Elena made.

3 groups of 4

$3 \times 4 = 12$

12 is the **product.**

Elena made 12 jars of salsa.

Working Together

You and your partner need 25 and .

▶ Use counters to make the groups.

▶ Draw dots to show the groups you made.

▶ Write the multiplication sentence.

1 2 groups of 5

_____ × _____ = _____

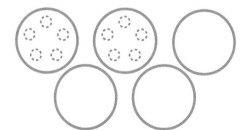

2 5 groups of 5

_____ × _____ = _____

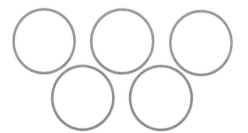

3 5 groups of 4

_____ × _____ = _____

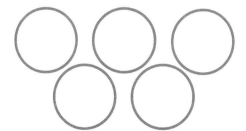

CHAPTER 12 *Lesson 2*

Try These!

Use counters if you want to.

Write the multiplication sentence.
Find the product.

1

1 group of 5

__1__ × __5__ = __5__

2

2 groups of 4

____ × ____ = ____

3

4 groups of 4

____ × ____ = ____

4

3 groups of 5

____ × ____ = ____

5

4 groups of 5

____ × ____ = ____

6

1 group of 4

____ × ____ = ____

7 You need 4 tomatoes to make 1 jar of salsa. How many tomatoes are needed for 3 jars of salsa?

____ tomatoes

 Write about how you multiply to find the product.

 We multiplied by 4 and 5. Ask your child to show 2 groups of 5 and find the product.

Name _____

Multiplication Patterns

2 groups of 3

3 groups of 2

$2 \times 3 = \underline{6}$

factor   factor   product

$3 \times 2 = \underline{6}$

factor   factor   product

Talk What happens to the product if you switch the order of the factors?

Working Together

You need 25 and .

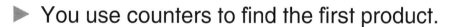

► You use counters to find the first product.

► Your partner uses counters to find the second product.

► Compare your work.

1 $3 \times 5 = \underline{}$ $4 \times 1 = \underline{}$ $4 \times 5 = \underline{}$

$5 \times 3 = \underline{}$ $1 \times 4 = \underline{}$ $5 \times 4 = \underline{}$

2 $5 \times 1 = \underline{}$ $3 \times 4 = \underline{}$ $2 \times 1 = \underline{}$

$1 \times 5 = \underline{}$ $4 \times 3 = \underline{}$ $1 \times 2 = \underline{}$

Critical Thinking When 1 is a factor, what do you notice about the product?

McGraw-Hill School Division

Try These!

Find the product.

1 $4 \times 2 =$ __8__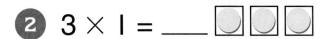

 $2 \times 4 =$ ___

2 $3 \times 1 =$ ___

 $1 \times 3 =$ ___

3 $5 \times 2 =$ ___

 $2 \times 5 =$ ___

4 $4 \times 3 =$ ___

 $3 \times 4 =$ ___

More to Explore   Algebra Sense

Look at the factors. Look at the products.

$0 \times 1 = 0$ $1 \times 0 = 0$

$0 \times 2 = 0$ $2 \times 0 = 0$

$0 \times 3 = 0$ $3 \times 0 = 0$

$0 \times 4 = 0$ $4 \times 0 = 0$

$0 \times 5 = 0$ $5 \times 0 = 0$

Look for a pattern.

 What do you notice about the factors and the products? Write about it.

 Use your own paper.

 At Home

Ask your child to tell you why 2×3 and 3×2 have the same product.

Oh, Beans!

You and your partner need 25 beans and 2 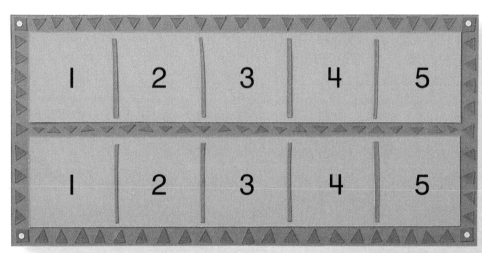 .

Take turns.

▶ Place 1 counter on each grid.

▶ Put that many beans in that many bowls below.

▶ Write the multiplication sentence.

Number of
bowls

| 1 | 2 | 3 | 4 | 5 |

Number of
beans for
each bowl

| 1 | 2 | 3 | 4 | 5 |

___ ✕ ___ = ___   ___ ✕ ___ = ___

___ ✕ ___ = ___   ___ ✕ ___ = ___

___ ✕ ___ = ___   ___ ✕ ___ = ___

Find the product.

1

3 groups of 1

$3 \times 1 =$ _____

2

3 groups of 4

$3 \times 4 =$ _____

3

4 groups of 5

$4 \times 5 =$ _____

4

5 groups of 4

$5 \times 4 =$ _____

5

3 groups of 2

$3 \times 2 =$ _____

6

1 group of 2

$1 \times 2 =$ _____

7

3 groups of 5

$3 \times 5 =$ _____

8

4 groups of 4

$4 \times 4 =$ _____

9

$2 \times 4 =$ _____

$4 \times 2 =$ _____

10

$5 \times 2 =$ _____

$2 \times 5 =$ _____

Name _____

Make a Table

Read Gabe is making 7 salads. He puts 3 cherry tomatoes in each salad. How many tomatoes does he need?

Read
Plan
Solve
Look Back

Plan You can **make a table** to solve. You can also draw a picture or use counters.

Solve Make a table.

Salads	1	2	3	4	5	6	7		
Tomatoes	3	6	9	12	15	18	21		

Gabe needs __21__ tomatoes for 7 salads.

Look Back Did you answer the question? Explain.

Make a table to solve.

1. Tess cooks 2 potatoes for each person. There will be 6 people at dinner. How many potatoes should Tess cook? _____ potatoes

People	1	2	3						
Potatoes	2	4							

2. What if 8 people came to dinner. How many potatoes should Tess cook? _____ potatoes

Try These!

Make a table to solve.

1 Marla makes 9 pizzas.
She slices 2 tomatoes for each pizza.
How many tomatoes does Marla need? _____ tomatoes

Pizzas	1	2								
Tomatoes	2	4								

2 Tony buys 6 eggplants.
He cuts each eggplant into 4 pieces.
How many pieces does Tony have? _____ pieces

Eggplants	1	2								
Pieces	4	8								

3 Louis uses 3 crates of lettuce each week. How many crates does he use in 8 weeks? _____ crates

Weeks	1									
Crates	3									

4 Write your own problem.
Have a partner solve it.

Use your own paper.

 We made tables to solve problems. Ask your child to explain how to solve problem 3 above.

Midchapter Review

Do your best!

Multiply.

1 2 groups of 5 _____

2 $2 \times 5 =$ _____

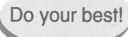 

3 4 groups of 4 _____

4 $4 \times 4 =$ _____

5 I group of 3 _____

6 $1 \times 3 =$ _____

7 $4 \times 2 =$ _____

8 $2 \times 4 =$ _____

Make a table to solve.

9 Casey buys 6 boxes of peppers.
Each box has 3 peppers.
How many peppers does Casey buy?   _____ peppers

Boxes						
Peppers						

10 What other way could you solve problem 9? _____

_____

How are 3×4 and 4×3 the same? How are they different?

Multiplication Table

You and your partner each need your own color  and I ◐ .

Take turns.

▶ Toss your counter on the multiplication table.

▶ Find the product for that space. Write it. Your partner checks.

▶ Color that space if you are correct. Your partner colors the space if you are wrong.

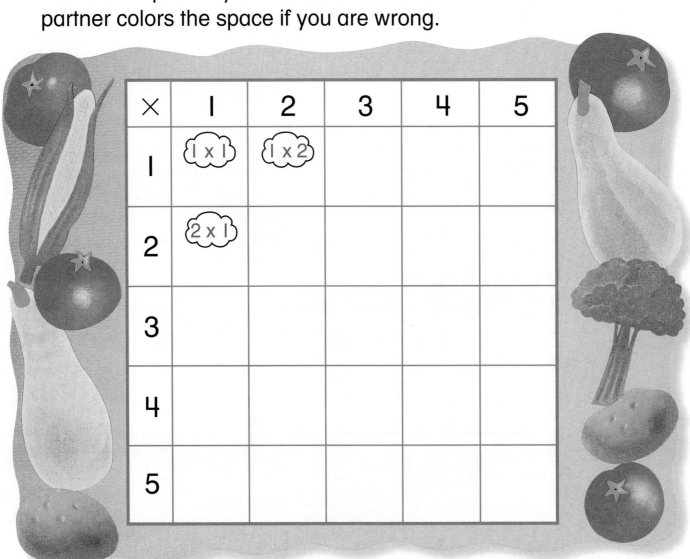

✕	1	2	3	4	5
1	⟨1 x 1⟩	⟨1 x 2⟩			
2	⟨2 x 1⟩				
3					
4					
5					

The winner is the player with more spaces colored.

Name

Plan a Garden

People in cities sometimes plant community vegetable gardens.

Then people share the vegetables they grow. The greater the **yield,** the more they have to share.

Working Together

Find the yield for two kinds of vegetable plants.

BUSH CUCUMBERS								
Plants	1	2	3	4	5	6	7	8
Yield each week	2	4						

TOMATOES								
Plants	1	2	3	4	5	6	7	8
Yield each week	3	6						

Decision Making

1. Plan a vegetable garden. Decide what vegetables to grow.

2. Find the yield for each kind of vegetable or choose a reasonable number.

3. Draw a map of your garden.

 Write a report.

4. Tell how you decided what to plant and how many plants you chose.

5. Explain your garden plan and tell how you will share the vegetables.

More to Investigate

PREDICT Choose a vegetable to grow. How long do you think it will take before you have a vegetable to pick?

EXPLORE Plant some seeds. Watch them grow.

FIND Keep track of the days until the first vegetable appears. Keep a record of the yield.

How many groups of 3 can you make from 12 counters?

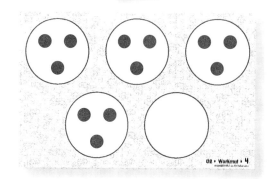

_**4**_ groups of 3

Working Together

You and your partner need 16 and .

▶ Use counters to make the groups.

▶ Draw dots to show the groups you made.

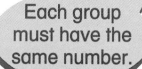

Each group must have the same number.

▶ Write how many groups.

1 Use 6 counters. Make groups of 2.

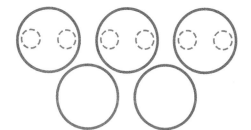

_____ groups of 2

---

2 Use 9 counters. Make groups of 3.

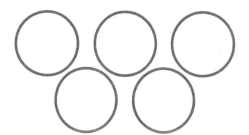

_____ groups of 3

---

3 Use 16 counters. Make groups of 4.

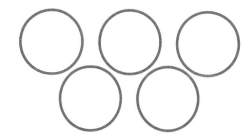

_____ groups of 4

Critical Thinking How can you check your answer?

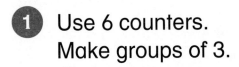 **Try These!**

Use counters to make groups.
Draw dots to show the groups.
Write how many groups.

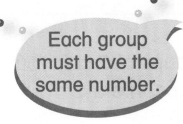 Each group must have the same number.

1 Use 6 counters.
Make groups of 3.

_____ groups of 3

2 Use 10 counters.
Make groups of 5.

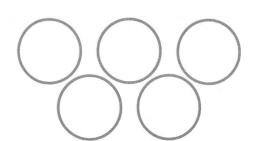

_____ groups of 5

3 Use 12 counters.
Make groups of 4.

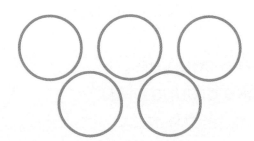

_____ groups of 4

More to Explore   Number Sense

You have 24 counters.

Number in each group	Can you make equal groups?	How many groups?	How many left over?
2	Yes.	12	0
5			
3			
7			

 At Home

We made equal groups today. Ask your child to explain exercise 3 above.

There are 12 crates to put in 3 trucks.
Each truck gets the same number of crates.
How many crates go in each truck?

There are ___4___ crates in each truck.

Working Together

You and your partner need 16 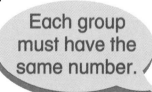 and  .

▶ Use counters to make the groups.

▶ Draw dots to show how many counters in each group.

Each group must have the same number.

▶ Write how many in each group.

1 Use 8 counters.
Make 2 groups.

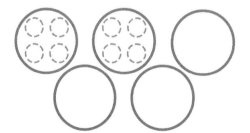

_____ in each group

---

2 Use 15 counters.
Make 5 groups.

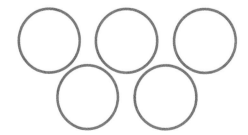

_____ in each group

Talk How do you make the groups equal?
Share your ideas.

Try These!

Use counters to make the groups.
Draw dots to show the groups.
Write how many in each group.

Each group must have the same number.

1 Use 6 counters.
Make 2 groups.

_____ in each group

2 Use 12 counters.
Make 2 groups.

_____ in each group

3 Use 10 counters.
Make 5 groups.

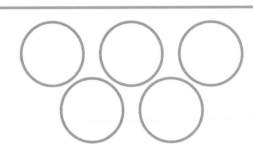

_____ in each group

Mixed Review

Add or subtract.

4

571	36	$1.45	362	525
− 329	+ 377	+ 4.90	− 9	+ 299

5

707	985	349	$6.38	921
+ 4	− 293	+ 343	− 4.86	− 17

At Home

We made equal groups of counters. Ask your child to explain or show how to solve exercise 3 above.

Name ______________________

Extra Practice
Activity !

Divide and Counters

You need 20  and 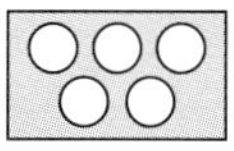.
Complete the table.

	Number of children	Number of teams	Number of children on each team
1	15	5	3
2		3	5
3	6		2
4		2	3
5	20		4
6		4	5
7	8	2	
8		4	2
9	12		4
10		4	3
11	16	2	
12		8	2
13	10		5
14		5	2

McGraw-Hill School Division

Draw dots to show
the counters.
Write how many groups.

1 8 counters
Make groups of 2.

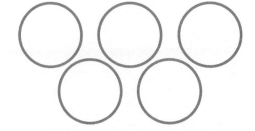

_____ groups of 2

2 20 counters
Make groups of 5.

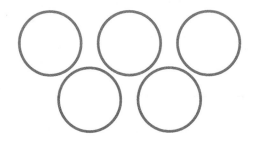

_____ groups of 5

Draw dots to show the counters.
Write how many in each group.

3 4 counters
Make 4 groups.

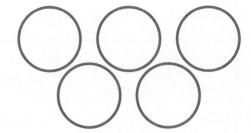

_____ in each group

4 9 counters
Make 3 groups.

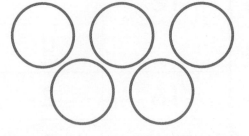

_____ in each group

5 20 counters
Make 5 groups.

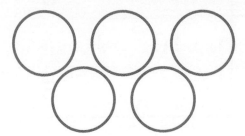

_____ in each group

Name _____

Use Models

Ellen picked 20 little pumpkins.
She wants to share them equally
among herself and 3 friends. How
many pumpkins will each person get?

Read
Plan
Solve
Look Back

You can use models to show groups.

Each person gets __5__ pumpkins.

 Tell about another
way to solve the problem.

Use models to solve.

1. The farm has 3 trucks.
   Each truck has 5 crates of peppers on it.
   How many crates of peppers are there
   altogether?   _____ crates

---

2. The farm has 10 crates of onions.
   Each van can carry 5 crates.
   How many vans are needed to
   carry the 10 crates of onions?   _____ vans

---

3. Each box holds 6 heads of cabbage.
   There are 3 boxes of cabbage.
   How many heads of cabbage
   is that in all?   _____ heads

McGraw-Hill School Division

Try These!

Solve.

1 There are 5 cars on the train. Each car holds 5 crates of vegetables. How many vegetable crates are on the train?

_____ crates

2 Tim picks 16 carrots. He puts them into 4 equal bunches. How many carrots are in each bunch?

_____ carrots

3 What if Tim puts 8 carrots in each bunch. How many bunches would he make?

_____ bunches

Write and Share

Nico wrote this problem.

The farm has 5 crates of apples. Each car carries 5 crates. How many cars carry the 5 crates of apples?

Nico Mooduto
P.S. 144
Forest Hills, New York

4 Solve Nico's problem. _____

What strategy did you use? _____

5 Write your own problem. Have a partner solve it.

Use your own paper.

What strategy did your partner use? _____

 At Home   We used models to help solve problems. Ask your child to explain how to solve the problem he or she wrote.

Name _____

Chapter Review

Find the product.

1

1 group of 4

$1 \times 4 =$ _____

2

2 groups of 5

$2 \times 5 =$ _____

3

2 groups of 4

$2 \times 4 =$ _____

4 $3 \times 5 =$ _____

$5 \times 3 =$ _____

Draw dots to show the counters.
Write how many groups.

5 9 counters
Make groups of 3.

_____ groups of 3

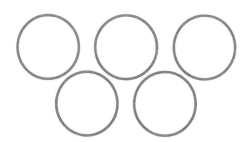

Draw dots to show the counters.
Write how many in each group.

6 12 counters
Make 4 groups.

_____ in each group

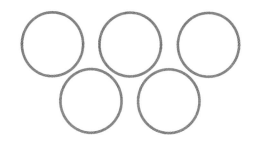

Make a table to solve.

7 A farmer fills 3 crates of corn each hour.
How many crates can he fill in 5 hours?   _____ crates

Hours	1									
Crates	3									

8 How many crates could the farmer
fill in 7 hours?   _____ crates

Solve.

9 Each truck holds 5 crates of corn.
How many crates can 4 trucks hold?   _____ crates

10 A farmer picked 16 carrots.
She put them into 2 equal bunches.
How many carrots were in each bunch?   _____ carrots

What Do You Think?

Which strategy would you use to find 3 groups of 2?
☑ Check one.

☐ Use counters.   ☐ Draw dots.   ☐ Draw a picture.

Why? _____

Journal   Write and show how to find how many
in each group.

Chapter Test

1

1 group of 5

$1 \times 5 =$ ___

2

2 groups of 4

$2 \times 4 =$ ___

3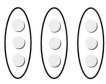

3 groups of 3

$3 \times 3 =$ ___

4

4 groups of 4

$4 \times 4 =$ ___

5

$3 \times 4 =$ ___

6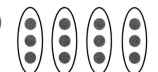

$4 \times 3 =$ ___

Draw dots to show the counters. Complete.

7

10 counters
Make groups of 2.

___ groups of 2

8

12 counters
Make 4 groups.

___ in each group

Make a table to solve.

9 Jed makes 8 pizzas.
He puts 2 meatballs on each pizza.
How many meatballs does Jed need?   ___ meatballs

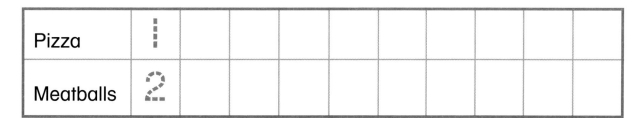

Pizza	1							
Meatballs	2							

10 What if Jed makes 10 pizzas.
How many meatballs does Jed need?   ___ meatballs

What Did You Learn?

Work with a partner. You need .

You have 2 bags with 9 ears of corn in each.
You want to share the corn with some friends.
Give each friend the same number of
ears of corn.

Show how many ears of corn each
friend gets.
Draw a picture or write a sentence.

 Talk What if you have more friends. Is there another
way you can share the corn equally?

 Portfolio You may want to put this page in your portfolio.

Name _____

Division Sentences

Sal makes sauce with 14 tomatoes. He uses 2 pots. He puts the same number of tomatoes in each pot. How many tomatoes go in each pot?

14 tomatoes in 2 equal groups

$$14 \div 2 = 7$$

14 **divided by** 2 equals 7.

Draw dots to show equal groups of tomatoes. Complete.

1 8 tomatoes
Make 2 groups.

$8 \div 2 = \underline{4}$

2 12 tomatoes
Make 3 groups.

$12 \div 3 = \underline{}$

3 12 tomatoes
Make 2 groups.

$12 \div 2 = \underline{}$

4 9 tomatoes
Make 3 groups.

$9 \div 3 = \underline{}$

Healthy Snacks

Here is a healthy snack your class can make.

Double the recipe so that you will have enough.

Party Mix

2 cups Wheat Chex _____

3 cups pretzel sticks _____

$1\frac{1}{2}$ cups peanuts _____

$\frac{1}{2}$ cup raisins _____

$\frac{1}{2}$ cup dried sliced apples _____

Talk What else could you add to the party mix? How much would you add?

Name _____

Cumulative Review

Choose the letter of the correct answer.

1

$$15$$
$$- \ \ 6$$

ⓐ 21
ⓑ 11
ⓒ 9
ⓓ 8

6

$$53$$
$$- 37$$

ⓐ 90
ⓑ 86
ⓒ 26
ⓓ 16

2 What number comes just before?

___?___, 75

ⓐ 70
ⓑ 74
ⓒ 76
ⓓ 85

7

ⓐ $\frac{3}{4}$
ⓑ $\frac{3}{6}$
ⓒ $\frac{1}{3}$
ⓓ not here

3

ⓐ $1.31
ⓑ $1.36
ⓒ $1.45
ⓓ $1.55

8

$$644$$
$$- 309$$

ⓐ 335
ⓑ 345
ⓒ 935
ⓓ 953

4

ⓐ 2:40
ⓑ 2:20
ⓒ 1:40
ⓓ 8:10

9

2 groups of 5

$2 \times 5 = $ ___?___

ⓐ 2
ⓑ 5
ⓒ 10
ⓓ 25

5

$$\$15$$
$$+ \ \ 48$$

ⓐ $62
ⓑ $53
ⓒ $33
ⓓ not here

10

2 groups of 3

$2 \times 3 = $ ___?___

ⓐ 3
ⓑ 6
ⓒ 23
ⓓ not here

11 3 groups of 4

$3 \times 4 = \underline{\ ?\ }$

(a) 7
(b) 9
(c) 12
(d) 34

12 10 counters
Make 2 groups.

$\underline{\ ?\ }$ in each group

(a) 20
(b) 12
(c) 8
(d) 5

13 It rains 148 days. It snows 39 days. How many days does it rain or snow?

(a) 187
(b) 177
(c) 119
(d) 109

14 Ann has 43 pumpkins. She uses 26 for bread. How many pumpkins are left?

(a) 69
(b) 27
(c) 17
(d) 16

15 Dan's pattern has 15 shapes. How many will be blue?

(a) 2
(b) 4
(c) 5
(d) 15

16 Luke reads the thermometer on a cold, windy day. About what temperature is it?

(a) 15°F
(b) 55°F
(c) 65°F
(d) 88°F

17 Lara spends $5.60 and $1.46 on food. How much does she spend in all?

(a) $4.14
(b) $6.06
(c) $6.96
(d) $7.06

18 There are 5 bags. Each bag has 5 peppers. How many peppers are there?

(a) 10
(b) 20
(c) 25
(d) 30

19 Ronnie picks 8 tomatoes. She puts 4 in each box. How many boxes does she fill?

(a) 2
(b) 4
(c) 12
(d) not here

20 Tito plants 4 seeds in each of 4 rows. How many seeds is that?

Row	1	2	3	4
Seeds	4	8	?	?

(a) 4
(b) 12
(c) 15
(d) 16

Name _____

Multiplication Game

PLAYERS 2 or more

MATERIALS 10 index cards, pencil

DIRECTIONS Make two sets of cards. Write the numbers 1 to 5, one number on one card in each set. Put the sets facedown on a table.

Take turns. Pick a card from each set. Multiply.

If your answer is correct, give yourself 2 points. Play until you have 20 points in all.

 Playing this game with your child will help him or her practice multiplication facts.

Picture Glossary

addend

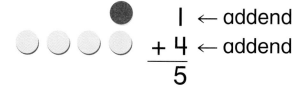

$$1 \leftarrow \text{addend}$$
$$\underline{+\ 4} \leftarrow \text{addend}$$
$$5$$

addition sentence

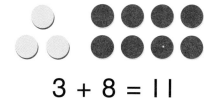

$$3 + 8 = 11$$

after

202   203

↑ just after 202

area

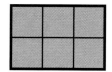

The area is 6 square units.

bar graph

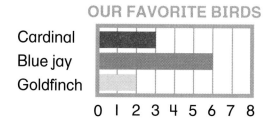

OUR FAVORITE BIRDS

Cardinal
Blue jay
Goldfinch

0 1 2 3 4 5 6 7 8

before

202   **203**

↑ just before 203

between

202   203   204

↑ between 202 and 204

calculator

calendar

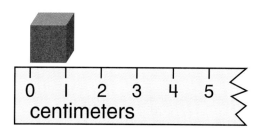

centimeter

circle

○

compare

$$978 < 987$$ is less than

$$838 > 818$$ is greater than

cone

congruent

Shapes that are the same size and shape.

count back

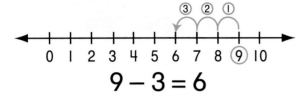

$$9 - 3 = 6$$

count on

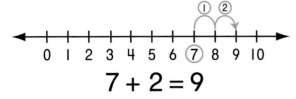

$$7 + 2 = 9$$

count up

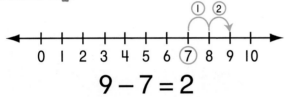

$$9 - 7 = 2$$

cube

cup

cylinder

difference

$$\begin{array}{r} 9 \\ -2 \\ \hline 7 \end{array} \leftarrow \text{difference}$$

digit

$$3\,5\,4$$
$$\uparrow\,\uparrow\,\uparrow$$
digits

dime

 10¢

division sentence

$$14 \div 2 = 7$$

dollar $1.00

doubles

$$\begin{array}{cccccc} 1 & 2 & 3 & 2 & 4 & 6 \\ +1 & +2 & +3 & -1 & -2 & -3 \\ \hline 2 & 4 & 6 & 1 & 2 & 3 \end{array}$$

equal parts

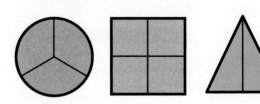

estimate

$$47 + 22$$

50 + 20

about 70 ← estimate

even

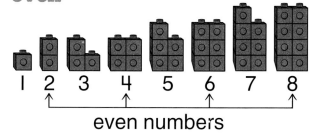

even numbers

fact family

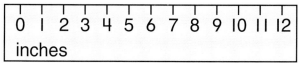

$5 + 6 = 11$ $11 - 6 = 5$

$6 + 5 = 11$ $11 - 5 = 6$

factors

$1 \times 7 = 7$

↑   ↑

factor   factor

foot

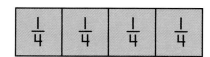

12 inches equal 1 foot.

fourths

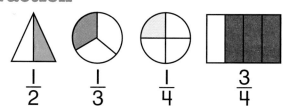

4 equal parts

fraction

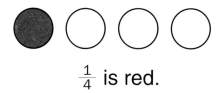

$\frac{1}{2}$ $\frac{1}{3}$ $\frac{1}{4}$ $\frac{3}{4}$

fraction of a group

$\frac{1}{4}$ is red.

half dollar

50¢

half hour

30 minutes

halves

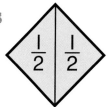

2 equal parts

hour

60 minutes

hundreds

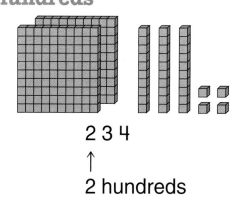

2 3 4

↑

2 hundreds

inch

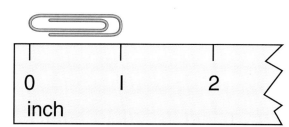

is greater than

26 > 24

is less than

11 < 18

kilogram

line of symmetry

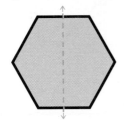

liter

mental math

Finding math answers in your head.

meter

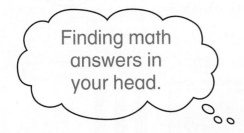

100 centimeters equal 1 meter.

minute

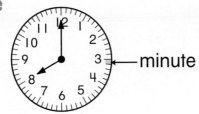

60 minutes equal 1 hour.

multiplication sentence

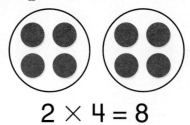

2 × 4 = 8

nickel

5¢

number line

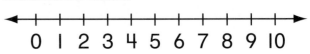

0 1 2 3 4 5 6 7 8 9 10

odd

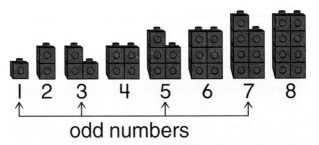

1 2 3 4 5 6 7 8

odd numbers

ones

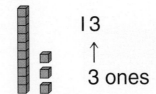

13

3 ones

order

57, 58, 59, 60, 61

These numbers are in order.

ordinal numbers

Jan is seventh in line.

part-part-total

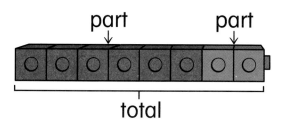

$$6 + 2 = 8$$

pattern

penny

1¢

perimeter

The distance around a shape.

pictograph

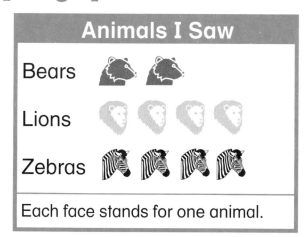

Animals I Saw	
Bears	
Lions	
Zebras	
Each face stands for one animal.	

pint

2 cups equal 1 pint.

pound

product

$$4 \times 3 = 12$$

↑ product

quart

2 pints equal 1 quart.

quarter

25¢

quarter hour

15 minutes

rectangle

rectangular prism

regroup

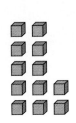 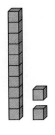 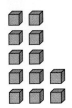

12 ones = 1 ten 2 ones = 12 ones

related facts

$3 + 7 = 10$ $7 + 3 = 10$

skip-count

5   10   15   20

sphere

square

square unit

1 square unit   4 square units

subtraction sentence

$10 - 2 = 8$

sum

$$\begin{array}{r} 14 \\ + 25 \\ \hline 39 \end{array} \leftarrow \text{sum}$$

tally marks

a way to keep track of counting

temperature

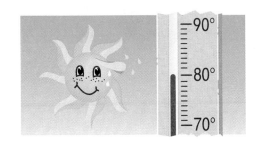

tens

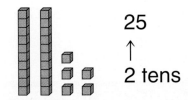

25
↑
2 tens

thirds

$\frac{1}{3}$	$\frac{1}{3}$	$\frac{1}{3}$

3 equal parts

triangle

yard

3 feet equal 1 yard.